Cognitive-Behavioral Therapy for Avoidant/Restrictive Food Intake Disorder

This practical, accessible manual, written by two of the leading experts in the emerging ARFID field, will be a very welcome addition to the clinician's library. I anticipate that it will quickly become a much used volume by anyone offering care and treatment to patients with this disorder. Until now there has been very little by way of guidance in terms of evidence-based treatments specifically for ARFID. This clearly written book, based on sound theoretical principles, enables the outstanding skills, expertise, and insights of its authors to be shared by a much wider audience, which can only benefit patient care.

Dr. Rachel Bryant-Waugh

It is rare that a newly conceptualized mental disorder is introduced into systems of nosology without an existing treatment approach with some evidence for efficacy; but, this was the case with ARFID. Now, from one of the leading eating disorders centers in the world comes a very well-conceived stage model of intervention that can be personalized for the individual patient, as well as the patient's family. Anyone treating eating disorders should find this new clinical manual invaluable.

Dr. David H. Barlow

ARFID sounds a little less unfamiliar today than when it was introduced by DSM-5 only five years ago. Since then, a small cadre of clinical researchers has devoted considerable energy to explore treatments for this patient population. Thomas and Eddy have been leaders in this domain. Through their focused efforts, the authors have put together an extraordinarily helpful treatment manual that everyone who wants to learn more about ARFID, whether a treating clinician, curious trainee, or worried parent, would be well advised to consult. This clinician manual first provides the reader with an excellent psycho-educational overview of ARFID, before delineating the four stages of CBT-AR. The authors round out this manual by demonstrating their treatment approach by way of five elucidating clinical case examples. This book is a most welcome addition to the small family of clinical treatment manuals for eating disorders.

Dr. Daniel Le Grange

As an ARFID advocate, author on the topic, and mother to a recovered child with ARFID, I couldn't be more thrilled with this book. Cognitive-Behavioral Therapy for Avoidant/Restrictive Food Intake Disorder is vital toward the education and treatment of ARFID. With comprehensive and detailed information, workable steps for treatment, and actual case studies, this book is desperately needed in the eating disorder community, and one that I wish had been available when our family was struggling to find answers.

For so many years, our daughter was misdiagnosed, misunderstood, and misheard until she received the proper treatment – and that treatment very much mirrors what authors/doctors Jennifer Thomas and Kamryn Eddy outline in their book. It was extremely encouraging to read about CBT-AR and to have so many of the techniques and stages feel familiar to what we experienced with our daughter's treatment.

There is much to learn about ARFID, but this manual is a terrific starting point in helping clinicians, physicians, therapists, and even parents learn more about this very prevalent and very mysterious eating disorder that affects children and adults of all ages.

I can't wait for this book to be published because I am going to single-handedly contact everyone I know who has struggled with ARFID and tell them they absolutely need this manual!

Stephanie Elliot, author of the young adult novel, *Sad Perfect*, ARFID advocate, and mother to a daughter recovered from ARFID

Cognitive-Behavioral Therapy for Avoidant/Restrictive Food Intake Disorder

Children, Adolescents, and Adults

Jennifer J. Thomas
Harvard Medical School

Kamryn T. Eddy
Harvard Medical School

CAMBRIDGE
UNIVERSITY PRESS

CAMBRIDGE
UNIVERSITY PRESS

University Printing House, Cambridge CB2 8BS, United Kingdom

One Liberty Plaza, 20th Floor, New York, NY 10006, USA

477 Williamstown Road, Port Melbourne, VIC 3207, Australia

314–321, 3rd Floor, Plot 3, Splendor Forum, Jasola District Centre, New Delhi – 110025, India

103 Penang Road, #05-06/07, Visioncrest Commercial, Singapore 238467

Cambridge University Press is part of the University of Cambridge.

It furthers the University's mission by disseminating knowledge in the pursuit of education, learning, and research at the highest international levels of excellence.

www.cambridge.org
Information on this title: www.cambridge.org/9781108401159
DOI: 10.1017/9781108233170

First published 2019
9th printing 2021

Printed in the United Kingdom by TJ Books Limited, Padstow Cornwall

A catalogue record for this publication is available from the British Library.

Library of Congress Cataloging-in-Publication Data
Names: Thomas, Jennifer J., author. | Eddy, Kamryn T., 1977– author.
Title: Cognitive-behavioral therapy for avoidant/restrictive food intake
    disorder : children, adolescents, and adults / Jennifer J. Thomas,
    Kamryn T. Eddy.
Description: Cambridge, United Kingdom ; New York, NY :
    Cambridge University Press, 2019. | Includes bibliographical
    references and index.
Identifiers: LCCN 2018023258 | ISBN 9781108401159 (pbk. : alk. paper)
Subjects: | MESH: Feeding and Eating Disorders–therapy | Cognitive
    Therapy–methods
Classification: LCC RC552.E18 | NLM WM 175 | DDC 616.85/26–dc23
    LC record available at https://lccn.loc.gov/2018023258

ISBN 978-1-108-40115-9 Paperback

For Asher and Colby

Contents

Foreword

This book starts with a very simple premise: If you give people a diagnostic label, it helps them identify that they or their loved ones have a legitimate problem, and they feel justified in seeking help. However, then you hit a quandary. You need a way of helping those people deal with that problem when there has not been time to come up with solutions. So, when Avoidant/restrictive food intake disorder (ARFID) was launched onto the world stage in 2013, it was great to have a label, but we had to face individuals with ARFID and their families with the news that we were not ready with any evidence-based treatment. All that we could offer were best guesses, and they were often far from adequate.

The cognitive-behavioral therapy for eating disorders (CBT-ED) approach that works well with many adults with eating disorders has not proven suitable for this group. However, now we have a well-thought-out treatment approach that can bring real hope to those with ARFID, whatever their age. The authors have given us a form of CBT that is adapted for ARFID – for Avoidant/Restrictive Food Intake Disorder (CBT-AR). In this book, it is made clear how CBT-AR differs from CBT-ED, as well as how they overlap.

This book is a true trailblazer, with its combination of clinical knowledge, sound theoretical reasoning, empirical support, and plenty of case material. It is no exaggeration to say that only this team could have produced such an excellent clinical protocol at this time. They have worked at multiple levels to understand ARFID, and have used that research and clinical evidence to develop the therapy that you are going to read about here.

What Jennifer Thomas and Kamryn Eddy have done here (along with their redoubtable team) is to find ways of doing this work with the person with ARFID or their family, according to what is most likely to fit the individual case. Their CBT-AR protocol is soundly based on cognitive-behavioral

principles, which have been honed and refined. In your hands, you have: a staged model that is adaptable to the nature of the individual case; clearly laid out psychoeducational materials; and a manual for parents that will help them get involved as active agents in the treatment process. The stages of therapy and the tasks within each stage are clear to the reader. The penultimate chapter gives vivid case material, showing the thinking that we need to do as we deliver CBT-AR. Anyone who has trouble in understanding how to make CBT-AR work in routine practice can learn from these excellent case examples.

The authors are very clear: The work of our field to understand and treat ARFID is not yet complete, and will be the subject of research and clinical innovation for decades to come. However, this book is the most significant step to date – a bringing together of research and clinical knowledge in order to provide clinicians with the knowledge and skills that they need to be able to work with this challenging clinical population. So now, when a parent or person with ARFID says, 'I have been given this diagnosis, so what can you do about it?,' we will have an answer and the tools that we need. We should be delighted, and I believe that you will be by the time you have read what follows in this manual and tried it with your patients.

This manual is written to be immediately accessible. It is certainly not going to spend much time on my shelves. It will be where it belongs – on my desk, and getting used. This manual deserves to be on the desks of all clinicians who work with such eating and feeding problems. Jennifer Thomas, Kamryn Eddy, and their team are a formidable group of clinical researchers. This book demonstrates not only their skills but also their dedication to the care of their patients and families.

Glenn Waller, DPhil
Professor of Clinical Psychology
University of Sheffield, UK

Preface

Avoidant/restrictive food intake disorder (ARFID) was introduced to the psychiatric nomenclature in 2013, with the publication of the *Diagnostic and Statistical Manual of Mental Disorders, fifth edition* (*DSM-5*; American Psychiatric Association, 2013). By naming and describing a syndrome that reflected the symptoms with which many patients and families had long been struggling, the American Psychiatric Association inspired a groundswell of hope for individuals with avoidant and restrictive eating and their loved ones. Indeed, naming a diagnosis implies that the condition may be treatable – that there may be a cure. Over the past five years, hopeful patients and their families have inundated clinics worldwide seeking help for avoidant and restrictive eating. Many of them have come to our own center, the Massachusetts General Hospital Eating Disorders Clinical and Research Program in Boston.

Unfortunately, in 2013, we as a field knew very little about the phenomenology and treatment of ARFID. Although there was already a robust literature on pediatric feeding disorders and classical eating disorders, ARFID itself was so new that there was no clear standard of care. That is, no psychological treatment had demonstrated clear efficacy in a randomized controlled trial. This created a conundrum for practicing clinicians: What were we to offer the hundreds of patients and families who, heartened by a new diagnosis, honored us with their trust by asking for help? This book describes a specialized form of cognitive behavioral therapy – CBT-AR – that we have developed, refined, and studied in response to this urgent clinical need. CBT-AR is designed for the treatment of children, adolescents, and adults ages ten and up who meet *DSM-5* criteria for ARFID (American Psychiatric Association, 2013) or exhibit clinically significant symptoms of avoidant or restrictive eating. While there is still much to be learned about the etiology, neurobiology, prevention, and treatment of ARFID, patients and their families need help now. It is for this reason that we wrote this book.

Acknowledgments

Developing this treatment was truly a team effort. We would like to thank all of our clinical colleagues, research collaborators, funders, and patients who helped us to better understand the specific psychopathology of ARFID and identify potentially successful interventions. Specifically, very special recognition goes to Dr. Kendra Becker, who served as a study therapist in the initial pilot trial of CBT-AR, provided invaluable feedback that helped us refine the treatment, and assisted in creating the patient education handouts included in this book. We are extremely grateful to our team dietitian, Laurie Manzo RD, for compiling the 'Common Nutrition Deficiencies Associated with ARFID' patient education handout based on her clinical experience with this group. We owe a debt of gratitude to all of the members of the Eating Disorders Clinical and Research Program (EDCRP) clinical and research team, who provided important feedback on earlier versions of this treatment, including Drs. Rachel Liebman, Lazaro Zayas, Audrey Tolman, Judy Craver, Cathryn Freid, and Debra Franko. We would also like to thank our current and former EDCRP research assistants, Kathryn Coniglio, Helen Murray, and Ani Keshishian, who helped us with many grant proposals and institutional review board submissions to support this project. This manual would not have been possible without our research collaborators – particularly those on our National Institute of Health–funded study 'Neurobiological and Behavioral Risk Mechanisms of Youth Avoidant/Restrictive Eating Trajectories' (1R01MH108595) – including Drs. Elizabeth Lawson and Nadia Micali (the study's co-principal investigators) and co-investigators Drs. Madhusmita Misra, Thilo Deckersbach, Franziska Plessow, Melissa Freizinger, Elana Bern, and Lydia Shrier. Special thanks go to our study nurse practitioners, Elisa Asanza and Meghan Slattery, and our study coordinators – Reitumetse Pulumo, Olivia Wons, Christopher Mancuso, Alyssa Izquierdo, and Jenny Jo – for their tireless work on the neurobiology study. We would also like to thank Dr. Sabine Wilhem, who provided invaluable consultation on treatment development and helped us design our CBT-AR pilot study. As we state in the text, it is important to collaborate with physicians who can provide monitoring to this patient group. As such, we wish to thank the physician colleagues who provided medical care for our patients with ARFID, including Drs. Mark Goldstein, Kathryn Brigham, Diana Lemly, Nupur Gupta, Jennifer Rosenblum, and Melinda Mesmer. We also wish to thank Drs. Rachel Bryant-Waugh, Lucy Cooke, and Nadia Micali for working with us on the development of the Pica, ARFID, and Rumination Disorder Interview, which clarified our understanding of the psychopathology of ARFID and its clinical heterogeneity. We are sincerely grateful to the American Psychological Foundation, Hilda and Preston Davis Foundation, and Global Foundation for Eating Disorders, which funded our CBT-AR pilot study; and the National Institute of Mental Health and Harvard University's Mind, Brain, and Behavior Initiative, which funded our investigation into the neurobiology of ARFID. Last and most important, we are grateful to all of our patients with ARFID and their parents. Each of them had the selflessness to undergo a new, experimental treatment and the vision to see how their study participation could ultimately improve the lives of others.

What Is ARFID?

ARFID made its diagnostic debut in the *DSM-5* (American Psychological Association, 2013) as a reformulation of *DSM-IV* feeding disorder of infancy and early childhood. Although *DSM-5* provides a fairly clear definition of ARFID, research on its prevalence, distinction from classical eating disorders, and etiology is still emerging.

Definition

ARFID is defined by a pattern of eating that is limited in variety (e.g., avoidance of specific foods) and/or volume (e.g., restriction of amount) and associated with important medical and psychosocial consequences (*DSM-5* criterion A). Individuals with ARFID typically attribute their avoidant or restrictive eating pattern to the sensory characteristics of food (i.e., sensory sensitivity), a fear of aversive consequences of eating (e.g., choking, vomiting), and/or a lack of interest in eating or food (e.g., low hunger, lack of enjoyment of eating). But ARFID is more than just picky eating or skipping a meal once in a while. To qualify for the ARFID diagnosis, a person's pattern of eating must be associated with significant negative consequences. These include one or more of the following: significant weight loss/growth fall-off, nutritional deficiencies, dependence on tube feeding or reliance on energy-dense supplements, or psychosocial impairment (*DSM-5* criterion A). Avoidant/restrictive eating in ARFID cannot be due to lack of available food or cultural norms (*DSM-5* criterion B), nor can it be motivated by weight and shape concerns (*DSM-5* criterion C). If avoidant/restrictive eating co-occurs with other psychiatric or medical illnesses, the eating disturbance must be severe enough to require independent clinical attention (*DSM-5* criterion D) to warrant a comorbid ARFID diagnosis.

As a diagnostic group, ARFID is very heterogeneous. It can include the low-weight, short-stature grade schooler with a low appetite whose babyhood reflux challenged his early feeding, and who now limits his diet to bland white foods he has learned are easy on his stomach. Mealtimes in his family are tense because he is unable to eat the meal that the rest of the family members are eating and his parents vacillate between vehemently pressuring him to eat more and exasperatedly leaving him alone. ARFID also includes the slender high schooler with celiac disease who, following a gluten-contamination episode, has significantly restricted her already narrow diet and precipitously lost weight and incurred vitamin deficiencies. It may also include the overweight young adult with an iron deficiency who has been reluctant to enter the dating world due to embarrassment about his intake of so-called kid foods and his avoidance of all fruits, vegetables, and meats. While these cases are unified by their avoidant/restrictive eating patterns, the rationales for restriction and the medical and psychosocial sequelae differ.

In 2013, ARFID supplanted *DSM-IV's* feeding disorder of infancy or early childhood, which was sometimes used in clinical practice but rarely studied in the scientific literature. Feeding disorder of infancy or early childhood had been defined by weight loss or failure to gain weight as expected; lack of medical or psychiatric comorbid diagnosis that could account for the feeding disturbance; and an onset before six years old. However, the diagnosis was too narrow to be clinically useful. For example, one diagnostic study of individuals presenting to a pediatric feeding disorders clinic found that just 12% met criteria for feeding disorder of infancy or early childhood (Williams, Riegel, & Kerwin, 2009). The others presented with clinically significant feeding difficulties that fell outside the confines of the diagnosis. In response to this diagnostic dilemma, the *DSM-5* Work Group used the new ARFID diagnosis to both revise and expand upon this earlier diagnostic category in several important ways. First, while low weight or failure to gain weight is a common sequela of avoidant/restrictive eating, other complications can occur. The ARFID diagnosis allows for the eating pattern to be associated with nutrition deficiencies, reliance on enteral feeding or nutrition supplements, or psychosocial impairment. Importantly, this diagnostic reformulation acknowledged that food avoidance/restriction does not always or only lead to weight loss, but can be associated with normal weight or even overweight or obesity. Indeed, some individuals with ARFID may remain in the healthy weight range via the use of tube feeding or energy-dense supplements, while others, reliant on carbohydrates or energy-dense processed foods, carry excess weight. Supportive evidence that feeding difficulties can occur across the weight spectrum includes results from one study of youth presenting to a pediatric feeding disorders clinic, which found that 71% were not underweight (Williams et al., 2009).

Notably, deletion of the age-of-onset criterion validated that individuals of all ages can have clinically significant avoidant/restrictive eating that does not always begin in early childhood. Many individuals with frank food avoidance/restriction who would now be diagnosed with ARFID were effectively diagnostic orphans of *DSM-IV*. For example, the adult who had been a relatively normal eater before the experience of a choking episode, which resulted in food avoidance and profound weight loss, may have straddled the *DSM-IV* eating disorder not otherwise specified (EDNOS) and specific phobia diagnoses. The EDNOS diagnosis would have been too vague to meaningfully capture his presentation, while the specific phobia diagnosis would have underemphasized his weight loss. By contrast, the ARFID diagnosis parsimoniously characterizes the full problem.

Finally, *DSM-5* noted that ARFID *can* occur in the context of medical or psychiatric comorbidity if the eating problem requires independent clinical attention. The ARFID diagnosis does not presume the etiology of the feeding disturbance, and thus promotes detection of clinically significant disturbances in groups that likely went unrecognized under *DSM-IV* feeding disorder criteria. Indeed while some psychiatric or medical populations may be at greater risk for eating or feeding difficulties than others, most of these issues do not warrant treatment that is outside the scope of what would be expected based on the primary diagnosis. In a recent record review of more than 2,000 youth ages 8–18 years presenting to 19

Boston-area pediatric gastrointestinal clinics for an initial evaluation, our research team found just 1.5% met criteria for ARFID (Eddy et al., 2015). Although eating and feeding issues were rife in this medical population, those with a frank avoidant/restrictive eating disorder stood out.

Feeding or eating difficulties are common in childhood, occurring in roughly 25% of youth (Chatoor, 2002; Micali et al., 2011). However, ARFID is distinguished by its persistence and clinical severity. Childhood selective eating is prevalent but often improves during middle childhood, even without treatment (Jacobi, Schmitz, & Agras, 2008; Mascola, Bryson, & Agras, 2010). By contrast, the more severe food avoidance or restriction in ARFID does not remit on its own. Instead, the food avoidance and restriction that define ARFID can lead to medical or mental health consequences that further exacerbate food avoidance and restriction and serve to maintain the illness (Thomas et al., 2017a). Risks of such eating patterns include poor growth, diabetes, cardiovascular disease, fatigue, poor self-esteem, family mealtime conflict, peer social isolation, and difficulties with relationships and work. Indeed, quality of life is significantly impacted in ARFID. In an epidemiological study, individuals with ARFID ($n = 46$, ages 24–60 years, living in Australia) had lower mental health–related quality of life and more days of being unable to function due to emotional or physical health problems than people without eating disorders (Hay et al., 2017). Similarly, in an online study, adults with symptoms of ARFID ($n = 82$) self-reported greater internalizing distress than those without ARFID, and comparable levels of distress to individuals with symptoms of other eating disorders (Zickgraf, Franklin, & Rozin, 2016).

Much of what is known about avoidant or restrictive eating is based on the feeding disorders literature prior to 2013. While the ARFID diagnosis is new, the research in this area is nascent and has proliferated since the publication of *DSM-5*.

Prevalence

Although little epidemiological research has been conducted to date, available data suggest that ARFID is as common as other better-known eating disorders. In an Australian population-based survey of male and female adolescents and adults ages 15 years and older, Hay et al. (2017) found that the three-month point prevalence of ARFID was 0.3% (95% confidence interval 0.1–0.5) in 2013 and 0.3% (95% confidence interval 0.2–0.6) in 2014. Notably, these prevalence estimates were similar to those for other specific eating disorders (0.4% and 0.5% for anorexia nervosa, and 1.1% and 1.2% for bulimia nervosa), and lower than for the heterogeneous other specified feeding or eating disorder (OSFED) category (3.2%). A second published study reported a point prevalence of 3.2% (i.e., 46 of 1,444) in children ages 8–13 years surveyed through schools in Switzerland in which students self-reported symptoms consistent with an ARFID diagnosis via questionnaire (Kurz et al., 2015). Youth with self-reported ARFID were more likely to be either underweight or overweight compared to youth who did not report ARFID symptoms (Kurz et al., 2015). In contrast to other eating disorders, which predominate in females, in both of these epidemiological studies, males and females were equally likely to be diagnosed with ARFID (Hay et al., 2017; Kurz et al., 2015). In fact, in our own team's study at Boston-area pediatric gastrointestinal clinics, the majority of youth with ARFID were male (22 of 33; 67%) (Eddy et al., 2015).

A handful of studies have examined ARFID prevalence in specialty services via medical record review, estimating that roughly 5% of children (Norris et al., 2014) and up to 15% of adolescents (Fisher et al., 2014; Forman et al., 2014; Ornstein et al, 2013) evaluated in pediatric or adolescent medicine eating disorder programs could be diagnosed with ARFID based on a retrospective application of criteria. ARFID was found even more frequently (22.5%) in a record review of 7–17-year-olds participating in a partial hospital (day) program for eating disorders (Nicely et al., 2014).

While less is known yet about the relative occurrence of ARFID within different racial or ethnic minority groups, ARFID has already been reported outside North America, Europe, and Australia. For example, Nakai et al. (2016) reported that between 9% and 11% of individuals aged 15–40 years seeking treatment for an eating disorder through a hospital-based eating disorder program in Japan could be diagnosed with ARFID. Similarly, among adults receiving inpatient eating disorders treatment in Japan, Tanaka et al. (2015) reported that 8.9% were diagnosed with ARFID. Further, a recent case report documented ARFID in a school-aged boy of Colombian descent presenting for treatment in Canada (Schermbrucker et al., 2017).

Thus, these emerging data demonstrate that ARFID occurs in males and females in the general pediatric, adolescent, and adult population, and furthermore that individuals with ARFID present to eating disorder services. Notably, the majority of these published studies capture patient encounters occurring before the publication of *DSM-5* and, therefore, prior to both clinical and popular recognition of ARFID. Taken together, these findings suggest that the actual prevalence of ARFID may be underestimated in published reports.

Distinction from Classical Eating Disorders

ARFID is different from anorexia nervosa, bulimia nervosa, binge eating disorder, and related forms of OSFED. The primary distinction is that, in ARFID, avoidant or restrictive eating behaviors are not motivated by shape or weight concerns. Whereas desire for a thin ideal drives typical dieting, and overvaluation of body shape and weight is considered to be a core feature of classical eating disorders, in ARFID, shape and weight concerns are typically absent or within the normal range. The prototypical low-weight patient with ARFID, characterized by lack of interest in eating, may endorse unhappiness about being so thin and feel proud and visibly happy with weight gain during treatment. By contrast, the low-weight patient with a classical eating disorder will express frank fat phobia or engage in behaviors that thwart weight gain, and will typically experience intense anxiety during weight restoration. Furthermore, the preferred foods for individuals with ARFID, which are often energy-dense, high-fat, and high-carbohydrate, differ vastly from those preferred by individuals with more classical eating disorders, which are often low-calorie and include foods that individuals with ARFID actively avoid (e.g., fruits and vegetables). Indeed, as part of an ongoing study of low-weight eating disorders, our team examined food records over a four-day period and found that individuals with ARFID consumed a significantly smaller percentage of their calories from protein compared to those with anorexia nervosa (Izquierdo et al., 2018). Notably, ARFID is also distinguished from other feeding disorders including pica – characterized by intake of non-nutritive, non-food substances – and rumination disorder, which is defined by repeated regurgitation and re-chewing, re-swallowing, or spitting out previously ingested foods.

Clinical impressions about the distinctions between ARFID and classical eating disorders are borne out in emerging data as well. Data from adolescent medicine clinic record reviews suggest that those with ARFID are generally younger (Forman et al., 2014; Norris et al., 2014) and more likely to be male (Forman et al., 2014; Norris et al., 2014) than those with other eating disorders. Compared to individuals with anorexia nervosa or bulimia nervosa, individuals with ARFID predictably score lower on measures of eating disorder psychopathology (Nakai et al., 2016; Nicely et al., 2014; Ornstein et al., 2017). One contrast of clinical interest with diagnostic implications exists between individuals with putative ARFID and those with anorexia nervosa who deny or minimize their experience of weight and shape concerns (non-fat phobic anorexia nervosa; Becker, Thomas, & Pike, 2009). Because both disorders present with low weight in the absence of frank body image disturbance, differential diagnosis can be challenging (Thomas, Hartmann, & Killgore, 2013). Recognizing that explicit endorsements (e.g., of fat phobia) do not always match internal beliefs, our team used measures of implicit associations with dieting to explore between-group differences. In a sample of low-weight adolescent females, we tested the hypothesis that individuals with anorexia nervosa, whether or not they explicitly express fear of weight gain, have implicit beliefs biased in favor of thinness and dieting, while those with ARFID do not. Consistent with our hypothesis, we found that implicit bias toward dieting was high among those with anorexia nervosa and did not differ between those who did versus did not endorse fat phobia. By contrast, in ARFID, bias toward dieting was lower than in anorexia nervosa and did not differ from healthy controls (Izquierdo et al., 2017).

Yet in spite of endorsing different rationales for food avoidance and restriction, a subset of individuals with ARFID are just as low weight as those with anorexia nervosa (Nakai et al., 2016; Nicely et al., 2014). Interestingly, available data suggest that individuals with ARFID and ARFID-like symptoms have typically lost less weight immediately prior to seeking treatment compared to individuals with anorexia nervosa or related presentations (Pinhas et al., 2017; Strandjord et al., 2015). Instead, those with low-weight ARFID appear to have been chronically low weight prior to seeking treatment, rather than experiencing the acute weight loss that so often characterizes anorexia nervosa (Strandjord et al., 2015).

Speaking to medical severity, one preliminary study found that at presentation for treatment, 77% of individuals with ARFID (20/26) had bone density Z-scores of < -1. A further 25% (7/26) had Z-scores of < -2, indicating they were already in the osteoporosis range (Norris et al., 2014). Bone loss was greater in the ARFID group than in those with anorexia nervosa in that particular study (Norris et al., 2014) but comparable to rates of osteopenia and osteoporosis in anorexia nervosa that have been reported in the literature (Misra & Klibanski, 2014).

The psychiatric comorbidity profiles of individuals with ARFID also differ somewhat from those of individuals with other eating disorders. Clinically speaking, anxiety and depression seem to co-occur in ARFID just as often as they do in anorexia nervosa or bulimia nervosa. However, other conditions including autism spectrum disorder, oppositional defiant disorder, and attention deficit/hyperactivity disorder may be more common in ARFID than in the other eating disorders. The high prevalence of eating and feeding difficulties in autism spectrum disorder is well documented (e.g., Berry et al., 2015; Buie et al., 2010; Emond et al., 2010; Lucarelli et al., 2017; McElhanon et al., 2014). However, little data about psychiatric comorbidity and personality styles in ARFID compared to the other eating disorders are available. In a sample of 36 children and adolescents presenting for one of our team's ongoing research studies of ARFID, we found that 39% met criteria for a comorbid psychiatric disorder via structured clinical interview, with anxiety disorders (9/36) and attention deficit/hyperactivity disorder (4/36) being most common. Our data may underestimate the comorbidity with lower functioning autism spectrum disorders, as IQ < 70 was an exclusion criterion for the study. Very little data speak to different cognitive styles in individuals with ARFID versus anorexia nervosa. In a second study, we compared low-weight females with ARFID to those with anorexia nervosa on a task of monetary delay discounting, that is, the degree to which the subjective value of a reward decreases based on delay of receipt. In anorexia nervosa, delay discounting is often low; in other words, those with anorexia nervosa have a tendency to forgo smaller immediate rewards (e.g., high-calorie foods) in favor of larger long-term rewards (e.g., a thin body). By contrast, our preliminary data suggest that those with ARFID are more similar to healthy controls in that they were more likely to choose immediate than delayed rewards, in comparison to those with anorexia nervosa. These findings suggest individuals with ARFID may have less self-control or greater impulsivity than those with anorexia nervosa (who are often abstemious) (Coniglio et al., 2017). These findings seem consistent with our clinical impression that, in ARFID, food restriction is less calculated and purposeful than in classical eating disorders.

Finally, diagnostic crossover among the classical eating disorders has been well documented (Eddy et al., 2008; Milos et al., 2005), but whether crossover from ARFID to any of the other eating disorders commonly occurs has not yet been studied. There are data to suggest that there may be continuity between childhood feeding problems and adolescent or adult eating disorders. Some longitudinal studies suggest that childhood digestive problems and selective eating (eating little, pickiness, eating slowly, low interest) increase the risk for anorexia nervosa, while digestive problems, pica, and dieting increase the risk for bulimia nervosa (Marchi & Cohen, 1990). Further, another study found that childhood conflicts around eating and difficulty with family meals, which were both associated with picky eating, also increased the risk of developing eating disorders in adolescence (Kotler et al., 2001). Conversely, it is possible that some of those with ARFID, particularly those who are low weight, may develop secondary body image disturbance during the course of illness or even treatment. In an ongoing National Institutes of Health (NIH)-funded study entitled 'Neurobiological and Behavioral Risk Mechanisms of Youth Avoidant/ Restrictive Eating Trajectories' (1R01MH108595), our team is actively exploring the course of illness for those with ARFID and thus more information on the potential for crossover is emergent.

Etiology

The causes of ARFID are unknown. Some data suggest that there may be biological contributors, but biomarkers have been largely understudied and their putative relationship to frank ARFID, versus picky eating, is not known. While there are no twin or adoption studies of ARFID specifically, twin and adoption studies of related traits suggest that taste preferences are at least partially genetic (Breen, Plomin, & Wardle, 2006). Anecdotally, many of our patients have shared that their first-degree relatives (e.g., parents, siblings) also have avoidant/restrictive

eating, further highlighting the possibility of a genetic component to risk. We hypothesize that certain biological factors reflected in sensory sensitivity, anxiety, and low appetite play an etiologic role, and these hypotheses are described more fully in Chapter 4.

A body of research has focused on the role of the family meal environment and family dynamics around eating as they relate to early feeding and development of healthy or unhealthy eating behaviors in typically developing youth (see Savage, Fisher, & Birch, 2007 for reviews). Indeed, parents provide the first models of eating, creating an atmosphere (e.g., warm and relaxed versus harsh and tense) and setting expectations for mealtimes in terms of food volume, variety, and pace. Ellyn Satter has described a *division in responsibility in feeding* in which parents set the expectation of *what*, *when*, and *where* meals will be served, and then children decide *whether* and *how much* to eat (Satter, 1986). To promote healthy eating in normally developing youth, parents can make a variety of healthy foods available and model eating them in variety and in healthy amounts (Savage et al., 2007). There is evidence to suggest that parents with greater food neophobia have children who have greater food neophobia and higher levels of picky eating (Dovey et al., 2008). Further, there are data to suggest that in population-level studies, parental pressure to eat is associated with child low weight, whereas parental restrictions on child eating are associated with increased weight gain (Birch & Fisher, 2000). However, we highly doubt that parents cause ARFID. Indeed, the application of these data and recommendations to youth with the more severe form of picky eating and frank ARFID is not clear. In our experience, by the time families present for treatment, they routinely describe having tried *everything* – pressure, no pressure; rewards, punishment – suggesting that the recommendations that may be useful for most healthy children cannot be readily applied to those with ARFID.

Indeed, other environmental factors including agricultural subsidies, fast-food advertising, busy two-career families, and the high cost of fruits and vegetables compared to processed foods make it difficult for parents to present their children with a wide variety of healthy foods at all eating opportunities (Brownell & Horgen, 2004). Furthermore, the rise of 'kids' menus' and child-targeted food products (e.g., pre-packed lunch packs, squeezable yogurts and purees) that encourage homogenized food choices in youth may also contribute to the development of avoidant or restrictive eating patterns.

At the intersection of biological and environmental contributors are medical and psychiatric comorbidities that can challenge eating and feeding, setting the stage for the development of ARFID. For example, food allergies that require certain restrictions may increase vulnerability in some to more food avoidance or restriction. Similarly, autism spectrum disorder, which is associated with increased sensory sensitivity and cognitive inflexibility, sets the stage for selective eating, which will become entrenched for some. In addition, medical advances have meant an increase in preterm births in the past few decades. Individuals who are born early are more likely to have low birth weight and medical complications that can challenge early nutrition (Kumar et al., 2017; Villar et al., 2018), which may also increase risk for feeding disorders.

In sum, the clinical significance of ARFID is evident in the pattern of nutritional and psychological compromise it leaves in its wake. All available evidence demonstrates that ARFID is a real, identifiable, and heterogeneous problem. ARFID appears to occur at rates similar to other eating disorders and to affect males and females of all ages. While it shares some commonalities with classical eating disorders – including patterns of aberrant food avoidance and restriction, medical risks, and comorbid anxiety – ARFID is also clearly distinct. Unlike the classical eating disorders, the core psychopathology of ARFID is not overvaluation of weight and shape, and clinical impressions coupled with preliminary data demonstrate comorbidity and personality characteristics that also separate ARFID from anorexia nervosa and bulimia nervosa. Of course, similarities between ARFID and feeding, eating, and anxiety disorders may also suggest the possible efficacy of similar treatment strategies.

2

Overview of Existing Treatments for Feeding, Eating, and Anxiety Disorders

ARFID exhibits similarities in clinical presentation to pediatric feeding disorders, classical eating disorders, and anxiety disorders. Because there is a strong evidence base supporting the efficacy of psychological treatments for these disorders, it logically follows that Cognitive-Behavioral Therapy for Avoidant/Restrictive Food Intake Disorder (CBT-AR) would draw from them both general principles and specific techniques (Table 2.1). However, because ARFID is a novel disorder that is itself quite heterogeneous, there are important limitations to applying existing therapies. In what follows we describe evidence-based interventions for feeding, eating, and anxiety disorders; discuss their potential application to ARFID; and highlight limitations to their adaptation that underscore the need for a novel approach (i.e., CBT-AR).

Pediatric Feeding Disorders

As ARFID is a reformulation of *DSM-IV* feeding disorder of infancy and early childhood, successful techniques for increasing food volume and variety in children could be relevant for individuals with ARFID across the life span. Existing interventions for pediatric feeding disorders vary but can be roughly divided into behavior therapy and play-based systematic desensitization techniques.

Existing approaches. Behavior therapy is the only treatment for pediatric feeding disorders with well-documented empirical support (Lukens & Silverman, 2014; Sharp et al., 2010). The majority of studies evaluating the treatment of pediatric feeding disorders are single-case designs (see Sharp et al., 2010 for review) or non-randomized studies (see Lukens & Silverman, 2014 for review). Typical pediatric feeding interventions from applied behavior analysis include extinction-based procedures, differential reinforcement, environmental enrichment, and antecedent manipulation (Sharp et al., 2010; Williams & Foxx, 2007; Williams & Seiverling, 2016). Most published

interventions involve a combination of these techniques. Extinction-based techniques involve persisting with a reasonable feeding demand while simultaneously ignoring problematic behavior. For example, if a child is refusing all food and crying and gagging during mealtime, the therapist might put the spoon to the patient's lips and not remove the spoon until the patient opens his or her lips and accepts a bite. In differential reinforcement, the therapist reinforces positive feeding behaviors (e.g., providing verbal praise or a reward for bite acceptance) and ignores undesirable behaviors (e.g., gagging, spitting out food). To create an enriched feeding environment, the therapist may provide non-contingent access to preferred items (e.g., books, toys, television) for the duration of a meal regardless of the patient's feeding behavior. Lastly, antecedent manipulation involves reducing the feeding demand to make bite acceptance more likely, such as by providing a puree rather than a solid form of the same food, or providing very small bites of a novel food. Nearly all pediatric feeding disorder treatments involve a parent-training component, to facilitate generalization of feeding skills from the clinic to the home environment.

Another technique commonly applied in clinical practice is systematic desensitization accompanied by play. The Sequential Oral Sensory (SOS) approach (Toomey Ross, & Kortsha, 2014) is one such example. Although SOS also includes multiple interventions from behavior therapy, occupational therapy, and speech therapy, the centerpiece is systematic desensitization to novel foods using play as a competing response to anxiety. In SOS, the therapist exposes patients to a variety of foods and gently shapes the patient toward consuming the foods through modeling and play starting with merely interacting with the food, then touching it, smelling it, licking it, and, finally, tasting it, thereby ascending a hierarchy depicting the steps to eating (Toomey et al., 2014).

Table 2.1 Existing treatments from which CBT-AR draws general principles and specific techniques

Disorder	Treatment	General principles and specific techniques drawn from each treatment to develop CBT-AR
Pediatric feeding disorders	ABA	Contingency management
		Positive reinforcement
		Antecedent manipulation (i.e., reducing demand on bite size)
	SysD	Gradual exposure to novel foods (e.g., look, touch, smell, taste)
		Repeated exposure to enhance liking
Eating disorders	CBT for eating disorders	Psychoeducation about the effects of being underweight
		Lengthening treatment for those who are underweight
		Self-monitoring of food intake
		Regular eating
		Cognitive-behavioral formulation
		Relapse prevention planning
	FBT for anorexia nervosa	Parental management of re-feeding and supervision of meals and snacks (for youth who are underweight)
		Family meal (for youth who are underweight)
Anxiety disorders	CBT for specific phobia	Psychoeducation about the ineffectiveness of avoidance in reducing long-term anxiety
		Fear and avoidance hierarchy
		Exteroceptive exposures to distressing external stimuli
		Self-rating of Subjective Units of Distress
	CBT for panic disorder	Psychoeducation about hypervigilance to internal stimuli
		Interoceptive exposures to distressing internal stimuli
		Self-rating of Subjective Units of Distress

Note: ABA = applied behavior analysis; SysD = systematic desensitization; CBT = cognitive-behavioral therapy; FBT = family-based treatment

For example, the therapist might pretend a slice of apple is a truck. First the therapist might play independently by driving the apple around the table, and then, when the child shows interest, the therapist might drive the apple up the child's arm. Once the child is comfortable touching the apple slice, it might become an airplane buzzing around the patient's head, getting closer and closer to his nose and mouth. The hope is that, with increasing exposure and proximity to the mouth, the patient will become progressively more comfortable with the novel food and increasingly willing to smell, lick, or taste it. In contrast to strictly behavioral approaches, the explicit feeding demand is low in this child-led approach. In other words, the SOS therapist does not apply direct pressure and instead follows the child's lead to determine readiness to take a bite. In one study, systematic desensitization was just as effective as operant conditioning in promoting the acceptance of novel foods in children with selective eating (Marshall, Hill, Ware, Ziviani, & Dodrill, 2015). However, other elements of SOS, such as play-based techniques, occupational therapy, and speech therapy, are commonly offered in the community but less well studied in comparison to behavioral treatments (Lukens & Silverman, 2014; Sharp et al., 2010).

Principles and techniques that appear in CBT-AR. Other groups have published case reports and case series on the application of contingency management (Murphy & Zlomke, 2016; Nicholls et al., 2001) and systematic desensitization (Nicholls et al., 2001; Zucker, Covington, & Petry, 2015) to ARFID and related presentations. Similarly, in CBT-AR, we borrow techniques from applied behavior analysis, including contingency management (e.g., rewards for practicing with novel foods), differential reinforcement (e.g., verbal praise for trying new foods in session), and antecedent manipulation (i.e., allowing patients to take small bite sizes for the first exposure to novel foods). We also utilize systematic desensitization for the introduction of novel foods (e.g., look, touch, smell, taste) and leverage repeated exposure to enhance liking (similar to Zucker et al., 2015 and Toomey et al., 2014).

The treatment of pediatric feeding disorders is not without controversy, particularly regarding the degree to which parents or therapists should place pressure on children to change their eating. While most behavioral therapies involve repeated exposure to non-preferred foods and positive reinforcement for food consumption, some clinicians contend that parents should not force their children to eat because it could damage the parent–child relationship and will ultimately only encourage further food refusal (e.g., Rowell, McGlothlin, and Morris, 2015; Satter, 1987). Our view reflected in CBT-AR is that while gentle approaches with no expectation for behavior change might be appropriate for normally developing children, ARFID is a psychiatric disorder that typically requires intensive intervention to change eating patterns that have become entrenched, impairing, and – at times – life-threatening.

Limitations in the application to ARFID. There are limitations in applying treatments for pediatric feeding disorders to individuals with ARFID. Perhaps most notably, existing interventions for feeding disorders and related presentations target infants, toddlers, and young children (Benoit et al., 2000; Byars et al., 2003; Chatoor, 2009; Cooke and Webber, 2015; Greer et al., 2007; Marshall, Hill, Ware, Ziviani, and Dodrill, 2015; Paul et al., 2007; Pizzo et al., 2009; Toomey, 2014; Williams et al., 2008). Interventions designed for young children typically include techniques that may not be developmentally appropriate for older children, adolescents, or adults. For example, applying non-removal of spoon assumes that a caregiver is physically feeding the patient. Similarly, the types of rewards employed in most contingency management programs for pediatric feeding disorders (e.g., stickers, additional playtime) are not attractive or appropriate for adolescents and adults. Also of note, treatments for pediatric feeding disorders are typically purely behavioral and do not address cognitive distortions that may maintain avoidant or restrictive eating in more cognitively mature patients.

Eating Disorders

Classical eating disorders such as anorexia nervosa and bulimia nervosa exhibit obvious similarities to ARFID, most notably restrictive eating and – in many cases – low weight. The best-studied evidence-based treatments for eating disorders include cognitive-behavioral therapy (CBT; Fairburn, 2008; Waller et al., 2007) for adolescents and adults with bulimia nervosa, binge eating disorder, and other OSFED; and family-based treatment (FBT) for children and adolescents with anorexia nervosa (Lock and Le Grange, 2015).

Existing approaches. Perhaps the most well-known form of manualized CBT for eating disorders is Fairburn's (2008) enhanced version (i.e., CBT-E). CBT-E comprises four stages over 20 sessions (up to 40 sessions for those who are underweight). In Stage 1, the patient is oriented to the treatment through psychoeducation on the link between dietary restraint and binge eating, the ineffectiveness of purging to subvert caloric absorption, and the predictable psychological and physical effects of under-eating. The therapist asks the patient to self-monitor all eating episodes as well as associated thoughts and feelings, in order to identify patterns. Based on this self-monitoring, the therapist facilitates the creation of an individualized formulation that identifies the maintaining mechanisms of the eating disorder, including areas for intervention. The therapist then prescribes a schedule of regular eating to prevent the patient from become so hungry that a binge is inevitable, and to provide opportunities to increase caloric intake if weight gain is necessary. In Stage 2, the patient and therapist evaluate progress to date, identify barriers to continued change, and select the maintaining mechanisms to target in Stage 3. During Stage 3, the therapist implements modules as necessary to the patient's specific presentation. For example, if the patient endorses overvaluation of weight and shape, the therapist will help the patient identify other areas of life that are being neglected due to the eating disorder and encourage the patient to actively seek out activities in those domains. Similarly, if the patient is engaging in frequent shape-checking behaviors, the therapist will help the patient reduce these. Depending on the patient's specific presentation, the therapist may also elect to address perfectionism, mood intolerance, low self-esteem, and/or interpersonal difficulties in Stage 3. In Stage 4, the patient focuses on relapse prevention and planning for the future. Other versions of CBT for eating disorders contain similar key interventions (e.g., Waller et al., 2007).

For youth with anorexia nervosa, FBT (Lock and Le Grange, 2015) is the best-studied approach. FBT is based on the premise that the young person cannot control his or her symptoms, making it imperative that the parents step in to take charge of re-feeding. FBT comprises three phases over 20 sessions. In Phase I, the therapist orchestrates a grave scene highlighting the seriousness of anorexia nervosa and the difficulty in recovering, and organizes an in-session family meal as an opportunity to coach the parents to support the patient in taking one more bite than the patient intended. The therapist asks the parents to supervise every meal and snack during this phase to ensure that the patient is eating sufficient calories for weight restoration. For the remainder of Phase I, the therapist supports the parents in externalizing the illness (i.e., identifying the healthy part of the patient as separate from anorexia nervosa), reducing criticism toward the patient, and supporting further weight gain. As the patient approaches a healthy weight, the therapist moves to Phase II, in which the parents experiment with handing some control back to the patient (e.g., allowing the patient to plate his or her own meals, eat snacks without parental supervision). Finally, in Phase III, the therapist helps the family recognize the developmental milestones that the patient may have missed due to the eating disorder, and helps the patient return to the pursuits of normal development (e.g., dating, going away to college).

Principles and techniques that appear in CBT-AR. Due to similarities between ARFID and other eating disorders, other groups have described the application of CBT techniques such as psychoeducation about the effects of underweight (Lesser et al., 2017) and self-monitoring of food intake and associated thoughts and feelings (Nicholls et al., 2001) to the treatment of ARFID and related presentations. Still others have adapted FBT for individuals with avoidant or restrictive eating (Fitzpatrick et al., 2015; Lesser et al., 2017; Murray et al., 2013; Ornstein et al., 2017; Rhodes, Prunty, and Madden, 2009). However, these applications have been described in case studies, case series, and retrospective chart reviews, and there are no published manuals available for dissemination. CBT-AR draws several principles and techniques from existing evidence-based treatments for eating

disorders. From CBT-E, CBT-AR incorporates psychoeducation about the effects of underweight, self-monitoring of food intake, creating an individualized formulation, regular eating, lengthening the treatment for those who are underweight, and relapse prevention planning. CBT-AR is also similar in structure to CBT-E in that both are modular treatments designed to treat a heterogeneous patient population, in which the therapist selects the Stage 3 modules most appropriate to the patient's specific symptoms.

From FBT, CBT-AR draws parental management of feeding and supervision of meals and snacks, as well as the family meal intervention, for the subset of youth with ARFID who are underweight. Furthermore, like FBT, the family-supported version of CBT-AR engages families to unite against the illness. In anorexia nervosa, engaging families is crucial due to the egosyntonic nature of food restriction. Although ARFID is typically less egosyntonic than anorexia nervosa, engaging families is equally important, because youth with ARFID often lack recognition that their eating is a problem and thus lack motivation to change.

Limitations in the application to ARFID. Due to important differences between ARFID and classical eating disorders, existing approaches cannot be applied to ARFID without significant modification. The fundamental premise of CBT-E is that the core psychopathology of the eating disorder is an inappropriate overemphasis on shape and weight in evaluating self-worth. Because body image disturbance is absent in ARFID, many of the CBT-E Stage 3 interventions are inappropriate. For example, exercises such as examining the frequency of body checking and evaluating the impact of breaking rigid dietary rules on one's weight are of little relevance to individuals with ARFID, who rarely have more than normative shape or weight concerns.

Similarly, FBT cannot be applied to ARFID without modification because the primary focus of FBT is weight restoration, and not all patients with ARFID are underweight. Even when patients are underweight, FBT for anorexia nervosa is predicated on orchestrating an acute crisis in which the therapist describes the patient as starving to death as a result of precipitous weight loss. In ARFID, the patient has often been chronically underweight, making the low-weight crisis at treatment presentation seem less acute to parents. Indeed, when treating individuals with ARFID who are underweight, the therapist must typically focus on frank weight *gain*, rather than weight *restoration*, making additional psychoeducation and motivational enhancement for the parents crucial to treatment success. Lastly, FBT focuses primarily on increasing the volume rather than variety. When a young person has AN, parents typically facilitate weight gain by increasing the portion size of a range of energy-dense foods that the patient already accepts (or at least previously accepted). By contrast, in ARFID, weight gain may be achieved through initial focus on increasing the volume of preferred (high-calorie) foods, but there is still often a need to introduce foods that are completely novel to achieve adequate variety.

Anxiety Disorders

Anxiety disorders are characterized by excessive fear or apprehension about a future threat. In ARFID, food restriction or avoidance is often driven by anxiety and has commonalities with specific phobias, post-traumatic stress disorder, and panic disorder. Individuals with sensory sensitivity describe food neophobia and worry that they will be disgusted by an unfamiliar food; those with fear of aversive consequences predict that eating will cause a traumatic event. Across ARFID presentations, particularly those with an apparent lack of interest in eating or food, individuals are often highly attuned to physiologic sensations (e.g., of fullness), which they perceive as uncomfortable or even dangerous. A normal reaction to anxiety is avoidance of the anxiety-provoking stimulus. Avoidance provides relief from fear in the short term by taking away the fear-inducing stimulus, but may ultimately increase anxiety in the long term. Namely, the immediate reduction in anxiety following avoidance reinforces avoidance behavior; further, it does not allow the individual the opportunity to face his or her fears and either disconfirm predictions or learn to cope with feared outcomes.

Existing approaches. CBT has strong support for the treatment of anxiety disorders (e.g., Craske, Antony, & Barlow, 2006; Craske & Barlow, 2007), in which the primary intervention is exposure to feared stimuli to promote new corrective learning. Exposure, in short, means facing fears. Exposure can be imaginal or *in vivo*, and can be to external (e.g., feared foods) or internal (e.g., physical fullness) stimuli. Exposure is an outgrowth of early work describing the practice of systematic desensitization as a

transdiagnostic treatment for anxiety. Systematic desensitization involved imaginal or *in vivo* exposure to a feared stimuli in concert with engagement in relaxation (e.g., deep breathing), thought to be a competing response. Subsequent literature demonstrated that even without relaxation, exposure reduced anxiety, and that *in vivo* exposures were more successful than imaginal ones (Barlow, Leitenburg, Agras, & Wincze, 1969). In what follows we review the practice of exteroceptive and interoceptive exposure in anxiety management. We highlight strategies featured in the treatment of specific phobias and panic disorder, appreciating that these interventions are often applied transdiagnostically across CBT for anxiety disorders.

Exposure has demonstrated strong evidence in the treatment of specific phobias. For specific phobias, defined as excessive fears of a specific stimuli or situation (e.g., snakes, spiders, enclosed spaces), exposure involves progressive approach to, rather than avoidance of, the feared stimuli. CBT for specific phobia begins with psychoeducation about anxiety and fear learning, and explaining the idea that humans are more likely to learn to be fearful of certain situations or stimuli, particularly those that may have conferred a survival advantage. For example, someone who developed a stomach flu may be vulnerable to developing a fear of the food eaten right before the vomiting started even if the food was unrelated to the illness, because taking care with eating might guard against future sickness. Explaining prepared fear and the pathways of fear acquisition can be instrumental in the formulation and setting up the frame for exposure as the key intervention.

Patients are asked to identify and rate – using a 0–100 subjective units of distress (SUDS) scale – the feared stimuli, associated physical sensations, and any avoidance or safety behaviors they may engage in to begin to inform the development of a fear and avoidance hierarchy. For each feared stimuli, they are asked to identify thoughts and predictions, which will be tested via behavioral experiments (i.e., exposure). Exposure is introduced as the most effective intervention for targeting specific fears. Understanding what the patient most fears will happen in any given situation on the hierarchy allows the therapist to most effectively support the patient in gaining exposure to his or her feared outcomes and thus engage in new learning. With therapist support, the individual creates a fear and avoidance hierarchy, ranking feared stimuli from most to least anxiety-provoking along with corresponding SUDS ratings.

Exposures must be long enough, or occur enough times, to promote new learning, giving the patient an opportunity to accept that his or her feared prediction is unlikely or that if it does occur, he or she can cope with it and the associated anxiety. Imaginal exposures may be helpful for some as a first step before *in vivo* exposure. While safety behaviors may be used for initial exposures, the patient must ultimately work to eliminate them in order to maximize the corrective learning. For individuals who also have a fear of fear-based physical sensations, interoceptive exposure to different bodily sensations (e.g., heart racing, shortness of breath) can also be an integral part of treatment, and can even be engaged during the exteroceptive exposures. With the support of a therapist, the individual gradually moves through a hierarchy of fears, giving a SUDS rating each time, and building a new understanding that his or her fears are exaggerated and/or that he or she would be able to cope with feared outcomes.

Note that there is no set number of exposures needed to treat specific phobias. In fact, even single-session exposures can be effective (Ollendick & Davis, 2013; Zlomke & Davis, 2008), but for gains to be maintained over the long term, ongoing exposure (or practice) is typically needed. Because it is now understood that fear conditioning is not extinguished, but rather new learning about the safety of the stimulus/situation occurs, strategies that maximize generalizability of new learning are encouraged to reduce risk that the original fear will return. For example, it is recommended that patients take all opportunities – big or small – to practice exposures whenever they arise, and to practice exposures across contexts (Craske et al., 2006).

Panic disorder is characterized by recurrent panic attacks, which are discrete episodes of intense fear associated with physical signs that represent a sudden activation of the fight-or-flight response and are often experienced as occurring out of the blue. When the fight-or-flight system is activated in the absence of any external threat, the individual misinterprets the signs themselves to mean that something internal is wrong (e.g., 'I must be dying'). Consequently, the individual with panic disorder becomes scared of the physical signs, which he/she perceive to be dangerous. In panic disorder, unexpected internal sensations have become cues for fear, which then intensifies the fear response (Boettcher, Brake, & Barlow, 2016). Treatment involves psychoeducation about anxiety and panic as naturally occurring states, framing the physical sensations experienced during a panic attack as adaptive responses to the body's detection of danger or fear. Rather than being dangerous, the signs of anxiety are reframed to be understood as survival mechanisms. Yet in the case of panic disorder, these internal signals are being hyper-attended to, over-interpreted, and then exacerbated by fearful interpretation. Following psychoeducation, treatment for panic disorder involves exposure to these physical sensations to lessen fear of the physical sensations themselves. Interoceptive exposures are carried out in the same graduated way as exteroceptive exposures with the objective of promoting habituation to the physical sensations and corrective learning.

Principles and techniques that appear in CBT-AR. Given the similarities between ARFID and anxiety disorders, other groups have published case reports and case series describing the application of CBT for anxiety techniques to ARFID and related presentations (Bryant-Waugh, 2013; Fischer, Luiselli, & Dove, 2015; King, Urbach, & Stewart, 2015; Lopes et al., 2014) or described their integration within the broader context of FBT (Lesser et al., 2017; Ornstein et al., 2017). In CBT-AR, we borrow principles of CBT for anxiety disorders, particularly for the treatment of fear of aversive consequences and apparent lack of interest in eating or food. Specifically, we provide psychoeducation about the ineffectiveness of avoidance in reducing long-term anxiety. We co-create a fear and avoidance hierarchy to facilitate practices of exposure to both external stimuli and internal sensations to promote new learning. Exteroceptive exposures are particularly useful for individuals who present with a fear of aversive consequences and exposure is used as the primary intervention for addressing this maintaining mechanism of ARFID. In Stage 3 of CBT-AR, those with a fear of aversive consequences are guided through graded exposures to feared foods. Interoceptive exposures can also be useful for the fear mechanism, for example, when individuals are avoiding eating due to fear of sensations of nausea (a cue for vomiting) or pain. As in CBT for specific phobia, we ask patients to make SUDS ratings during all exposures. From CBT for panic disorder, we borrow psychoeducation about hypervigilance to internal sensations as a maintaining mechanism of anxiety. In Stage 3 of CBT-AR, for individuals with an apparent lack of interest in eating or food as a maintaining mechanism, interoceptive exposures can often be instrumental in helping them increase tolerance of physical bloating, fullness, and nausea. Further, in these individuals with restricted intake, such interoceptive exposures often have the salutary side effect of facilitating appetite increase as well. As in the treatment of panic disorder, individuals are asked to make SUDS ratings during interoceptive exposures to track habituation.

Limitations in the application to ARFID. Of course, there are limitations to the application of CBT for anxiety disorders to ARFID. First, although the hallmark feature of ARFID is the avoidance of specific foods or the restriction of overall amount, it is unclear whether this avoidance is always driven by anxiety. In some cases, patients cite disgust or unfamiliarity as reasons for avoiding specific foods, or overall lack of appetite. Thus anxiety techniques are likely to apply only to a subset of cases. Second, even in cases where anxiety is clearly present, the application of a fear and avoidance hierarchy is rarely sufficient for symptom resolution; most patients need additional support to establish a regular schedule of eating, gain weight, and improve appetite. Lastly, because individuals with anxiety disorders typically describe hypersensitivity to sympathetic nervous

system activation more generally, some interoceptive exposures (e.g., hyperventilation) are not relevant for ARFID, in which patients more often describe heightened reactivity to gastrointestinal sensations (e.g., bloating, fullness, nausea) specifically.

The Need for a Novel Approach

Due to similarities in clinical presentation, CBT-AR borrows basic principles and specific techniques from existing evidence-based treatments for feeding, eating, and anxiety disorders. However, because of the clinical heterogeneity of ARFID, these techniques are neither necessary nor sufficient to resolve ARFID symptoms fully, and a novel approach is clearly needed. CBT-AR is distinguished by its focus on ARFID specifically, combining selected interventions from prior treatments as well as novel interventions developed by our team. Moreover, whereas prior applications of existing treatments have been described in case reports, case series, and retrospective chart review, CBT-AR is a manualized treatment appropriate for prospective testing in randomized controlled trials. Lastly, CBT-AR is a single treatment approach that can be applied across the life span and widely disseminated, obviating the need for busy clinicians to learn multiple therapies.

Chapter 3

Assessment of ARFID

A comprehensive psychiatric and medical evaluation is crucial to determine the appropriateness, format, and interventions of CBT-AR. Specifically, the purpose of the psychiatric evaluation is to assess the presence and severity of ARFID, including the primary ARFID maintaining mechanism(s). The purpose of the medical evaluation is to ensure that the avoidant or restrictive eating is not entirely due to a co-occurring medical condition, confirm that the patient is medically stable for outpatient care, and inform treatment goals (e.g., weight gain and repletion of nutrition deficiencies).

Assessing the Specific Psychopathology of ARFID

Before beginning CBT-AR, we recommend that the therapist conduct a comprehensive psychiatric evaluation. Given the relative newness of the disorder, there are few measures of the specific psychopathology of ARFID. Published structured interviews that can be used to confer the ARFID diagnosis include the Eating Disorder Assessment for *DSM-5* (EDA-5; Sysko et al., 2015) and Structured Clinical Interview for *DSM-5* (SCID-5; First, Williams, Karg, & Spitzer, 2015). Available self-report measures that assess the severity of the specific psychopathology of ARFID include the Eating Disorders in Youth Questionnaire (EDY-Q; Hilbert, & van Dyck, 2016) and Nine Item Avoidant/Restrictive Food Intake disorder screen (NIAS; Zickgraf & Ellis, 2018). Our team has recently also developed a structured interview that not only diagnoses ARFID but also provides continuous severity ratings, called the Pica, ARFID, and Rumination Disorder Interview (PARDI; Bryant-Waugh, Micali, Cooke, Eddy, & Thomas, in press).

The PARDI is a clinical interview designed to assess the presence and severity of ARFID as well as disorders involving the consumption of non-nutritive/non-food substances (pica) and persistent regurgitation (rumination disorder). The PARDI is available in four versions suitable for (1) the parents/carers of 2–3-year-olds; (2) the parents or carers of 4-year-olds and up; (3) children (8–13-year-olds); and (4) young people or adults (14 years and up). To date, our team has completed the PARDI with more than 100 patients at three clinics and is currently evaluating its psychometric properties in an international multisite trial. Although data collection is ongoing, preliminary findings suggest adequate reliability (i.e., internal consistency values greater than or equal to 0.70 for all three ARFD profiles) and validity (i.e., individuals with ARFID score significantly higher than healthy controls) (Bryant-Waugh et al., in press). Importantly for the purposes of CBT-AR, the PARDI includes subscales evaluating sensory sensitivity, fear of aversive consequences, and apparent lack of interest in eating or food, which enable the assessor to create a profile of ARFID symptoms to facilitate individualized treatment planning. A comprehensive assessment allows the therapist to envision the patient's ARFID symptoms in a three-dimensional space based on the severity of sensory sensitivity, fear of aversive consequences, and apparent lack of interest in eating or food (Fig 3.1) (Thomas et al., 2017a). This is important given that the three classic ARFID presentations do not appear to be mutually exclusive (as in previous categorical models of feeding disorders; see Fig 3.1), but instead often co-occur in the same individual (Norris et al., 2017; Pulumo et al., 2016; Thomas et al., 2017a).

Food avoidance and restriction. It is helpful to begin the assessment by asking the patient whether he or she feels there is a problem with his or her eating, and to describe the difficulty. Some patients will readily label their avoidant or restrictive eating as problematic whereas others have limited insight. In such cases, it can be very helpful to get collateral information from significant others such as parents. That being said, the therapist should listen carefully to both

a

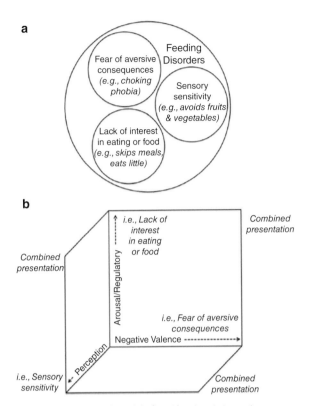

b

Fig 3.1 (a) Categorical model of avoidant/restrictive eating. (b) Dimensional model of avoidant/restrictive eating. *Note:* Reprinted with permission of Springer (Thomas et al., 2017a).

accounts, as in some cases, parents are extremely concerned about an eating pattern in their child that the therapist would deem to be run-of-the-mill picky eating. Getting an example of a typical day of eating in the past week can thus be very telling, as it will provide information about the frequency of eating as well as the amount, and provide an overview of variety. Next, it is helpful to ask the patient about the foods he or she consistently eats across the five basic categories of fruits, vegetables, protein, dairy, and grains. Importantly, the assessor should inquire about foods that are eaten consistently (e.g., in the past week or month) rather than rarely or inconsistently (e.g., once in the past two years). If it becomes apparent from this line of questioning that the patient is consuming a narrow variety or inadequate volume, the therapist should inquire about the reason. At a minimum, the therapist should ask about weight and shape concerns as a primary rationale (to rule out a classical eating disorder as a differential diagnosis) as well as the characteristics of the three primary ARFID presentations:

Sensory sensitivity. To evaluate the presence and severity of sensory sensitivity, the therapist should ask whether the patient avoids certain foods due to their taste, texture, smell, temperature, appearance, or other sensory properties. Patients with sensory sensitivity typically describe reluctance to try novel foods, which they view as disgusting (one 10-year-old patient told us that her non-preferred foods tasted like 'tree bark' and 'roasted rat'). It is often helpful to assess the number of foods the patient eats within each of the five categories and the types of food that he or she typically avoids. Sharp and Postorino (2018) have suggested the following categories to define the severity of food selectivity ranging from ordinary picky eaters through ARFID: *mild* (diet involves at least three items from each food group, but more than half of items fall into one food group and the patient consistently accepts food from all five groups); *moderate* (consumes two or fewer items in one or more food groups and accepts at least one item across all five food groups at least weekly); and *severe* (complete rejection of one or more food groups and accepts five or fewer food items). In our experience, individuals with the sensory sensitivity presentation of ARFID typically fall within or between these moderate or severe categories. A common pattern of eating for individuals with this clinical picture is the white diet, consisting, for example, of white-colored dairy and grains (e.g., pasta with butter, vanilla ice cream, crackers, breakfast cereal) and few or no fruits, vegetables, or proteins.

Fear of aversive consequences. To evaluate the presence and severity of fear of aversive consequences, the therapist should ask whether the patient avoids certain foods because he or she is worried something bad might happen. The therapist should inquire about the nature of the feared outcome (e.g., choking, vomiting, gastrointestinal discomfort, allergic reaction) and how certain (0–100%) the patient is that the outcome will occur. The therapist should then ask about any safety behaviors that the patient employs to prevent the feared outcome from happening (e.g., avoiding certain foods or eating situations). The therapist should consider whether the avoidance is *mild* (e.g., avoiding one food associated with a negative experience, such as avoiding chicken after choking on it), *moderate* (e.g., avoiding a whole class of foods associated with a negative experience, such as avoiding all nuts or foods that the patient is worried could contain nuts despite evidence to the contrary, after having an allergic reaction to just one type of nut), or *severe* (e.g., no oral intake or only eats a handful of foods he or she considers to be safe). Again, the moderate-to-severe presentations are prototypical for this presentation of ARFID.

Lack of interest in eating or food. To evaluate the presence and severity of lack of interest in eating or food, the therapist should ask about low appetite (e.g., whether the patient forgets to eat or rarely feels hungry), premature fullness (e.g., whether the patient feels full more quickly than others or typically stops meals after a few bites), and lack of pleasure in eating (e.g., whether the patient finds eating to be a chore rather than looking forward to it). The therapist should consider whether this lack of interest is *mild* (e.g., skipping some meals or eating small portions at most meals), *moderate* (e.g., skipping many meals or going long periods without eating), or *severe* (e.g., little to no oral intake, must be fed by tube or supplement drinks).

Psychosocial impairment. Although many of the sequelae of ARFID are medical, the psychosocial consequences cannot be underestimated. Many social activities revolve around eating, and individuals with ARFID are often left out. The therapist should ask the patient about the extent to which his or her avoidant or restrictive eating gets in the way of daily activities. For example, patients may avoid lunch at school or work, or decline invitations to social events such as holiday parties, dates, or sleepovers. Older patients may lose self-esteem due to embarrassment over eating what they consider to be child-oriented foods. Some may become so depressed due to their eating habits that they become socially isolated, withdraw from school or other important activities, or engage in self-harm. Families may provide helpful examples in the event that a child patient minimizes his or her symptoms. For example, many families feel they cannot travel or visit relatives because they worry that there will be nothing for their child to eat, or that their decision to accommodate their child's abnormal eating habits will invite criticism from family and friends. Other families may travel long distances or visit multiple grocery stores in order to track down a specific brand of a food item, only to find that their child will not accept it and goes hungry anyway.

Rule-outs for the ARFID diagnosis. Many of the diagnostic criteria for ARFID describe rule-outs for the diagnosis. The therapist should therefore inquire

about medical history, cultural background, and shape or weight concerns. Specifically, individuals with avoidant or restrictive eating whose pattern of eating is due solely to a medical condition (e.g., restricting only food to which one is allergic), socially sanctioned cultural practice (e.g., fasting during Ramadan), or another eating disorder (e.g., anorexia nervosa, bulimia nervosa) should not receive a diagnosis of ARFID.

Contraindications for CBT-AR. Another key component of an evaluation for ARFID is the assessment of comorbid psychiatric disorders. Individuals with most psychiatric disorders (e.g., depression, anxiety, attention deficit/hyperactivity disorder, oppositional defiant disorder) are appropriate for CBT-AR. However, there are some contraindications. For example, a patient at acute risk for suicide should first be treated for that problem before addressing his or her ARFID. Similarly, patients with substance use disorders who are actively misusing drugs or alcohol may not be appropriate for CBT-AR. In our experience, some individuals with ARFID use cannabis as a way to increase their appetite. There is no evidence that cannabis is an effective treatment for ARFID and, furthermore, active substance use can interfere with session comprehension and homework compliance. Lastly, patients with autism spectrum disorders can receive CBT-AR, but they must be verbal and functioning at a high enough level to engage in therapy tasks, even if family support is required.

Assessing the Medical Sequelae of ARFID

Patients must undergo comprehensive medical assessment with a pediatrician or primary care physician before initiating CBT-AR to ensure medical stability and further elucidate treatment goals. The medical evaluation is critical to determine the appropriateness of the current weight and height and identify any nutritional deficiencies, both central to the diagnostic criteria for ARFID. Patients must be medically stable and appropriate for outpatient treatment before beginning CBT-AR. The physician can refer to the Academy for Eating Disorders medical care standards guideline to determine whether hospitalization is necessary (Academy for Eating Disorders Medical Care Standards Committee Guide, 2016). Patients who are not medically stable, or those who are currently not taking in any calories at all (e.g., due to an acute food-related trauma), will require inpatient hospitalization prior to initiating outpatient care. Furthermore, patients who are tube-fed must be weaned from the tube before initiating CBT-AR. These patients should be transitioned to solid foods and be maintaining a healthy weight under the care of a physician or dietitian before potentially initiating CBT-AR to expand dietary variety. By contrast, patients who are reliant on energy-dense supplement drinks are appropriate to begin CBT-AR.

Height and weight assessment. The physician should screen for faltering growth in children and evaluate appropriateness of current weight for height in children, adolescents, and adults. Whether a patient is at an appropriate weight for his or her age, height, and growth trajectory is up to clinical judgment. Indeed, there are many different methods of determining expected body weight for individuals with eating disorders (Kandemir et al., 2017; Thomas, Roberto, & Brownell, 2009). Physicians need to carefully review medical records including charts of height, weight, and body mass index (BMI) history to guide determination of whether weight gain is needed in treatment. For many individuals with ARFID, stunted growth or low weight may be long-standing, which can at times make it more difficult to convince patients or parents that growth/weight have been compromised due to food avoidance or restriction patterns. When a patient is underweight, the physician can use a combination of BMI norms and the patient's individualized growth trajectory to determine an appropriate weight gain target for CBT-AR.

Vitamin deficiencies. Also of critical importance for treatment planning is the identification of any micro- or macro-nutrient deficiencies. The physician may choose to do blood tests for all potential deficiencies or evaluate through dietary recall whether the patient is at risk for specific deficiencies and test specifically for those. For example, patients who avoid meat or animal products may be at risk for B12, zinc, iron, or protein deficiency. Those who avoid dairy will be at risk for deficiencies in calcium and vitamin D. Those who avoid citrus fruits will be at risk for vitamin C deficiency. Those with low-fat or low-protein diets will be at risk for low vitamin A, vitamin K, and folate.

Data from the 2003–2006 US National Health and Nutrition Examination Survey indicate that 49% of American children and adults take dietary supplements (including individual supplements or multivitamins) – the majority of them (79%) daily (Bailey et al., 2010). This has two implications for the diagnosis and treatment of ARFID. First, just because a patient is taking a vitamin supplement does not mean that he or she has a frank deficiency. Many individuals self-select to take vitamins or are taking them prophylactically. Second, nutrition deficiencies may be masked if patients are supplementing with vitamins what they lack in their diets. While replenishing specific deficiencies is important, there is controversy regarding whether prophylactic use of individual supplements or multivitamins is helpful, and there may be iatrogenic effects of toxicity. Thus the decision as to whether the patient should receive vitamin supplements should be left to the physician. The ultimate goal of CBT-AR is to help a patient take in a wider variety of macro- and micro- nutrients with food alone, so that supplementation becomes unnecessary.

Use of supplement drinks. Many individuals with inadequate diets attempt to get additional calories and nutrients through high-energy supplement drinks (e.g., Boost, Ensure). Such drinks may be prescribed by a physician or self-started by parents or patients themselves. Individuals who take at least 50% of their daily calorie requirements through supplement drinks should be considered to meet criteria for supplement dependence. Patients with supplement dependence are appropriate for CBT-AR, and in such cases an important goal of treatment will be to reduce reliance on supplements by increasing the variety and volume of food.

Tube feeding. There are several methods of tube feeding that individuals with ARFID may receive to correct malnutrition and promote weight gain, including nasogastric, percutaneous endoscopic gastrostomy, and percutaneous endoscopic gastrojejunostomy. Available data suggest that individuals with ARFID are more likely to require tube feeding than those with anorexia nervosa (Ornstein et al., 2017; Strandjord et al., 2015). If patient is partially or fully tube-dependent, CBT-AR is not appropriate. Although there are many methods of weaning (e.g., Dunn-Klein & Morris, 2007; Nowak-Cooperman & Quinn-Shea, 2013; Sharp et al., 2010), transitioning from tube feeding to oral intake is typically done in an inpatient or day hospital setting under the care of a physician and dietitian (Sharp et al., 2010), whereas CBT-AR is an outpatient treatment.

Other medical considerations. Other assessments may be necessary, depending on the nature of the ARFID presentation. For example, depending on the patient's signs and symptoms, the pediatrician or primary care physician may need to refer the patient to a specialist physician for allergy testing (to determine previously unknown allergies may be contributing to food selectivity), an upper endoscopy (to detect inflammation and ulcers), pH probe study (to diagnose gastroesophageal reflux), an upper gastrointestinal series or barium swallow study (to detect inflammation, ulcers, or dysphagia), or a gastric emptying study (to determine whether a slowed emptying rate is causing nausea, vomiting, or excessive fullness) (Williams & Foxx, 2007). Similarly, the physician should consider any comorbidities that could make eating painful, including eosinophilic esophagitis.

Medication. The physician should ask about current medications, particularly those that may impact appetite. The United States Food and Drug Administration has not approved any medications for the treatment of ARFID, and there have been no randomized controlled trials of medications to treat its primary symptoms. Case reports and case series have described the use of lorazepam (Kardas et al., 2014) and mirtazapine (Thomas et al., 2017b) to decrease anxiety, and olanzapine to facilitate weight gain and decrease cognitive rigidity (Brewerton & D'Agostino, 2017), in ARFID and related presentations. Cyproheptadine is sometimes prescribed in clinical practice for individuals with lack of interest in eating or food. The evidence for the efficacy of cyproheptadine is mixed. Whereas some studies have found this medication to be effective in increasing appetite and facilitating weight gain, not all studies have had control groups or standardized dosing (e.g., Sant'Anna, Hammes, Porporino, Martel, Zygmuntowicz, & Ramsay, 2014). Furthermore, the medication has side effects (e.g., drowsiness) that may make functioning at school or work difficult. Clearly more research is needed. At the very least, the physician should consider stopping medications for other medical problems that may have a significant impact on appetite. For example, in one study, 12.5% of youth with ARFID were taking medication for attention deficit/hyperactivity disorder at treatment presentation (Ornstein et al., 2017). Due to the possibility of appetite suppression with stimulant medication, for underweight patients it may be necessary to discontinue stimulants and switch to a medication with less impact on appetite.

Assessment of oral-motor difficulties. Some individuals with ARFID find eating difficult due to structural or functional oral-motor difficulties, leading feeding specialists to recommend assessment of chewing and swallowing problems prior to initiating treatment (Morris & Klein, 1987). However, in our clinical experience with patients ages 10 and up, a clear inability to chew and swallow is rarely the sole cause of ARFID-like symptoms. On the contrary, apparent difficulties in chewing may actually be related to lack of experience with tough or fibrous foods. Similarly, swallowing difficulties commonly onset de novo after a traumatic experience with food in individuals who previously swallowed without difficulty. In both cases, the difficulty can be remedied by repeated exposure and practice with novel foods, in the absence of formal speech or occupational therapy. However, presenting novel foods to a patient with bona fide chewing or swallowing problems could be dangerous and lead to adverse consequences such as aspiration, which may make the problem worse. If the physician suspects oral-motor difficulties, he or she should refer the patient to a speech pathologist or occupational therapist for further assessment.

Using the Assessment to Plan Treatment

In summary, early psychiatric and medical assessment is crucial so that patients, their families, and providers can agree on diagnosis and treatment goals. This is particularly important for patients who may have been exhibiting ARFID symptoms for most of their lives and thus may not even recognize some of these as problems or even treatable targets. For the duration of CBT-AR, the patient should be medically monitored by a physician who is familiar with the principles of the therapy. The necessary frequency of medical visits will depend on the patient's degree of nutritional compromise. For example, low-weight patients with multiple nutritional deficiencies may require weekly visits, whereas normal- or overweight patients with few or no nutritional deficiencies may require less frequent visits (e.g., every one to three months). In youth patients, nutrition can improve such that patients grow several inches, thus necessitating a commensurate gain in weight, highlighting the importance of regular medical monitoring even among patients who are improving as a result of the treatment.

Many clinical guidelines for individuals with pediatric feeding disorders suggest that treatment requires a large multidisciplinary care team (e.g., a primary care physician or pediatrician, gastroenterologist, dietitian, speech therapist, occupational therapist, social worker, psychiatrist, and/or behavioral psychologist) (see Dodrill, 2014). Indeed, patients with very severe presentations may require input from all of these professionals. However, this may be excessive for patients ages 10 and up who can safely be treated on an outpatient basis. In our view, such a diverse and complex team is not readily attainable for all patients in the current health care environment and, importantly, can have the unintended consequence of well-intentioned providers from different disciplines working at cross-purposes. Thus we recommend starting with a pediatrician or primary care physician and behavioral health provider (e.g., psychologist), and then using the psychiatric and medical assessment to determine whether other members of the team should be added. In our experience, many patients can be successful with these team members alone. Indeed, because CBT-AR incorporates concepts from different disciplines, it is designed as a stand-alone treatment implemented by a trained therapist in conjunction with a pediatrician or primary care physician. CBT-AR's time-limited, less-is-more approach is sufficient for a large subset of ARFID cases and sets the stage for a stepped care approach in which complementary treatments (e.g., speech therapy, pharmacotherapy) can be added via thoughtful treatment planning if the patient does not fully respond.

Cognitive-Behavioral Model of ARFID

For decades, the treatment of avoidant/restrictive eating has been hampered by the lack of a conceptual model that explains core symptoms. To fill this need, we have developed the following generalized cognitive-behavioral model of ARFID (Fig 4.1). According to our model, individuals with ARFID are born with a biological predisposition that leads to a predictable cascade of negative feelings and predictions about the consequences of eating that perpetuate their initial food restriction or avoidance. Some individuals with these underlying biological risk factors will initially restrict their intake but ultimately develop more adaptive eating behaviors, perhaps due to other personality (e.g., openness to new experiences, low emotional reactivity) or environmental (e.g., repeated presentations of novel food during childhood) factors. However, for others – particularly those who do not test their predictions about eating – the food restriction will become chronic. Chronic food restriction – whether applied to food volume or variety – has physical and psychological effects manifested in nutritional compromise and limited opportunities for exposure. Depending on the individual patient, nutritional compromise can be characterized by low weight and a range of nutritional

deficiencies, which can in turn reinforce food avoidance and restriction. Limited opportunities for exposure – including, for example, social avoidance and reduced salience of hunger cues (and/or increased salience of fullness cues) – mean that the individual does not have the chance to disconfirm his or her negative predictions. Thus, the primary implication of our model is that, although the initial food restriction may have been triggered by a predisposition (e.g., high concentration of taste buds) or event (e.g., a choking episode) that cannot ultimately be changed, *it is now the pattern of food avoidance or restriction itself that serves to maintain the patient's negative predictions about eating and its attendant physical and psychological consequences. In turn, these physical and psychological factors serve to further reinforce food restriction, in a reciprocal feedback loop.* The obvious treatment implication for CBT-AR is that, by directly targeting food avoidance or restriction, the associated negative feelings, predictions, and consequences can be reduced or eliminated, thus interrupting the vicious cycle of ARFID symptoms.

We present in Figs 4.2–4.4 example formulations for the three most common ARFID presentations. Given that, in many cases, an individual with ARFID

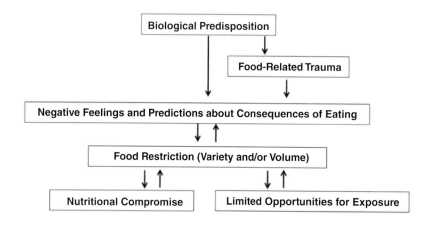

Fig 4.1 General cognitive-behavioral model of ARFID

can present with two or even all three of these presentations, any given patient's formulation must be individualized, and may include elements from one, two, or even all three example formulations.

Sensory Sensitivity Formulation

We hypothesize that individuals with sensory sensitivity are born with a predisposition that causes them to perceive the sensory properties of food (e.g., taste, texture, smell, temperature, and appearance) more intensely than do others (Fig 4.2). For example, there is evidence that children with picky eating are more likely to be supertasters (i.e., have a greater concentration of fungiform papillae, the structures that hold taste buds, on their tongues) compared to children without picky eating (Golding et al., 2009). Supertasters experience bitter tastes as strong and aversive, and thus may be unlikely to accept certain foods high in bitterness, such as dark green vegetables. Others with sensory sensitivity are hyper-attuned to textures, often showing clear preference for dry or crunchy foods and aversion to mushy or lumpy foods. These individuals may evidence a visceral disgust or fear reaction to the sight, touch, or smell of such foods, characterized by shuddering or gagging, for example. Still others experience extreme sensitivity to smell and cannot be in the same room when a non-preferred food is being prepared or consumed. Because of this biological predisposition, such individuals become suspicious, or disgusted by the prospect, of novel foods. For example, individuals will say, 'I won't try it because I know I wouldn't like it anyway.' Or, 'Five years ago I tried a similar food and it was disgusting so I'm never trying anything like it again.' They predict that they are very unlikely to like or even tolerate new foods, which leads them to consume a very limited diet consisting of foods they have come to view as safe and familiar.

This restriction has predictable consequences worth highlighting, which can maintain the avoidant/restriction pattern. First, if the individual's diet is very limited, it may result in nutritional compromise (i.e., weight loss or weight gain, nutrition deficiencies). Due to a reliance on starchy energy-dense processed foods, some individuals – particularly those who present with sensory sensitivity as a singular maintaining mechanism – are overweight or obese. However, others will lose weight. Importantly, some deficiencies (e.g., B12, zinc) can result in further reductions in appetite or changes in taste perception (e.g., https://www.nhlbi.nih.gov/health-topics/pernicious-anemia; https://ods.od.nih.gov/factsheets/Zinc-HealthProfessional/). Further – and this is particularly the case for individuals who present with both the sensory sensitivity and apparent lack of interest in eating or food phenotypes – individuals typically eat less when there is reduced variety in their food, due to a mechanism called sensory-specific satiety (Rolls, Rowe, & Rolls, 1982). A subset of these patients may

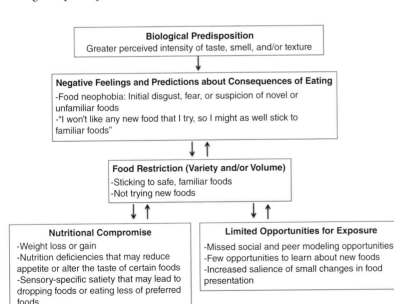

Fig 4.2 Cognitive-behavioral model of ARFID with sensory sensitivity

then be vulnerable to low weight. The idea behind sensory-specific satiety is that even when one sense is sated, another may not be: After a large savory meal, many of us can still miraculously find room for dessert! However, for highly selective eaters whose taste preferences are limited, sensory-specific satiety can be a mechanism that operates to further reduce intake. These individuals may eat less of preferred foods over time or drop preferred foods after a given time. For example, some individuals will eat the same foods for lunch and dinner every day and then, one day, simply tire of those foods and stop eating them altogether.

The second consequence of limited dietary variety is that there is little opportunity for exposure and habituation to novel tastes. Due to their limited diet, individuals with the sensory sensitivity type of ARFID often avoid social situations that involve eating, which further limits their opportunities to try novel foods and to watch others taste and enjoy these foods. If an individual with sensory sensitivity is invited to a party or social meal in which he or she predicts that preferred foods are unlikely to be available, he or she might decline the invitation altogether, reducing the possibility for gaining familiarity with any novel foods that might be served at the gathering. These individuals may also begin to develop a personal identity as selective eaters. In turn, they may not believe that it is even possible to change their eating pattern, and/or feel concerned that any changes to their current eating pattern would be highly salient to family and peers and then lead to unwanted pressure for further change.

They may also become less confident about or not develop skills for approaching, manipulating, or preparing novel foods. For example, it is very difficult to eat broccoli for dinner if one does not know how to chop, steam, or sauté it. Similarly, one might feel wary of eating an orange, especially in a social setting, if one does not know whether and how to peel it. One of our young adult patients who had never eaten any type of fruit or vegetable before presenting for treatment asked, when faced with an unpeeled orange, 'Do I just bite into it?' Perhaps most simply, if one has never heard of quinoa, one has no schema for seeking it out and purchasing it at a grocery store. These inexperience-based knowledge deficits can lead to shame or embarrassment that in turn beget continued food avoidance.

Further, a heavy reliance on safe foods – particularly if an individual's safe foods are primarily processed or packaged foods, with very little

variation in preparation, and which typically share similar sensory properties – results in non-preferred foods seeming increasingly novel and unfamiliar, thus causing individuals to become even more anxious about the prospect of changing their diets. In other words, their threshold for detecting a just noticeable difference between their preferred foods and any variation is reduced, and their perception of the magnitude of difference between familiar and unfamiliar foods is increased. This phenomenon is known as Weber's law, which states that the perceived difference between two stimuli is a function of the percentage difference between the two stimuli, rather than the absolute difference between them. For example, for the patient who has only two accepted foods, adding an additional food means an increase in food number of 50%, whereas for the healthy person who eats hundreds of foods, adding an additional food to his/her diet is a change of <1%. For the patient with the sensory sensitivity presentation of ARFID, the percentage of change being made with each novel food is substantial, particularly in the early stages of treatment.

Fear of Aversive Consequences Formulation

Because not everyone who has gastrointestinal distress, a choking event, or a vomiting episode will develop ARFID, we hypothesize that individuals with the fear of aversive consequences presentation have a preexisting anxious temperament and an increased sensitivity to bodily sensations (Fig 4.3). Thus, in the wake of an acute food-related trauma (e.g., choking on a piece of meat, vomiting, an allergic reaction, or pain), their initial fear quickly grows from normative and transient to intense and chronic. This fear leads them to overestimate the probability that eating (either a specific food or any food at all) will lead to a repeat trauma (e.g., another choking episode). For example, one young patient with ARFID who had choked on a bell pepper told us, 'If I have any food with any kind of skin on it, I'm scared I'll choke again.' After an experience with a vomiting norovirus, another stated, 'I'm terrified that if I feel even the slightest bit nauseous, I'll vomit, and I'm sure eating will make me nauseous.' Based on these negative predictions, these individuals begin to restrict their intake. Depending on the trauma (e.g., choking on steak), the individual might restrict only the food

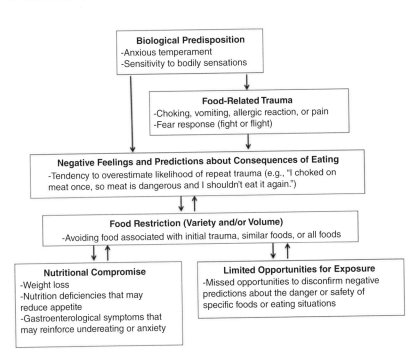

Fig 4.3 Cognitive-behavioral model of ARFID with fear of aversive consequences

(e.g., steak) or class of food (e.g., all meat) associated with the trauma, or may generalize their restriction to all solid food, or even all food and drink. Often patients who have had choking experiences will restrict their intake to soft or liquid foods that are easier to chew, while those who are fearful of vomiting will stick to bread or cracker-like foods that they think will be easier on their stomachs.

Those individuals who significantly limit their diet or reduce the volume of intake can experience weight loss and nutrition deficiencies, which may impact appetite or taste perception, as previously described. An additional consequence of both food restriction and anxiety can be the exacerbation of gastrointestinal symptoms (e.g., early satiety, constipation, nausea; Benini et al., 2004; Mascolo et al., 2017). Such gastrointestinal symptoms may be particularly salient to these individuals whose food avoidance is driven by fear of aversive consequences of eating and who are in turn hyper-attentive to their internal bodily cues, and thus likely to persist in restricting.

Avoidance of foods associated with feared outcomes leads to missed opportunities to test negative predictions about the danger or safety of specific foods or eating situations. Further, when these individuals do eat, they may engage in safety behaviors (e.g., taking extremely small bites, chewing for much longer than needed, using the front biting teeth rather than the back grinding teeth to chew, chasing every bite with water, eating only when close to home/the bathroom, carrying anti-nausea medicine) that further maintain anxiety and interfere with opportunities to disconfirm their catastrophic predictions that eating is unsafe. Furthermore, avoidance prevents the individual from having the opportunity for corrective experiences of successfully coping in the unlikely event of that an aversive consequence occurs.

Apparent Lack of Interest in Eating or Food Formulation

According to the CBT-AR model, individuals with the lack of interest in eating or food presentation of ARFID are born with a predisposition for low homeostatic appetite (i.e., physiologic hunger) and/or find food less hedonically rewarding (i.e., pleasurable/tasty) (Fig 4.4). For example, one patient with this presentation shared with us that 'I never feel hungry ... Ever.' Another shared that 'I don't look forward to eating like other people do.' Our preliminary data demonstrate that after an eight-hour overnight fast, low-weight females with ARFID have similar levels of ghrelin (a hunger-stimulating hormone) to healthy controls, in contrast to higher levels seen in females with anorexia nervosa (Mancuso 2017). Typically, ghrelin levels are high in wasting

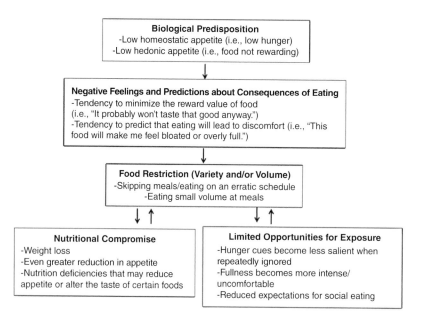

Fig 4.4 Cognitive-behavioral model of ARFID with apparent lack of interest in eating or food

diseases, which is thought to reflect a biological adaptation to promote hunger and eating in those who are low weight (Solomou & Korbonits, 2014). In our low-weight ARFID sample, ghrelin levels did not differ from those in healthy controls, which suggests dysregulation and substantiates reported low appetite by our ARFID patients. In the same study, even after an overnight fast, brain-derived neurotrophic factor (an appetite-decreasing hormone) was higher in individuals with ARFID compared to individuals with anorexia nervosa or healthy controls. These data suggest that neurobiological factors may underlie the experience of low appetite in ARFID. Thus it is understandable that these patients do not predict that eating will be pleasurable, and instead see it as a chore. Further, because they experience less physiologic hunger, they may predict that eating will make them feel full, bloated, or nauseous rather than satisfied. Because they do not often feel hungry and do not predict that eating will be pleasurable, they may skip meals, eat on an erratic schedule, and/or eat a limited volume of food at mealtimes.

Unfortunately, this chronic restriction will have predictable consequences of nutritional compromise and limited opportunities for exposure that only serve to reinforce this pattern of limited volume intake. The prototypical patient with lack of interest in eating or food is underweight and may have long-standing low weight or even early failure to thrive. However, it is also possible for individuals who are normal weight

or overweight to present with lack of interest. An example is the patient with primary sensory sensitivity who goes long periods without eating early in the day because preferred foods are not available but then eats larger amounts later in the day to compensate for the calorie deficit. This fasting schedule may disrupt normal appetite signals over time. Most individuals with lack of interest in eating or food will chronically under-eat, becoming accustomed to eating very little and, as a result, experience further reductions in appetite, and start to feel full on smaller amounts of food. This is similar to the starvation syndrome in anorexia nervosa described by Fairburn (2008). Their restricted diet may create vitamin deficiencies that can exacerbate low appetite or alter the taste experience, as described earlier. For these individuals, limited calorie intake is also likely to result in low mood, diminished energy, and decreased motivation to engage in pleasurable activities, including eating. Although for some individuals – such as those with bulimia nervosa or binge eating disorder – food restriction ultimately leads to increased food intake in the form of binge eating, it is important to note that individuals with this form of ARFID typically find food less hedonically rewarding, possibly protecting them from overeating, but also keeping them locked in a restrictive pattern. The less they eat, the more likely they are to develop negative predictions about eating, including underestimating even the minimal pleasure that they used to get from eating (similar to how individuals with major depressive disorder lose interest or pleasure in activities that they used to enjoy).

In the context of chronic under-eating, for these individuals, hunger cues become less salient when repeatedly neglected or ignored, and fullness cues become more salient when full-stomach sensations are avoided. Further, these individuals become recognized as being light eaters by family and peers alike. In time, the social expectations for them to eat an adequate intake fade. For example, one adult described, 'My parents pushed me to try foods when I was a little kid but then they stopped. Growing up, all my friends knew I didn't have much of an appetite and no one expected me to eat a lot. Since middle school, I never ate at the table with my family since I usually ate something different or wasn't hungry anyway.' As with other forms of ARFID, it is the restriction itself that reinforces these physical and psychological consequences, in a reciprocal feedback loop.

Putting It All Together

It is important to note that the example presentations of ARFID provided in *DSM-5* are not exhaustive. In clinical practice individuals may present with other presentations that do not map clearly onto sensory sensitivity, lack of interest in eating, and fear of aversive consequences (e.g., rigid food preferences without clear sensory sensitivities). However, when providing CBT-AR, these patients should be treated with the interventions described for the closest match to the *DSM-5* presentation. For example, patients with rigid food preferences will benefit from exposure to novel foods regardless of whether or not sensory sensitivity was the initial reason for food avoidance, as the CBT-AR model hypothesizes that it is now the *food avoidance itself* that maintains the ARIFD symptoms.

In sum, the CBT-AR model posits that biological vulnerabilities including sensory sensitivity, anxiety, and/or low appetite, with or without a negative experience with eating, contribute to negative feelings and predictions about eating, which lead to food avoidance or restriction. Avoidant/restrictive eating has a series of physical and psychosocial consequences that maintain the maladaptive cycle. Regardless of whether the patient has one, two, or all three primary presentations, CBT-AR challenges avoidant/restrictive eating head-on in order to interrupt and correct the maintaining mechanisms.

Overview of CBT-AR

As illustrated by the cognitive-behavioral model of ARFID, the symptoms that unify all clinical presentations are food avoidance and restriction. Thus avoidance and restriction are the primary targets for intervention in CBT-AR. However, because ARFID is so heterogeneous, CBT-AR is designed to be flexible enough to apply to the broad range of patients who present for care. To address heterogeneity in age at presentation, CBT-AR can be applied in either a family-supported or individual format. To address heterogeneity in maintaining mechanisms, CBT-AR always proceeds through four stages, but Stage 3 features three optional modules that the therapist can implement depending on the primary maintaining mechanism(s) of the individual patient. Lastly, to address heterogeneity in weight status and clinical complexity, the treatment spans 20–30 sessions in length, affording additional time for patients who have significant weight to gain or must address multiple maintaining mechanisms. Regardless of the version of the treatment employed, all forms of CBT-AR include important common features such as a structured session format, at-home practice assignments, common therapeutic goals, and consistent therapist stance.

Family-Supported vs. Individual Formats

CBT-AR can be delivered in one of two ways: family-supported therapy or individual therapy. Both versions rely on the same basic principles and follow the same 20- to 30-session, four-stage format. Family-supported therapy is generally recommended for patients ages 10–15 years, but also for older adolescents and young adults who are living at home and have significant weight to gain, or those with autism spectrum disorder or other developmental disabilities who may require additional support to make the desired behavioral changes. Individual therapy is generally recommended for patients ages 16 years and

above who are not underweight. Fig 5.1 provides a decision tree for determining whether family-supported or individual CBT-AR is most appropriate for a particular case. Determining whether the individual or family-supported format will be used is absolutely critical to decide in advance of treatment. It can be discouraging to patients who expect to be in individual treatment to be told part way through treatment that they require family support.

In family-supported CBT-AR, the patient's parents or primary caregivers attend all sessions with the patient, and it is the parents or caregivers who hold the primary responsibility for change. Specifically, the parents either support the patient in selecting treatment goals or select treatment goals themselves, and the parents support the patient in completing at-home practice tasks. Given our understanding that ARFID often persists within the context of a family system, the importance of family intervention for younger children and adolescents with ARFID cannot be overstated. Not only is it important to engage the parents because it is difficult for patients to gain weight on their own; it is also helpful to determine to what extent the parents may be accommodating or exacerbating the ARFID symptoms. For example, they may become short-order cooks at the moment the patient looks askance at the dinner on offer. Or they may allow the patient to graze on snack foods during the day because they are so worried that the patient is not taking in sufficient calories at meals and snacks. Alternatively, they may present the patient every day with non-preferred foods that the patient feels completely unequipped to consume. This is not to criticize parents at all. Rather, parents often feel helpless or confused about how best to help their child with ARFID. Indeed, many parents have been given unclear or diverging opinions on how to handle their child's eating, particularly as the ARFID diagnosis is so new. Whereas a normally developing child with picky eating might eventually eat a non-preferred meal, a child with ARFID may gag, vomit,

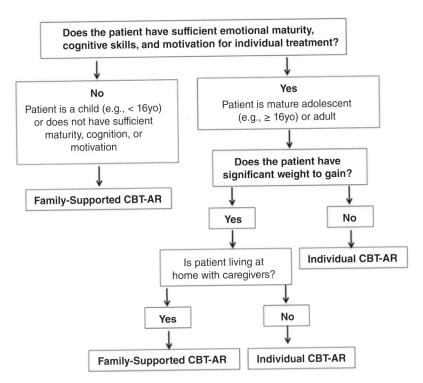

Fig 5.1 Decision tree for when to use family-supported versus individual CBT-AR

leave the table, or storm out of the room. Similarly, whereas a normally developing child may eventually become hungry and eat, a child with ARFID may hold out for many meals until the parents offer a preferred food out of desperation.

If both parents live at home, it is ideal for both to participate in all sessions. However, we appreciate the diversity of modern family arrangements and know from experience that it may be difficult for all family members to take part. Thus if only one parent is able to attend sessions (i.e., if parents are divorced or one parent has a challenging work or travel schedule), the therapist can allow this as long as the patient is progressing successfully toward achieving treatment goals. Even in such cases, both parents should attend the 2–4 sessions in Stage 1, to set the stage for joint management of their child's eating problem. In our experience, it is not usually necessary for siblings to participate in CBT-AR.

In individual CBT-AR, the patient attends sessions alone and bears primary responsibility for change. In other words, the patient him- or herself selects treatment goals and plans and completes at-home practice assignments. Parents, caregivers, or significant others may be invited by the patient or at the recommendation of the therapist to discuss how they can support the patient in making at-home changes but, again, the

patient is responsible for implementing these changes. For example, the parent of an adolescent living at home may be included for the last 10–15 minutes of each session to discuss how the parent can purchase specific foods *that the patient has selected* to practice tasting during the upcoming week or to learn about in the next session. This can be quite useful, as parents are typically still in charge of grocery shopping, meal preparation, and finances for adolescent children. The patient may also request that his or her parents prompt him or her to practice the selected foods, but the parents are discouraged from encouraging the patient to eat foods that he or she has not selected for intervention. Similarly, adult patients who live independently may wish to invite a significant other to attend a full session or two midway through treatment to learn more about ARFID and brainstorm how to support the patient in making changes. Significant others are typically less involved in CBT-AR for older patients, who are able manage day-to-day meal planning and food shopping on their own.

Four Stages of CBT-AR

CBT-AR is a structured treatment divided into four broad stages (Table 5.1). In Stage 1, the therapist provides psychoeducation on ARFID and its maintaining

Table 5.1 Four stages of cognitive-behavioral therapy for avoidant/restrictive food intake disorder (CBT-AR)

Stage	Primary interventions
1. Psychoeducation and early change (2–4 sessions)	• **Psychoeducation** on ARFID and its treatment • **Self- or parent-monitoring** of food intake • Establishing a pattern of **regular eating** to normalize hunger cues • **Increasing volume of preferred foods** (for patients who are underweight) **and variety** (for all patients) • **Individualized formulation** of mechanisms that maintain avoidant/restrictive eating (i.e., sensory sensitivity, fear of aversive consequences, lack of interest in eating or food)
2. Treatment planning (2 sessions)	• **Continue increasing volume and/or variety** • Reviewing intake from **Primary Food Group Building Blocks** and selecting foods to learn about in Stage 3
3. Maintaining mechanisms in order of priority (14–22 sessions)	• **Sensory sensitivity:** Systematic desensitization to novel foods by repeated in-session exploration of sight, touch, smell, taste, and texture; specific, detailed plans for out-of-session practice with tasting and incorporation • **Fear of aversive consequences:** Psychoeducation about how avoidance maintains anxiety, development of fear/avoidance hierarchy, graded exposure to feared foods and situations in which choking, vomiting, or other feared consequence may occur • **Apparent lack of interest in eating or food:** Interoceptive exposure to bloating, fullness, and/or nausea; in-session exposure to highly preferred foods
4. Relapse prevention (2 sessions)	• **Evaluating** whether treatment goals have been met, identifying treatment strategies to continue at home, developing a plan for maintaining weight gain (if needed), and continuing to learn about novel foods

mechanisms and helps the patient create an individualized formulation of how his or her ARFID works. The therapist also supports the patient (or parents) in making early change by significantly increasing volume (for underweight patients) and beginning to increase variety (for all patients). Stage 1 lasts as few as two sessions, but up to four sessions if the patient is underweight. In Stage 2, the therapist helps the patient (or parents) determine which maintaining mechanisms will be addressed in Stage 3, and helps the patient determine which novel foods will be introduced to increase representation from the five basic food groups. If the patient is underweight, the therapist continues to support the patient's (or parents') efforts toward weight gain. Stage 2 lasts two sessions. In Stage 3 – the heart of the treatment – the therapist supports the patient (or parents) in addressing the relevant maintaining mechanisms in order of priority, as determined by the individualized formulation. Each maintaining mechanism (sensory sensitivity, fear of aversive consequences, and lack of interesting in eating or food) has an optional module that can be offered in Stage 3. Stage 3 is the most variable part of the treatment in terms of content and length. It may last as few as 14 sessions (if the patient is not underweight and has just one or two maintaining mechanisms) or as many as 22 sessions (if the patient is underweight and has multiple maintaining mechanisms). Lastly, in Stage 4, the therapist assists the patient (or parents) in making a detailed plan to maintain treatment gains and prevent relapse. Stage 4 lasts two sessions.

Variable Treatment Length

Similar to enhanced CBT-E for eating disorders (Fairburn, 2008), which bases treatment length on the degree of underweight, the basic course of CBT-AR is 20 sessions. For a patient with a single maintaining mechanism who is highly motivated to make changes, the treatment may be abbreviated to fewer than 20 sessions. On the other hand, the treatment can also be extended up to 30 sessions if the patient is underweight, particularly if the underweight patient also has multiple ARFID maintaining mechanisms. In deciding on the exact number of sessions to offer to underweight patients, the therapist should consider the severity of underweight. Patients who are extremely underweight (e.g., those needing to gain >15 lbs) may require 30 sessions to gain as much as necessary, whereas those who are mildly underweight may only require 25 sessions, similar to recent treatment trials for anorexia nervosa, which stratified treatment length based on degree of underweight (Andony et al., 2015). However, not all patients who are very low weight will require the full 30 sessions.

Fig 5.2 is a visual schematic of how CBT-AR can be tailored to heterogeneous patient presentations based on weight status and number of maintaining mechanisms. The first example illustrates how the 20-session version would be applied to a normal-weight patient with a single maintaining mechanism (e.g., sensory sensitivity only). This patient would spend two sessions in Stage 1, two sessions in Stage 2, up to 14 sessions in Stage 3, and two sessions in Stage 4. The second example illustrates how the 20-session version would be applied to a normal-weight patient with two maintaining mechanisms (e.g., fear of aversive consequences and sensory sensitivity). This patient would spend the same amount of time in each stage, but Stage 3 would be tailored to address both maintaining mechanisms in order of clinical priority. For example, if the patient presents with a history of mild selective eating but has recently curtailed his or her intake to comprise only purees and other soft foods following an acute choking incident, that patient would likely need to address fear of aversive consequences first (4–6 sessions) before moving on to sensory sensitivity (8–10 sessions). Finally, the third example illustrates how the 30-session version would be applied to an underweight patient with all three maintaining mechanisms. This patient would require an extended Stage 1 (i.e., four sessions rather than just two) to support weight gain, and an extended Stage 3 (i.e., to continue increasing weight to a normative level, and to address all three maintaining mechanisms in order of clinical priority). For example, if the patient has a history of selective eating and multiple vomiting episodes that have led to avoidance of a small subset of foods, but is currently citing lack of appetite as the primary barrier to consuming sufficient calories, the therapist may choose to start Stage 3 by addressing lack of interest in eating or food (2–6 sessions), then fear of aversive consequences (4–8 sessions), then sensory sensitivity (8–16 sessions), all the while supporting continued weight gain.

Example Presentation #1: ARFID with 1 maintaining mechanism; not underweight

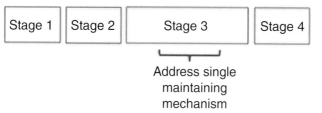

Address single
maintaining
mechanism

Example Presentation #2: ARFID with 2 maintaining mechanisms; not underweight

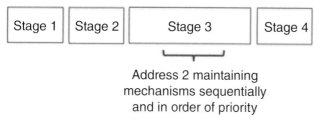

Address 2 maintaining
mechanisms sequentially
and in order of priority

Example Presentation #3: ARFID with 3 maintaining mechanisms; underweight

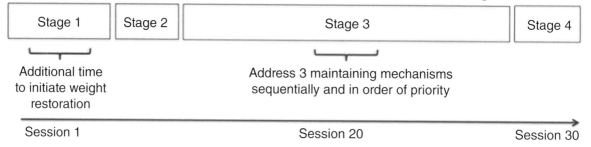

Additional time
to initiate weight
restoration

Address 3 maintaining mechanisms
sequentially and in order of priority

Session 1   Session 20   Session 30

Fig 5.2 Visual schematic of how CBT-AR can be tailored to heterogeneous patient presentations based on weight status and number of maintaining mechanisms

Outline of a Typical CBT-AR Session

Because CBT-AR is time-limited, there is no time to waste. The therapist should therefore make the best use of time by structuring each session as follows:

1. Verbally set the session agenda (the therapist should highlight the CBT-AR items to be covered in the session, and inquire about any relevant agenda items that the patient wishes to discuss, which should be added only after primary CBT-AR items)
2. Weigh the patient (regardless of whether weight gain is a treatment goal, all patients should be weighed at the beginning of session)
3. Review homework from last session (e.g., self- or parent-monitoring, checking on at-home practice or number of novel foods tasted and/or incorporated at home that week)
4. Implement intervention related to current treatment stage (e.g., individualized formulation, exposure to novel or feared food, interoceptive exposure)
5. Review any agenda items brought in by patient and/or family
6. Plan at-home practice task(s) to be completed before next session

At-home practice (i.e., homework) is critical to meeting treatment goals. In Stage 1, many of the at-home practice tasks are predetermined by the treatment itself (i.e., starting self-monitoring). However, as the treatment progresses, we recommend that the therapist involve the patient (and/or family, if implementing the family-supported version) in goal-setting. After agreeing on a goal, if the patient seems ambivalent about following through, the therapist should assess motivation by asking the following: 'On a scale of 0–100%, how likely is it that you'll do the homework?' If the patient is <90% likely, the therapist should work on reducing barriers to homework completion or consider reducing the demands of the task. Once the patient has established the expectation that homework goals will be realistic and attainable, the therapist will no longer need to inquire about the likelihood of homework completion at each session.

CBT-AR Treatment Goals

Some patients seek treatment in hopes of making extremely specific changes to their eating. For example, parents may want their child to eat broccoli or a specific holiday dish that the family enjoys. A patient may want to 'enjoy food again' or 'look forward to mealtimes.' However, it is important to be realistic about the types of changes that are (1) achievable given our hypotheses about the underlying biology of the disorder and (2) sufficient to reverse the physical sequelae of ARFID and enhance or restore quality of life. Here is what we believe can feasibly be achieved by the completion of CBT-AR:

- Patient no longer meets criteria for ARFID and/or symptom severity has markedly decreased
- Patient is able to eat several foods in each of the major food groups, and incorporates these foods into his or her diet (i.e., eats them on a regular basis)
- Patient's growth (height and weight) has increased to that expected (e.g., patient is back on pre-illness trajectory, and/or is no longer underweight)
- Nutritional status is replete (i.e., deficiencies have been corrected or are on their way to being corrected, or patient is taking appropriate vitamins as prescribed by a physician and is no longer exacerbating deficiencies with his or her diet)
- Patient no longer experiences clinically impairing psychosocial consequences of food avoidance or restriction, and has a plan for managing food-related social situations

Note that the primary goals of CBT-AR do not include becoming a foodie, enjoying very unusual foods, or eating a specific food (e.g., broccoli), but rather eating a wider variety of foods in general, with less associated distress. Similarly, a goal is also not necessarily to get the patient to enjoy food, as homeostatic appetite and hedonic response to food

may be at least partly genetic. Instead, in CBT-AR we support patients to consume enough food to meet their nutritional needs, even if the task at times still feels like a chore.

Rapid response. A recent major development in the cognitive-behavioral literature is the discovery that rapid change in the first four weeks of treatment predicts positive outcomes at the end of treatment, as well as at subsequent follow-ups. A recent meta-analysis of 34 studies indicated that this was particularly true of eating-disorder treatments (Linardon, Brennan, & de la Piedad Garcia, 2016). To that end, CBT-AR is designed to produce the following rapid changes in the first four weeks:

- In patients whose food variety is limited, (1) reincorporate previously preferred foods that may have been dropped from their diets; (2) reduce reliance on the eating the same food items for the exact same meal or snack each day (i.e., alternating between two or three preferred breakfasts rather than relying on just one); and (3) promote small changes in presentation of preferred foods (e.g., whole rather than sliced apples, different flavor of prepackaged snack food)
- In patients who report fear of aversive consequences, to begin incorporating at least some foods that produce anxiety, even if the most anxiety-provoking or target food is not yet being consumed
- In patients who present with a lack of interest in eating and food, and underweight, facilitate a weight gain of at least 4 lbs (i.e., a rate of 1–2 lbs per week)

For patients with multiple maintaining mechanisms, the therapist should focus on a single maintaining mechanism only for gauging rapid change. To achieve these goals, it is very important for the therapist to push for early change from the very first session, and reinforce behaviors that will lead to sustained change, such as therapy attendance and daily completion of at-home practice tasks.

CBT-AR Therapist Stance

Many individuals with ARFID come to treatment having felt criticized by family, friends, and health professionals for their picky eating and food refusal. In a 2015 article in the *Boston Globe*, Sally Sampson, the editor of a children's cooking magazine, added to the impression that ARFID symptoms are willful, stating that, 'picky eating is the privilege of the privileged.' In CBT-AR, it is important that the therapist does not reinforce this negative self-view. After all, if the patient believes himself to be a 'picky eater' or 'stubborn,' he or she may feel disempowered to make changes. Having worked in the mental health field for many years, we have observed that when new disorders are defined, a common first response among professionals and the lay public is to blame the patient for his or her symptoms, or else to blame his or her family for causing them. Note that there is a long history of stigmatizing and blaming parents for a panoply of psychiatric disorders including autism, schizophrenia, and anorexia nervosa. In all cases, research has ultimately identified a strong underlying biology to these disorders, and often gone on to highlight how parenting behaviors that may seem unusual at first blush are likely a consequence rather than a cause of the illness. (Parenthetically, we have often wondered whether self- or parent-blaming serves a self-protective function for the blamers; if people view the person or family with the disorder as being at fault for having it, those without the disorder can take comfort in the illusion that they themselves could never develop it.)

Thus in CBT-AR, the therapist takes an empathic, non-blaming, and nonjudgmental stance. The CBT-AR therapist assumes that the avoidant/restrictive eating makes perfect sense for this patient, given his or her genetic taste preferences, feeding experiences, and/or past history of reinforcement. Of course, this empathic stance should not let the patient off the proverbial hook for making changes. Instead, the therapist should view the problem as malleable (even if long-standing), and express curiosity about the patient's experience that may lead the patient to increased self-understanding. While the therapist uses praise and encouragement to support behavioral change, the therapist and patient should always be on the same team, collaborating to solve an issue that both view as problematic. Some programs for picky eating have discouraged parents or clinicians from praising children for trying new foods (e.g., Rowell et al., 2015; Satter, 1987). However, this advice is inconsistent with data suggesting that operant conditioning via verbal or object reinforcement is a successful strategy for helping youth with feeding difficulties accept new foods (Marshall et al., 2015). In our experience, it is also usually at odds with parents' and therapists' natural inclination to offer encouragement and praise to the patient for meeting new challenges.

Conclusion

CBT-AR is structured in its delivery yet flexible in its approach. While providing the treatment, the therapist may wonder how successfully he or she is implementing its general principles. Appendix 1 ('CBT-AR Competence Ratings') provides the competency measure that our group used to evaluate our own delivery of CBT-AR in the first clinical trial. The form provides a structured opportunity for the therapist to reflect on how competently he or she has brought across the key points of CBT-AR such as remaining collaborative, involving family, keeping focused on therapy tasks, presenting optimism about change, and avoiding common pitfalls. We include it here so that interested readers can evaluate their delivery of any given session. Drilling down further, Appendix 2 ('CBT-AR Adherence: Session-by-Session Ratings') provides an opportunity for the therapist to rate his or her fidelity to the content of CBT-AR. Because the content differs by session, for each session we have provided a checklist of tasks to be completed, as well as an option to rate how successfully the tasks were performed. Again, we used these forms to rate our own fidelity to CBT-AR in the first clinical trial, and have provided them here in hopes that readers will find them useful. For example, we often found it handy to check off tasks in real time as we completed them during each session, to ensure that nothing important was forgotten.

Stage 1: Psychoeducation and Early Change

The primary purpose of CBT-AR Stage 1 (two to four sessions) is to help the patient (or family) learn more about ARFID and the patient's specific presentation of it, and to foster urgency for achieving early changes in eating behavior. In session 1, the therapist provides psychoeducation about ARFID, assigns self- or parent-monitoring of daily food intake, and encourages early change by asking the patient (or family) to make their first increase in volume or variety. In session 2, the therapist works collaboratively with the patient (or family) to co-create an individualized formulation of the patient's eating problem, establish a pattern of regular eating, continue to support increases in volume or variety, and (if the patient is underweight) plan for the therapeutic meal that will take place in session 3. If the patient is underweight, session 3 will comprise a therapeutic meal designed to help the patient and/or family learn strategies for increasing volume at home. Session 4 will then include further brainstorming about how to support continued weight gain. If the patient is not underweight, he or she will skip the last two sessions of Stage 1 and move directly to Stage 2.

Stage 1, Session 1

Introductions. If the therapist has not yet met the patient or family (i.e., if another clinician performed the initial assessment), the therapist should begin the first session by introducing him- or herself to the patient (or family). In turn, the therapist should ask the patient to share a little bit about what has brought him or her to treatment. In family-supported CBT-AR, the therapist should greet each family member individually and ask the same question. Because there is so much to cover in session 1, the therapist should spend no more than five minutes on this initial task.

Set agenda. The therapist will begin each session by verbally setting an agenda. In doing so the therapist models that session time is valuable and there is no

time to waste in this time-limited approach. After listing the topics to be covered in the session, the therapist should ask if the patient (or family) has anything else he or she (or they) would like to discuss. If so, the therapist should make sure to respectfully address the patient's agenda item(s) before the end of the session, either by weaving them into a topic that is already on the agenda, addressing them as separate agenda items at the end of the session, or deferring them to a future session where they can be more appropriately addressed. However, it is important that the therapist not let irrelevant topics (i.e., those not related to ARFID) dominate the session.

Weigh patient. After setting the agenda, the therapist should take the patient's weight and share it with the patient (or family). In the patient for whom weight gain is a treatment goal, taking the patient's weight at the beginning of the session will enable the therapist, patient, and/or family to remain accountable for weekly weight gain and assess progress toward the target weight. For the non-low-weight patient, weight assessment is also important to ensure that the recommended changes in the patient's eating are not adversely affecting the patient's weight in either direction. For the overweight patient, it is possible that expanding dietary variety to include more fruits and vegetables and lean proteins may lead to weight loss, but this is not an explicit goal of CBT-AR. For the patient who is neither underweight nor overweight, it is important to ensure that prescribed dietary changes (e.g., reduction in reliance on supplement drinks or other high-calorie staple foods such as macaroni and cheese) do not lead to unhealthy weight loss or failure to grow as expected.

Provide psychoeducation on ARFID in general. The therapist should begin by asking the patient (or family) what he or she knows about ARFID. It is important that the therapist not assume a great deal of prior knowledge about the disorder, given its relative newness to the psychiatric nomenclature. Using this initial knowledge as a base, the therapist should review the patient education handout depicted in Fig 6.1 ('What is ARFID?'). Important points to emphasize include that ARFID is a psychiatric disorder and that individuals with ARFID have underlying biological traits that initially made limiting their eating a logical choice. Once established, this pattern of food restriction and avoidance becomes self-reinforcing and highly resistant to change. Fortunately, there are helpful steps that patients and families can take to interrupt this pattern. During this collaborative review, the therapist should ask the patient to highlight any aspects of the handout that feel especially relevant to his or her current situation. The therapist should also encourage the patient (or family) to ask questions.

Psychoeducation is crucial to support treatment engagement, regardless of the patient's current weight or nutritional status. For example, patients who have ARFID with sensory sensitivity may feel powerless to expand their low-variety diet. Thus helping them understand that they are trapped in a vicious cycle that limits their opportunities for exposure is critical. In contrast, those with fear of aversive consequences may believe that their inability to eat without choking represents a physical problem rather than a psychological one. Lastly, some patients and/or parents might need additional support to push for weight gain because they do not see low weight as a problem, particularly if the patient has not fallen off the growth curve (as in AN), but rather always been slight. Similarly, eating insufficiently or irregularly may become part of the core identity of a person with ARFID – rather than viewed as the symptoms of a disorder – thus limiting insight into negative consequences.

Provide psychoeducation on all maintaining mechanisms relevant for the patient. Although the therapist should review Fig 6.1 ('What is ARFID?') and 6.5 ('How is ARFID treated?') with all patients, Figs 6.2, 6.3, and 6.4 should be presented only if they are relevant to the patient's primary maintaining mechanisms established in the initial assessment. For example, the therapist would only need to present Fig 6.2 ('What happens when you eat a limited variety of food?'), but not Figs 6.3 ('What happens when you become more careful about your eating after a negative experience with food?') or 6.4 ('What happens when you eat a limited volume of food?'), for a patient with sensory sensitivity alone. In contrast, for a patient with all three maintaining mechanisms, the

therapist would present Figs 6.2, 6.3, and 6.4. If the patient has just one maintaining mechanism to address, the review process may be quite leisurely. However, if the patient presents with two or three maintaining mechanisms, the therapist will necessarily need to cover the main points and move fairly quickly on to the next handout. Any material that is not covered in session 1 can be assigned as reading for at-home practice, and patients or families should always be encouraged to review handouts in-between sessions.

In reviewing Fig 6.2, the therapist should highlight that flavor preferences are partly genetic and begin developing before we are even born. In one study, children of mothers who consistently drank carrot juice during the third trimester of pregnancy or during breast-feeding were more likely to accept carrots as babies than were children of mothers who did not drink carrot juice (Mennella, Jagnow, & Beauchamp, 2001). Even if someone's mother eats a highly varied diet during pregnancy, all babies show an initial preference for sweet foods and a dislike for bitter foods. Indeed, some people, called supertasters, who are born with a higher concentration of taste buds on their tongues, have an even more intense dislike of bitter foods, like vegetables. Evolutionarily, it makes sense that young children would prefer foods that are familiar, safe, and available. Indeed, foods that are usually disliked by individuals with ARFID – like fruits, vegetables, and meats – were those most likely to be poisonous when our ancient ancestors were hunting and gathering. According to Cooke and Webber (2015, p. 81) the foods avoided by children with selective eating make 'perfect sense if you consider that plant and protein foods pose the most significant risk of poisoning to young children. Toxins are present in many plants (fruits, vegetables), while animal foods (meet, fish and eggs) are primary sources of bacteria, causing poisoning.'

However, most people who do not go on to develop ARFID ultimately learn that many foods are safe, and even tasty, through a process called *exposure*. In other words, once they eat a new food several times, they realize that they will not get sick. They also start to find that an initially novel or strange taste starts to feel familiar, and even enjoyable. On the other hand, people with ARFID may be so careful about their eating that they never get to benefit from this mere exposure effect. They typically limit their diet to very few foods, prepared in exactly the same

What is ARFID?

Avoidant / Restrictive Food Intake Disorder

- People with ARFID eat a very limited variety or amount of food and it causes problems in their lives

- These problems may be health-related, like losing too much weight, or not getting enough nutrients

- These problems may be social, like not being able to eat meals with others

ARFID is different from other eating disorders, like anorexia nervosa, because people with ARFID do not worry much about how they look, or how much they weigh. Instead, people with ARFID might have one, two, or all three of these important concerns:

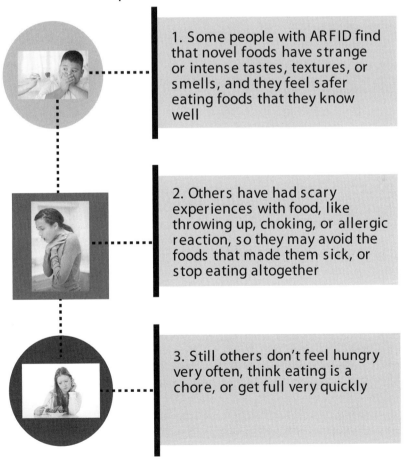

1. Some people with ARFID find that novel foods have strange or intense tastes, textures, or smells, and they feel safer eating foods that they know well

2. Others have had scary experiences with food, like throwing up, choking, or allergic reaction, so they may avoid the foods that made them sick, or stop eating altogether

3. Still others don't feel hungry very often, think eating is a chore, or get full very quickly

Fig 6.1 Patient education handout: 'What is ARFID?'

ARFID is a Psychiatric Disorder

It's important to understand that someone with ARFID is not just being "picky" or "stubborn"

People with ARFID have underlying biological traits that initially made their eating habits a logical choice

Once established, a pattern of food avoidance can become long-standing and highly resistant to change

GOOD NEWS!

There are helpful steps patients and families can take to interrupt these patterns of behavior

Thomas, J.J. and Eddy, K.T. (2018). *Cognitive-Behavioral Therapy for Avoidant/Restrictive Food Intake Disorder: Children, Adolescents, & Adults.* Cambridge: Cambridge University Press.

Fig 6.1 *(cont.)*

What happens when you eat a limited variety of food?

*Flavor preferences are partly genetic

*You may even be a "supertaster" - meaning you could have been born with a high concentration of taste buds on your tongue and dislike bitter foods, like vegetables

*There may be evolutionary advantages to food preferences

*Foods like fruits, vegetables, and meats were those most likely to be poisonous when our ancestors were hunting and gathering

How does a limited diet keep ARFID going?

*Eating the same foods all the time makes new foods taste even more different

*Certain nutrition deficiencies can change the way food tastes, making new food even less appealing

*Eating a particular food over and over may also make you tired of that food and stop eating it, further limiting your diet

*Eating a very limited diet can also cause serious health problems. Eating preferred foods high in sugar and fat has been associated with diabetes and heart disease. Avoiding non-preferred foods, like fruits and vegetables, is associated with certain cancers

*It may be hard to eat with others, causing you to miss out on opportunities to learn about new foods

Thomas, J.J. and Eddy, K.T. (2018). *Cognitive-Behavioral Therapy for Avoidant/Restrictive Food Intake Disorder: Children, Adolescents, & Adults.* Cambridge: Cambridge University Press.

Fig 6.2 Patient education handout: 'What happens when you eat a limited variety of food?'

What happens when you become more careful about your eating after a negative experience with food?

*Negative experiences with food such as choking, vomiting, an allergic reaction, or pain after eating can be traumatic

*These experiences might cause you to limit your diet to prevent further trauma

*You might even avoid any food that reminds you of the traumatic experience or stop eating altogether

How does avoiding foods or eating altogether keep ARFID going?

*You may be using "safety behaviors" to try and prevent another traumatic experience from happening
 -Taking very small bites
 -Chewing for much longer than needed
 -Only eating at familiar restaurants
 -Not eating at all

*Safety behaviors prevent you from testing negative predictions about eating

*The more you avoid eating, the scarier it becomes!

Thomas, J.J. and Eddy, K.T. (2018). *Cognitive-Behavioral Therapy for Avoidant/Restrictive Food Intake Disorder: Children, Adolescents, & Adults.* Cambridge: Cambridge University Press.

Fig 6.3 Patient education handout: 'What happens when you become more careful about your eating after a negative experience with food?'

What happens when you eat a limited volume of food?

*How hungry you feel and how much pleasure you get from eating is partly due to your genes

*Eating very little can cause you to feel full quickly, even though you are not getting enough nutrients

*Eating without a regular schedule of meals and snacks can dull hunger cues, especially if you go long periods without eating

*Eating too little can promote excessive fullness when you do eat an adequate amount because your stomach capacity decreases with chronic food restriction

How does eating very little keep ARFID going?

*Even if you are born with a smaller appetite than others, eating very little may further reduce your appetite. This is particularly true if you also limit food variety

*Eating a limited variety can decrease your ability to eat a sufficient volume of food because you get bored of eating the same things and then eat less of them

*You may experience low mood, irritability, anxiety, apathy, difficulty concentrating, or social isolation

*You may also experience significant weight loss, osteoporosis, loss of menses, muscle wasting, decreased heart rate, or other medical problems

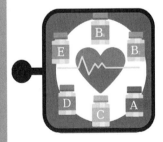

Thomas, J.J. and Eddy, K.T. (2018). *Cognitive-Behavioral Therapy for Avoidant/Restrictive Food Intake Disorder. Children, Adolescents, & Adults.* Cambridge: Cambridge University Press.

Fig 6.4 Patient education handout: 'What happens when you eat a limited volume of food?'

way. Eating these same foods over and over causes individuals to get used to food tasting a certain way, making the taste of novel foods even more different. Also, eating a particular food repeatedly may result in an individual becoming tired of that food and dropping it entirely, further limiting their diet. All of these factors make the person with ARFID even more reluctant to try new foods, keeping them locked into their disorder.

In reviewing Fig 6.3, the therapist should note that, although eating is often conceptualized as a pleasant activity, many people will at some point have a negative experience related to food, such as choking, vomiting, having a food-related allergic reaction, or experiencing pain after eating. For some, these experiences feel traumatic and lead the person to become more careful about his or her eating going forward. While some degree of extra care is adaptive following an adverse event, some people become so careful that it interferes with their ability to get adequate nutrition. For example, a person might avoid any food that reminds him or her of the traumatic experience, or even stop eating altogether. Further, when they do eat, they may engage in safety behaviors that further interfere with opportunities to disconfirm their catastrophic predictions. The problem with these strategies is that they can backfire: the more a person avoids something, the more anxiety-provoking the avoided object or situation becomes.

In reviewing Fig 6.4, the therapist should note that how hungry people feel and how much pleasure they derive from eating varies across individuals and is partly due to genetic factors. However, some people who do not feel hungry very often or find eating to be a chore eat less and less over time. Eating a limited volume of food has important effects on a person's appetite that, paradoxically, make eating more difficult. For example, eating erratically throughout the day, without a regular schedule of meals and snacks, may dull hunger cues. This is particularly true when people go long periods of time without eating. Eating too little can also promote excessive fullness – and even pain – when an adequate amount is finally eaten, because the stomach capacity can decrease to accommodate chronic food restriction. Eating a limited variety may further decrease a person's ability to eat a sufficient volume. This happens in part because decreases in variety (even perceived variety) make people eat less. For example, people will eat fewer M&Ms (small chocolates covered in a candy shell)

when the experimenter puts just one color of M&Ms (e.g., green) in a bowl, versus when the experimenter puts M&Ms of all colors in the same bowl (Kahn & Wansink, 2004). This occurs even though all colors of M&Ms taste virtually the same! As described in Chapter 4, eating a limited variety can also limit volume through a process called *sensory-specific satiety*. This occurs when a person gets tired of a particular taste (e.g., savory, salty) and stops eating, even though the person may still have an appetite for foods of a different taste (e.g., sweet). You may have had this experience yourself if you have ever finished dinner and felt full, but suddenly had room for dessert when a sweet treat arrived. A subset of people with limited intake will also experience significant weight loss, which further entrenches the problem. Findings from the Minnesota Starvation Study in which 36 men lost 25% of their body weights in the 1940s suggested that limited intake has predictable negative consequences on feelings, thoughts, and behavior (Garner, 1997). Specifically, experimenters observed low mood, irritability, anxiety, apathy, hypochondriasis (body-focused anxiety), difficulty concentrating, social isolation, ritualistic eating behaviors, and eating very slowly. A crucial point to emphasize – particularly for patients who are underweight – is that many of the side effects of starvation can be reversed once the patient begins eating a sufficient volume of food and gains to a healthier weight. It is important to presage that, because of the patient's unique biological vulnerabilities (e.g., low appetite, lower reward value of food), it is unlikely that the patient will simply increase intake on his or her own. In other words, therapist or parent support will be crucial to facilitate this process.

Provide psychoeducation on CBT-AR. After introducing ARFID and its maintaining mechanisms, the therapist should present Fig 6.5. Specifically, the therapist should emphasize that CBT-AR is based on the theory that although we cannot necessarily change the biological traits that caused the ARFID in the first place, we can help the person escape the ARFID cycle. The first step is helping the patient understand how his or her ARFID works. Next, the therapist and patient will work together to achieve early increases in variety and/or volume. Then the therapist will carefully plan with the patient (or family) which foods or situations to introduce in treatment. The heart of the treatment is a series of repeated exposures to novel foods or eating situations, to facilitate new learning about the safety and tolerability of these

How is ARFID treated?

★ CBT-AR ★

How does Cognitive-Behavioral Therapy for ARFID work?

 ## Main treatment goals:

1. Achieve or maintain a healthy weight

2. Correct any nutritional deficiencies

3. Eat foods from each of the five basic food groups (i.e., fruits, vegetables, proteins, dairy, grains)

4. Feel more comfortable eating in social situations

 ## What treatment is not:

1. Trying to change your personality

2. Making you eat very unusual foods

3. Force feeding

Fig 6.5 Patient education handout: 'How is ARFID treated?'

What Does CBT–AR look like?

4 stages over 20-30 sessions

1

LEARN ABOUT ARFID AND MAKE EARLY CHANGES

Keep records to figure out what maintains your symptoms; if you are underweight, increase the volume of your preferred foods; make early changes to variety

2

CONTINUE EARLY CHANGES AND SET BIG GOALS

Set goals to face your fears; continue increasing volume and/or food variety

3

FACE YOUR FEARS

Gain exposure with new or feared foods; taste small amounts at first, then incorporate larger amounts

4

PREVENT REPLASE

As part of completing treatment, develop a skills plan to keep practicing on your own

Treatment is Active!

*You have to attend sessions weekly

*Depending on your age and treatment goals, your parents may also need to attend

*Each week you will have at-home practice tasks. Examples include:
   -Keeping food logs to track your progress
   -Trying and practicing new foods at home

If you are interested in CBT-AR for yourself or a loved one, you should consider whether now is the right time for you to make this commitment

Thomas, J.J. and Eddy, K.T. (2018). *Cognitive-Behavioral Therapy for Avoidant/Restrictive Food Intake Disorder: Children, Adolescents, & Adults.* Cambridge: Cambridge University Press.

Fig 6.5 *(cont.)*

experiences. The overall goal of the treatment is not to change the patient's personality or to get him or her to eat very unusual foods, but rather to help the patient eat the types of foods that will support healthy weight, correct any nutritional deficiencies, and feel comfortable eating with others. The treatment takes 20–30 sessions and involves a high degree of commitment from the therapist, patient, and/or family. Not only does the patient need to attend sessions regularly, but the therapist will ask the patient to do regular at-home practices, like recording what he or she is eating and making changes to his or her diet. Importantly, the therapist will never assign busywork; all of the at-home practices are designed to bring the person closer to escaping the ARFID cycle.

Assign at-home practice tasks. At the conclusion of session 1, the therapist should assign two important at-home practice tasks. The first is self- or parent-monitoring of food intake, and the second is the first change to volume and/or variety. We will discuss each in turn.

In individual CBT-AR, the therapist asks the patient to begin to self-monitor all food and drink taken during the day (including all meals, snacks, or grazing/picking opportunities), as well as associated thoughts, feelings, and physical sensations. While some patients may wish to use a smartphone app to streamline the process, Table 6.1 provides a blank self-monitoring form for patients who prefer to keep paper records. In the 'thoughts, feelings' box of the self-monitoring form, patients should be asked to note avoidance of specific eating situations, and avoidance of places where others are eating non-preferred foods. The patient should also pay special attention to timing, volume, variety, and intensity of any sensory reactions to food. Lastly, in the 'physical sensations' box, the patient should begin recording hunger and fullness, nausea, and/or physical sensations of anxiety. Table 6.2 depicts a worked example of a self-monitoring record for a patient participating in the early stages of CBT-AR.

In family-supported CBT-AR, the therapist asks that the parents (rather than the patient) monitor all of the patient's meals and snacks, using a smartphone app or paper record. This is because, in family-supported CBT-AR, the parents (rather than the patient) bear primary responsibility for change. If the patient in family-supported CBT-AR has significant weight to gain, it will be imperative that the parents also plan to supervise all of the patient's

eating opportunities in Stages 1–2, similar to FBT for AN (Lock & Le Grange, 2015). In most cases, this will require substantial commitment on the part of the parents, who may need to take time off from work or school, or make alternate arrangements for care of other children or household duties, so that they can be present during all-important breakfasts, lunches, dinners, and snacks. Because session 1 already includes a great deal of material, the therapist can set this expectation now, but will likely need to return to it in session 2 for further discussion and troubleshooting.

The final task of session 1 is to support the patient in embracing early change by asking him or her to make the first change in volume or variety. For patients who are underweight, the therapist should focus on *volume*. Specifically the therapist should share the expectation that the patient will gain 1–2 lbs/week during CBT-AR and ask the patient (or parents) to increase the patient's daily calorie intake by approximately 500 calories per day. The therapist should emphasize that the patient need not make any changes yet to variety but should instead focus only on increasing the volume of preferred foods – particular those that are high enough in calories (e.g., ice cream, pizza, supplement drinks) to support weight gain. There will not be a great deal of time to discuss exactly what the patient will eat (which will be the focus of later sessions), but the patient (or family) should be encouraged to get started on this important task right away, to the best of their ability.

For patients who are not underweight, the therapist should instead focus on *variety*. This first change can be small, as it will be built on in future sessions. Examples include: (1) changing the presentation or flavor of a preferred food (e.g., biting into a food whole that is normally chopped; trying a different flavor of a preferred cereal; eating a chicken nugget after peeling off the breading); (2) reintroducing a previously preferred food that has recently been dropped or is eaten at very low frequency (e.g., the patient states that he or she eats bananas, but has not eaten one in several months); (3) reducing a minor safety behavior related to food presentation (e.g., blending a puree to a slightly thicker consistency than the patient is currently tolerating; eating a food to which the patient knows he or she is not allergic and is packaged in an allergen-free facility, but which the patient has not eaten before); or (4) rotating meals or snacks by day (e.g., if the patient has the same

Table 6.1 Self-monitoring record for CBT-AR

Time	Food/drink consumed	Thoughts, feelings	Physical sensations

Table 6.2 Self-monitoring record for CBT-AR (worked example)

Time	Food/drink consumed	Thoughts, feelings	Physical sensations
7:30 AM	2 pieces of toast with butter, 2 cups of tea	Trying to eat at least something small	Not hungry
12:00 PM	Skipped lunch	Ugh. I couldn't bring myself to eat lunch at work today.	Tired
4:15 PM	1 order of chicken nuggets (one with breading peeled off) and 1 order of French fries from McDonalds, 1 glass of water	Finally after work I got some McDonalds nuggets. I don't feel comfortable eating other nuggets except the ones from McDonalds. The other ones have a weird texture. I tried peeling the breading off one nugget like we talked about, and it was OK but not great.	
8:20 PM	1 order of chicken nuggets, 1 glass of water	My roommate was cooking pasta with garlic in our apartment tonight. It made my stomach turn because it was so strong. I went to my room so I could eat my leftover McDonalds nuggets in my room in peace.	Hungry, but stomach upset from garlic smell

morning snack every school day but a different snack on the weekends, incorporating the weekend snack into the weekday repertoire, and vice versa). The patient need not introduce a totally novel food (as will be done in later sessions), but rather agree to at least one slight, manageable change. The purpose here is to increase flexibility just enough to set the stage for further change.

Stage 1, Session 2

Because every session of CBT-AR begins with setting the agenda and weighing the patient (described in detail earlier), the therapist should do both of those tasks as a matter of course at the beginning of each session. Only then should the therapist move on to the tasks unique to each session, to which we now turn.

Review at-home practice tasks. After setting the agenda and taking the patient's weight, the therapist should review the patient's self- (or parent-) monitoring. In our experience, if the therapist does not reinforce the importance of the self-monitoring by reviewing it with the patient at every session, the patient will sooner or later stop completing it. This review will necessarily be more detailed at the beginning of treatment (e.g., checking for adherence to regular pattern of eating as well as gathering data to support the individualized treatment formulation that is created in session 2), and may take a different form later in treatment as the therapist is checking on at-home practice tasks (e.g., tasting or incorporating a new food). The therapist should begin by praising the patient's (or family's) efforts at completing the monitoring, and then move on to discussing the content of the records. The therapist should ask clarifying questions (e.g., if the amount of a food is unclear) and share relevant observations (i.e., if the patient is not yet taking in adequate calories, or is eating the same meals and snacks at every eating opportunity).

In reviewing the monitoring, the therapist should look for a recording of the first change to volume or variety that was agreed on in the last session. If the patient was successful in increasing volume or variety, the therapist should provide praise and reinforce any changes as well as inquire about the patient's willingness to continue making that change during the upcoming week. If the patient was not successful, the therapist should identify barriers. For example, if the underweight patient has not gained weight

as expected, during review of the self- or parent-monitoring, the therapist should identify meals or snacks in which the patient can increase calories, even if still relying on preferred foods.

Create individualized formulation. The therapist should then move on to creating the individualized formulation. The primary maintaining mechanisms of ARFID listed in *DSM-5* and assessed on the PARDI include sensory sensitivity, fear of aversive consequences, and apparent lack of interest in eating or food. The patient may have one, two, or all three of these issues as primary maintaining mechanisms. Based on the patient's initial assessment, self-monitoring, and discussions of psychoeducational materials, the therapist builds an individualized formulation collaboratively with the patient (or family). The formulation should be based on the generalized formulation presented earlier (Fig 4.1), but created collaboratively with the patient on a blank piece of paper and written in the patient's (or family's) own words. The emphasis in building the formulation is on highlighting for the patient a reciprocal feedback loop in which maintaining factors not only promote food restriction and avoidance, but the restriction and avoidance themselves actually strengthen the maintaining factors, which then feed back into further restriction and avoidance.

To start out, the therapist should ask the patient, 'What is the most upsetting part about your eating?' or 'What part of your eating brought you into treatment?' Typically, the patient's response will fall into one or more of the constructs in the CBT model of ARFID. For example, if a patient with both sensory sensitivity and apparent lack of interest in eating or food responds with 'not being able to go to parties,' the therapist should write this response word-for-word in place of 'social avoidance.' If the response does not fit into one of the categories, the therapist should continue to explore with the patient, in a downward-arrow fashion, until they collaboratively hit on one of the relevant constructs. From there, the therapist should begin asking questions that might direct the patient to uncover other pieces of the formulation. In the case of social avoidance, the therapist might ask, 'What makes you not want to go to parties?' If the patient responds, for example, that 'There's nothing there I can eat; all of the food at parties is usually gross,' the therapist can write this in place of 'negative feelings and predictions about food.' From there, the therapist can continue to ask

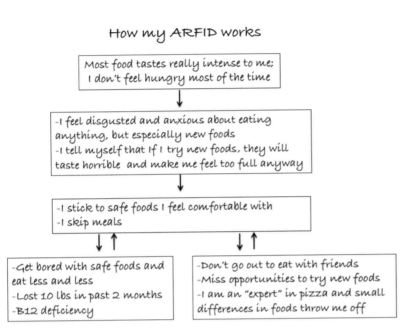

How my ARFID works

Most food tastes really intense to me;
I don't feel hungry most of the time

-I feel disgusted and anxious about eating
anything, but especially new foods
-I tell myself that if I try new foods, they will
taste horrible and make me feel too full anyway

-I stick to safe foods I feel comfortable with
-I skip meals

-Get bored with safe foods and
eat less and less
-Lost 10 lbs in past 2 months
-B12 deficiency

-Don't go out to eat with friends
-Miss opportunities to try new foods
-I am an "expert" in pizza and small
differences in foods throw me off

Fig 6.6 Example of CBT-AR formulation in patient's own words (worked example for ARFID with sensory sensitivity and apparent lack of interest in eating or food)

directed questions so as to fill in the remaining gaps in the formulation. Fig 6.6 depicts an example formulation of patient who has ARFID with both sensory sensitivity and apparent lack of interest in eating or food.

Once the individualized formulation is complete, the therapist should hand it to the patient (or family) and ask whether the patient (or family) feels it resonates with their own experience. The therapist should invite the patient (or family) to edit, amend, or embellish the formulation, as appropriate. Then the therapist should emphasize the primary take-home message, as described in the CBT model of ARFID: Regardless of the preexisting biological vulnerabilities, *it is now the avoidance itself that serves to maintain the patient's negative predictions about eating and its attendant physical and psychological consequences. In turn, these physical and psychological factors serve to further reinforce food restriction, in a reciprocal feedback loop.* The therapist should then share the treatment implication for CBT-AR – i.e., that by targeting food restriction itself, the associated negative thoughts, feelings, and consequences that the patient finds aversive (e.g., social avoidance) can be reduced or eliminated.

Prescribe a schedule of regular eating relying on preferred foods. The second major task of session 2 is to prescribe a schedule of regular eating. At this early stage in treatment, the patient can continue eating his or her preferred foods. The key here is to establish a regular schedule of eating opportunities, including three meals and two to three snacks each day. If the patient does not have significant weight to gain, two snacks may be adequate. If the patient is underweight, three snacks are nearly always necessary. The schedule is important because, regardless of their clinical presentation, many individuals with ARFID go for long periods without eating. For example, those with sensory sensitivity may avoid eating entirely at mealtimes if preferred foods are not available. Similarly, those with fear of aversive consequences may have stopped eating entirely secondary to a choking or vomiting episode. Those with apparent lack of interest in eating or food may forget to eat without frequent prompting. Such patterns may paradoxically reduce hunger overall, encourage hunger at inappropriate times, and/or discourage hunger at mealtimes when nutritious foods are being presented. Thus implementing a regular pattern of eating is a crucial intervention in CBT-AR. In order to establish a regular eating pattern, we recommend eating every three to four hours. Similar to Fairburn's CBT-E, we discourage grazing or otherwise eating during the gaps in order to shape the development of healthy appetite. For example, a patient who wakes up early and eats breakfast at 7:00 AM may need a morning snack at 10:00 AM, lunch at 1:00 PM, afternoon snack at 4:00 PM, dinner at 6:30 PM, and evening snack at 9:00 PM. In contrast, a patient who wakes up later might have breakfast at 9:00 AM, lunch at 12:00 PM, afternoon snack at 3:00 PM, dinner at 7:00 PM, and evening snack at 9:00 PM. It is helpful for the therapist to review with the patient the specific timing of meals and snacks that will work with the patient's individual schedule, to promote adherence. The therapist should assist the patient (or family) in creating a daily schedule that will coincide with school and work activities. If the patient is low weight, it will additionally be important to identify which parent(s) or caregivers (s) can supervise each meal and snack throughout the day. Creating this daily schedule may require trouble-shooting around whether parents need to request time away from work, or whether other caregivers (e.g., school nurse, grandparent) can be educated about CBT-AR and engaged to provide supervision in place of the parents.

It is important to note that eating by the clock is particularly helpful for patients who present with apparent lack of interest in eating or food. Studies suggest that the appetite-stimulating hormone ghrelin is entrained with habitual meal patterns in humans. For example, individuals who typically eat lunch 2.5–3.5 hours after eating breakfast will hit their peak ghrelin concentrations and experience their highest levels of subjective hunger within 2.5–3.5 hours of eating breakfast, whereas those who usually wait 5.5–6.5 hours between meals will experience peak ghrelin concentrations and hunger much later (Frecka & Mattes, 2008). The implication for CBT-AR is that individuals with apparent lack of interest in eating or food can take advantage of this hormonal entrainment by eating their three meals and two or three snacks at roughly the same times each day, thereby training their bodies to secrete appetite-stimulating hormones at these times. To that end, the therapist should briefly explain the concept of ghrelin entrainment (to the parents in family-supported CBT-AR, and to the patient in adult CBT-AR) and encourage the patient to follow his or her usual eating schedule as closely as possible, varying meals and snacks by no more than 30 minutes each day. For patients who forget to eat, this will almost always require the creative implementation of external cues as reminders for eating (e.g., setting alarm on smartphone; setting the breakfast table the night before).

Discuss critical importance of gaining weight (underweight patients only). If the patient is underweight, the therapist should emphasize the importance of weight gain as a primary treatment goal of CBT-AR by referring to the handout 'Why do I need to gain weight and how do I do it?' (Fig 6.7). Some patients (or families) will need the therapist's help in appreciating the critical importance of weight gain for ARFID recovery. This is particularly true if the patient has been chronically underweight, so the current low weight is not experienced as an acute crisis. This may also be true if the patient (or family) has come to treatment specifically to work toward increasing dietary variety and therefore does not see insufficient volume as problematic.

First, if the patient (or family) cites the patient's chronic underweight as a reason not to gain, the therapist should refer back to the pretreatment medical evaluation and highlight the physician's recommendation that the patient gain weight and approximately how much. The therapist can remind the patient (or family) that the goal of CBT-AR is to restore the patient with ARFID to his or her individual growth trajectory. Rather than expecting all patients to achieve 50th percentile height, weight, and BMI for age and gender, the therapist will support the patient in returning to whichever percentile the patient was previously following, or should be following to avoid the medical sequelae of malnutrition. In some cases this may mean restoring a patient whose BMI is less than the 1st percentile to just the 5th or 10th percentile. If the patient (or family) cites other family members who are thin as a rationale for allowing the patient to maintain an unhealthily low weight, the therapist might gently inquire whether these other family members have also had doctors express fear of their weight being too low. If not, the therapist should emphasize that the patient's own physician has expressed concern – and indeed the therapist him- or herself is gravely concerned – about the patient's low weight. In other words, the therapist should emphasize that the purpose of weight gain is not to force the patient to conform to a predetermined social or family norm, but rather to help the patient achieve and sustain optimal health.

Second, in the case that the patient (or family) is eager to increase dietary variety and does not see insufficient volume as problematic, the therapist should explain that a major philosophy of CBT-AR is *volume before variety*. This is because eating a limited volume of food typically leads to health consequences that are usually more acute and severe (e.g., underweight, stunted growth, amenorrhea,

WHY DO I NEED TO GAIN WEIGHT? and HOW DO I DO IT?

Being at a low weight is <u>DANGEROUS</u> to your health! It can lead to:

| Feeling sad or irritable | Feeling tired all the time | Your brain shrinking | Stunted Growth | For females: losing or never getting your period | For males: low testosterone | Low bone density and increased fracture risk | Death |

Your therapist will work with your physician to determine the most appropriate weight for you given your height, age, and prior growth trajectory

HOW DO I DO IT???

Ways to gain weight at a rate of 1-2 lbs per week:

Eat more of the preferred foods you like. Its OKAY to eat cookies, candy, and ice cream every day if those are the foods you prefer!

Eat on a regular schedule throughout the day (3 meals and 3 snacks)

Even snacks should have multiple components (e.g., crackers AND peanut butter AND milk)

500 Increase your caloric intake by AT LEAST 500 calories a day

Eliminate or reduce your physical activity OR replace the calories you burn by eating EVEN MORE

For children and adolescents, let your parents help by supervising your meals and snacks

Examples of meals and snacks with at least 500 calories:

*Large milkshake

*3 small-to-medium chocolate chip cookies and 10 ounces of whole milk

*Bagel with 2 slices of cheese

*2-3 pieces of cheese pizza

*2-3 frozen waffles with 2 tablespoons of syrup and 6 ounces of juice

*12 ounces of hot chocolate and 2 doughnut holes

REMEMBER: You need to eat this amount in addition to whatever you are already eating!

Thomas, J.J. and Eddy, K.T. (2018). *Cognitive-Behavioral Therapy for Avoidant/Restrictive Food Intake Disorder. Children, Adolescents, & Adults.* Cambridge: Cambridge University Press.

Fig 6.7 Patient education handout: 'Why do I need to gain weight and how do I do it?'

bradycardia, osteoporosis) than those associated with eating a limited variety (e.g., nutrition deficiencies, social difficulties). Furthermore, the foods that individuals with ARFID already prefer (e.g., refined carbohydrates, dairy foods) are perfect for supporting weight gain because they are typically high in calories. In contrast, the foods that the patient (or family) would like to learn about in Stage 3 (e.g., lean proteins, fruits, vegetables) are usually low in calories and may actually interfere with weight gain by making the patient feel full before he or she has consumed a sufficient amount of food. Indeed, a patient would need to eat five apples in order to equal the number of calories in just one cup of ice cream! Lastly, focusing on volume and variety simultaneously is challenging because CBT-AR addresses low weight and selective eating with different treatment strategies. In this way CBT-AR differs from FBT for anorexia nervosa, which focuses on increasing variety and volume simultaneously. This is because an important difference between anorexia nervosa and ARFID is that individuals with anorexia nervosa tend to abhor the very foods that their counterparts with ARFID adore, namely the refined carbohydrates and processed dairy foods that are ideally suited to supporting weight gain.

In order to achieve the expected weight gain of 1–2 lbs/week, the patient must eat at least an additional 500 calories per day above and beyond his or her daily maintenance calorie needs. Given that the therapist will have already prescribed a schedule of regular eating (i.e., three meals plus two or three snacks per day), we recommend that the therapist now suggest increasing the portion size of the patient's preferred foods at each eating opportunity (in line with the approaches of Toomey et al. [2014] and Williams and Foxx [2007]). For example, if the patient is currently eating plain pasta with butter for dinner, the patient (or family) should greatly increase the portion of pasta and perhaps double or triple the amount of butter.

Patients and families may balk at this suggestion if the patient's preferred foods are considered unhealthy by societal standards. Indeed, it is rare that a doctor would give a patient carte blanche to eat as much pizza, ice cream, and chicken nuggets as possible, yet that is exactly what the CBT-AR therapist does when the patient is underweight. If the patient (or family) protests, the therapist should point out that many of our contemporary conceptions of which foods are healthy versus unhealthy have been shaped in the setting of a global obesity epidemic. Certainly it is not healthy for someone who is normal weight or overweight to eat only processed carbohydrate foods and eschew fresh fruits and vegetables. However, if someone is starving and desperately needs to gain weight, consuming high-calorie foods is actually the healthiest step he or she can take. Some patients' diets are so limited that, in order to gain weight as expeditiously as possible, they will need to eat a very unusual diet. For example, one 14-year-old female patient in our treatment trial with a BMI of 15.9 started her 20-lb weight gain trajectory by consuming chocolate milk, candy bars, sugar cookies, and chocolate hazelnut spread at most meals and snacks! It is often helpful if the therapist frames the increase in consumption of preferred foods as a temporary measure, usually lasting no more than a few weeks or months. If the patient (or family) remains concerned, the therapist can point out that the patient is already consuming these foods, and that simply increasing the volume of foods that the patient is already eating is unlikely to lead to worse health outcomes than if the patient were to remain dangerously underweight. Indeed, the long-term goal of CBT-AR is that the patient will regularly consume a variety of foods across the five basic food groups. By way of example, after achieving a healthy weight and initiating her menses in Stage 2, the 14-year-old with the penchant for chocolate milk and candy bars ultimately incorporated salad and almonds into her diet in Stage 3.

Patients (or families) may wonder if they can take (or give their child) high-energy drinks (e.g., Ensure, Boost) to support weight gain. Because dependence on dietary supplements (including high-energy drinks) is part of the diagnostic criteria for ARFID, we do not recommend introducing them *de novo* if the patient is not already taking them. Since the ultimate goal of CBT-AR is for the patient to maintain his or her weight without relying on supplements, introducing them early in treatment will create extra work for the patient at later stages. However, if a patient's diet is quite limited and he or she is already drinking high-energy drinks, increasing the number of drinks each day may be a straightforward way of achieving early weight gain. If high-energy drinks will be used, we suggest that they only be provided at preplanned meal and snack times. Parents may be tempted to offer the drinks at any time the patient seems likely to accept them (e.g., in the car, while watching television), or patients may wish to sip on them throughout a busy day at work or school. However, we discourage grazing on supplements between meals and snacks, as it will prevent the patient from developing predictable hunger cues at preplanned meal and snack times.

Planning the therapeutic meal (underweight patients only). If the patient is underweight, the final task of session 2 is planning the therapeutic meal that will take place in session 3. Patients (and families) are often surprised at the large volume of food that the patient will need to consume in order to put on weight. Many worry that the therapist is asking them to stuff themselves (individual CBT-AR) or force-feed their child (family-supported CBT-AR). Thus the purpose of the therapeutic meal is to help the parents and therapist get on the same page about the volume of food required for weight gain, and for the therapist to provide *in vivo* coaching to the patient (or family) on how to consume it. If the patient is underweight, the therapist should conclude the first session of Stage 2 by inviting the patient (or family) to bring a meal to the next session. The meal could be breakfast, lunch, or dinner, depending on the timing of the session. The only requirement for the meal is that it be (1) composed primarily or even solely of preferred foods (recall that when the patient is underweight, Stages 1 and 2 address volume, whereas Stage 3 addresses variety) and (2) of sufficient volume or calorie density to facilitate weight gain. The therapist should also ask that the patient (or family) bring one item to the next session that would increase the patient's eating flexibility (e.g., a different presentation of a preferred food, or a previously preferred food that was recently dropped). The purpose of bringing a less preferred (though not completely novel) food to the therapeutic meal is for the patient (or family) to experience success in making small changes in variety that can be built on in Stage 3.

Assign at-home practice tasks. In closing, the therapist should confirm the patient's understanding of the at-home practice tasks for the week. For all patients this will include self- or parent-monitoring of food intake. For those who are underweight, this will include continuing to increase intake of preferred foods by 500 calories per day, and bringing to session 3 a high-calorie meal and a food that will increase eating flexibility. For those who are not underweight, this will include continuing to increase eating flexibility by making a small change in food presentation,

reintroducing a previously eaten food, eliminating a minor safety behavior, or rotating preferred meals throughout the week. Also for those who are not underweight, session 2 will be the last session of Stage 1, and the therapist will move on to Stage 2. For those who are underweight, the therapist will continue on to session 3 of Stage 1.

Stage 1, Session 3 (underweight patients only)

If the patient is underweight, the therapist continues with the third session of Stage 1 as usual by setting the agenda, weighing the patient, and reviewing the patient's progress with at-home practice tasks. In particular, the therapist will want to check how the patient is doing with self- or parent-monitoring, regular eating, and increasing eating volume. Perhaps most importantly, the therapist should discuss the patient's progress toward gaining 1–2 lbs/week by adding at least 500 calories per day. If the patient has not gained, the therapist should brainstorm with the parents and family how calories can be further increased. After these tasks are complete, the therapist should initiate the primary task of session 3 – the therapeutic meal. In line with the CBT-AR mantra *volume before variety*, the therapist will focus the majority of the therapeutic meal on supporting the patient to increase volume. Only once this task has been accomplished should the therapist move on to a more modest intervention designed to introduce variety.

Increase volume with the therapeutic meal. The therapist should initiate the therapeutic meal by encouraging the patient (or family) to begin eating as they normally would at home. Similar to the family meal in FBT for anorexia nervosa (Lock & Le Grange, 2015), the therapist will not eat, but rather will observe the patient's eating and any helpful or unhelpful strategies that the patient (or family) employs in the early stages of the meal. For example, did the patient (or family) follow the therapist's instructions to bring a high-calorie meal? Given that patients and families are often surprised at the volume that is necessary, the therapist should take note if the portion is inadequate and provide gentle corrective feedback. Did the patient (or family) follow the therapist's guidance to bring a meal comprising primarily preferred foods? If so, what are the preferred foods? The therapist may note that the meal is a bit unusual (e.g., cereal for dinner; a panoply of snack foods without any main dish), but this is fine as long as the foods are preferred and the patient is able to eat them. Does the patient (or family) plate the meal (enabling the patient or family to monitor how much is being eaten while the meal is in progress) or does the patient eat out of larger bags or containers? Does the patient eat very slowly? In family-supported treatment, do the parents ignore this or do they encourage the patient to increase eating speed? Does the patient complain of nausea or premature fullness? If so and if the patient is in family-supported treatment, do the parents reinforce the behavior and reduce the volume the child is required to eat? Finally, through direct observation, the therapist will begin determining which of the ARFID maintaining mechanisms appears to be the biggest barrier to increasing volume. Does the patient express fear of aversive consequences (e.g., vomiting) as the primary rationale for ending the meal, or lack of interest in eating (e.g., getting bored or no longer feeling hungry)?

Partway through the session, the therapist should move from simple observation to active coaching of the patient (or family). Specifically, using behavioral principles, the therapist should either begin coaching the patient (in individual CBT-AR) or the parents (in family-supported CBT-AR) to help the patient increase volume. Variety should not yet be addressed. Specifically, the therapist (or parents) should begin making very specific requests of the patient encouraging him or her to take another bite (e.g., 'Here, have another bite of pizza') or to finish a portion (e.g., 'You're almost done with your mashed potatoes; just one bite to go!'). It is important that the therapist (or parents) empathize with any challenges but not allow them to get in the way of the primary task of the session, which is helping the patient eat more volume than he or she originally intended (e.g., 'We know you are feeling really full right now, but it's very important for your health that you keep drinking your chocolate milk'). Finally, the therapist (or parents) should praise any successes (e.g., 'Great work eating all of your pasta!'). Importantly, the therapist should ensure that the parents are on the same page and take turns encouraging the patient to eat, rather than letting just one parent bear the full responsibility of this monumental task. The therapist should also discourage the parents from expressing criticism or anger toward the patient, whom the therapist views as ill rather than picky or stubborn.

Once the patient declines to eat any additional food, the therapist (or parents) should support the patient in eating just one more bite than he or she had originally intended. This is similar to the 'one more bite' intervention of FBT (Lock & Le Grange, 2015). The purpose of this intervention is to empower the patient to see that he or she is able to eat just a bit more than he or she previously thought (in individual CBT-AR) and/or (in family-supported CBT-AR) to empower the parents to see that they can support the patient in increasing volume, even when the patient says he or she cannot possibly eat another bite.

Increase variety with one bite of novel presentation. After the patient has eaten what the therapist (or parents) deems to be an adequate volume, or has at the very least eaten one more bite than the patient originally intended, the therapist (or parents) should switch the focus to increasing variety. Specifically, the therapist (or parents) should use the same strategies to support the patient in taking at least one bite of the novel presentation of the preferred food, or previously dropped food, that the patient (or family) brought to session. The amount can be quite small – even a pea-sized bite of a solid food or very small sip of a liquid will do. For example, if the patient typically drinks only chocolate milk and brought in regular milk, taking a small sip of regular milk is sufficient to complete the task. Similarly, if the patient used to eat apples but has not eaten them for several months, just one bite of an apple will suffice. Indeed, the purpose of this intervention is for the patient (or family) to experience success in making small changes in variety that can be built on in Stage 3. Again, the therapist (or parents) should make specific requests, empathize with any challenges, and praise any successes. In family-supported CBT-AR, the therapist should note whether the parents have unrealistic expectations for such an early stage of the treatment (e.g., that the patient will eat a large amount of a novel food; that the patient will immediately like the novel food) and provide corrective feedback.

Assign at-home practice task. In closing, the therapist should invite the patient (or family) to continue with self- or parent-monitoring for the upcoming week, and to continue eating sufficient volume to support a weight gain of 1–2 lbs/week. This will typically involve keeping calories the same if the patient has gained weight and increasing them further if the patient has not gained. If the patient responded positively to the bite of non-preferred food, the therapist can also encourage the patient to continue practicing small bites or sips in the upcoming week. If the patient had a difficult time with the non-preferred food, further increases in variety can be deferred to future sessions as the primary focus for Stage 1 for underweight patients is increasing volume.

Stage 1, Session 4 (underweight patients only)

For underweight patients, the last session of Stage 4 will begin as usual by setting the agenda, weighing the patient, and reviewing the at-home practice tasks of self- or parent-monitoring, regular eating, and increasing volume by at least 500 calories per day. The therapist will then spend the majority of the session engaged in brainstorming with the patient (or family) about how to help the patient continue to substantially increase volume. If the patient has successfully begun to gain weight, the therapist may broach the topic of modest increases in variety.

Continue to focus on weight gain. If the patient has been successfully gaining weight, the therapist should inquire about how this is being done and reinforce any positive changes (e.g., eating three meals and three snacks per day, including multiple components per snack, relying on energy-dense preferred foods). If the patient has not been gaining weight, the therapist should brainstorm with the patient (or family) how to increase eating opportunities throughout the day and/or increase the energy density of meals and snacks that are already taking place. To facilitate this discussion, the therapist may wish to refer back to the patient education handout 'Why do I need to gain weight and how do I do it?' It is common, for example, for a patient to feel that he or she is trying very hard to add energy-dense foods but is not seeing positive changes on the scale. In such cases, the therapist should praise the changes that the patient has begun to make, but emphasize that further changes must be made. For example, if a patient has added a high-calorie milkshake on two evenings in the past week, the therapist should praise this effort but strongly recommend that the patient add the milkshake or other high-calorie dessert every night during the upcoming week. In many cases, small changes are salient to the patient (or family) because they are difficult to implement. However, the therapist should explain that, when it comes to weight gain, it is much more effective to put in 100% effort for

several weeks or months than 80% effort for several months or years.

Continue to focus on increasing eating flexibility (optional). If the patient has begun to gain weight and once the therapist has established a plan for the upcoming week to continue to significantly increase volume to support further weight gain, only then should he or she shift focus to a modest increase in variety. Specifically, the therapist should encourage the patient to work toward increasing eating flexibility while continuing to rely on energy-dense preferred foods. For example, the patient may vary meals and snacks each day, even while sticking with preferred foods. Alternatively, the patient may wish to reintroduce previously eaten or very-low-frequency foods during the upcoming week. These changes will not only presage larger changes in variety in Stage 3 but will also help ensure that the patient does not get bored of eating the same energy-dense foods for all meals and snacks and begin eating less of them. Furthermore, the patient (or family) can be encouraged to vary tastes (e.g., salty versus sweet) within a single meal to combat sensory-specific satiety.

Assign at-home practice tasks. The therapist should conclude the session by asking that the patient continue with self- or parent-monitoring and regular eating. If the patient has been gaining weight, the therapist should assign tasks relating to increasing both volume and variety. However, if the patient has not been gaining weight, the therapist should focus the at-home practice task on volume specifically, and defer variety until a later session when weight gain has been better established.

Troubleshooting Stage 1

What if the patient (or family) doesn't do the self-monitoring? The therapist should react at first with nonjudgmental curiosity. Explore with the patient (or family) what got in the way. For example, was the patient worried that monitoring would only increase anxiety and make the problem worse? Did the family feel they didn't have time to keep such detailed records? The therapist should then shift his/her focus to problem solving around these barriers. The therapist can reassure the patient that, although an initial increase in anxiety is possible, most patients habituate to the monitoring. The therapist should reinforce the importance of the monitoring and identify strategies to make it more convenient, such as completing it on a smartphone.

Since CBT-AR is a specific behavioral treatment for ARFID, can the patient concurrently see another therapist for more general therapy? CBT-AR is meant to be a stand-alone treatment and it's our experience that doing CBT-AR concurrently with another psychotherapy is *almost always* problematic, no matter how complex the case or the degree of comorbid psychopathology. Not only does it divide the patient's attention between two therapies and reduce focus CBT-AR; it can also lead to splitting if the other therapist is not familiar with CBT-AR and provides the patient with conflicting advice. This is particularly true when the patient is ambivalent about doing important therapy tasks, such as gaining weight, or doing exposures. For patients who are in long-term therapy, we suggest framing CBT-AR as a break from their regular therapy and an opportunity for a fresh start. The patient is certainly welcome to return to the long-term therapy to support relapse prevention after completing CBT-AR. For patients who wish to seek additional short-term treatment for comorbid symptoms (e.g., depression, anxiety), we suggest that the patient prioritize the treatments and participate sequentially rather than simultaneously. Some patients will be taking medications for comorbid conditions, which is allowable in CBT-AR. We encourage discussion with the pediatrician or primary care provider about possible effects of such medication on eating or appetite, in order to determine the potential impact on treatment.

Should the patient see a dietitian concurrently with CBT-AR? In our initial case series, we did not incorporate concurrent dietary counseling as we were testing the efficacy of CBT-AR alone. However, in clinical practice, we have often found dietitians to be extremely helpful with ARFID cases, provided that they are familiar with CBT-AR and provide advice consistent with this manual. Specifically, if the dietitian can support the implementation of regular eating, identify opportunities for increasing intake by 500 calories/day (in patients who are underweight), and brainstorm ideas for increasing dietary variety, the collaboration is likely to support treatment progress. However, if the dietitian is unfamiliar

with certain philosophies of CBT-AR (e.g., focusing on increasing volume before variety), this may feel confusing to the patient, lead to splitting, and interfere with goal attainment.

What if the patient is not gaining weight? The therapist should consider offering a second therapeutic meal to provide additional coaching to the parents (in family-supported CBT-AR) or patient (in individual CBT-AR) on increasing food intake at supervised meals (Lock et al., 2015). Although we suggest four sessions for the underweight patient in Stage 1, it is sometimes appropriate to lengthen Stage 1 to allow additional time for weight gain before moving on to Stage 2. The therapist can also consider with the parents whether a brief stay in a higher level of care is necessary (e.g., partial hospitalization, inpatient hospitalization).

Checklist for Moving on to Stage 2

By the end of Stage 1, the patient should have accomplished the following tasks. These expectations are implicit in the psychoeducation and homework tasks already presented in Stage 1; however, it is sometimes also helpful to reiterate them to the patient and family at this juncture. If the patient is having difficulty with any of these tasks, the therapist may consider extending Stage 1 beyond the expected 2–4 sessions.

- The patient (or family) expresses an understanding of ARFID and what will happen in CBT-AR
- The patient (or family) expresses an understanding of his or her specific ARFID presentation
- The patient has established self-monitoring (or parent-monitoring) of daily food intake
- The patient is eating at regular intervals (i.e., every 3–4 hours), typically three meals and two to three snacks per day, even if relying mostly on preferred foods or supplement drinks
- The patient has begun increasing volume (by 500 calories/day, if underweight) or variety (by making small changes in food presentation)

Stage 2: Treatment Planning

The purpose of CBT-AR Stage 2 (two sessions) is to continue the focus on increasing volume and variety, to learn how to prevent or ameliorate nutrition deficiencies with a varied diet comprising the five basic food groups, and to plan Stage 3. Stage 2 is designed to last two sessions. The first session presents psychoeducation about nutrition deficiencies and helps the patient continue to increase eating flexibility. In the second session, the patient will review his or her current intake from the five basic food groups and identify new foods to learn about in Stage 3.

Stage 2, Session 1

The therapist will begin the first session of Stage 2 by setting the agenda, weighing the patient, and reviewing the at-home practice tasks. For all patients, the at-home practice review will include self- or parent-monitoring, regular eating, and progress toward increasing eating flexibility and/or volume. For patients who are underweight, the at-home practice review will also include progress with increasing the patient's daily food intake by at least 500 calories per day. For patients who are underweight and not gaining, the therapist should continue to emphasize the importance of increasing *volume before variety*, identify barriers to increasing volume, and strategize potential solutions using the same techniques reviewed in sessions 3–4 of Stage 1.

Psychoeducation on nutrition deficiencies. The next task is a discussion of nutrition deficiencies, which are common among individuals with ARFID. Based on the patient's medical assessment, the therapist and patient (or family) should discuss any micro- or macro-nutrient deficiencies that have been identified. Even if the patient's medical workup has not identified any deficiencies (which is common if the patient has been prophylactically taking a multivitamin), the therapist should emphasize that the patient is at risk for developing deficiencies in the

future if ARFID is left untreated. To that end, it is important to review the patient education handout entitled 'Common nutrition deficiencies associated with ARFID' (Table 7.1). For each deficiency, the therapist should discuss the primary symptoms and whether the patient has experienced them; any treatments that a physician might prescribe to correct the deficiency (e.g., pills, drops, powders); and, most importantly, how the deficiency can be corrected by increasing the consumption of specific foods that are high in that particular nutrient.

Linking deficiencies to non-preferred foods can provide additional motivation for incorporating novel foods for patients who are otherwise reluctant to expand their diets. For example, a patient with a vitamin C deficiency may recall that he or she used to drink orange juice regularly but has recently dropped it. The therapist could inquire whether the patient is willing to reintroduce orange juice during the upcoming week as a way of increasing eating flexibility. Conversely, a patient with no known deficiencies might determine from reviewing the handout that he or she is not currently eating any iron-rich foods, and set an intention to learn about beef and lentils in Stage 3 to prevent the development of a future deficiency.

Continue to increase eating flexibility. After reviewing the material on nutrition deficiencies, the therapist should continue to emphasize the importance of increasing eating flexibility. In-session review of the self- or parent-monitoring will often highlight rigidity around eating behaviors. For example, the patient may eat exactly the same foods at each meal or snack, and/or only rarely incorporate a food viewed as tolerable though not preferred. Stage 2 is an opportunity to enhance flexibility around eating while keeping the task demands manageable. Making small changes now will prepare the patient for the harder work in Stage 3 (i.e., introducing totally novel foods). To that end, the therapist can make two suggestions.

Table 7.1 Patient education handout: 'Common nutrition deficiencies associated with ARFID'

Deficiency	Signs and symptoms	Possible treatments your doctor may prescribe	Foods rich in this nutrient (in order of nutrient density)
Calcium	Weak or broken bones (even when blood levels may be normal)	Pills, chews, wafers	Milk, cheese, yogurt, canned sardines, fortified fruit juices or cereals, milk substitutes (e.g., soymilk, almond milk), tofu, collard greens, kale, ice cream, blackstrap molasses
Folate	Persistent exhaustion or weakness, poor concentration, increased irritability, heart palpitations, shortness of breath, headaches, mouth soreness or ulcers, pale appearance, increased risk of birth defects, weight loss	Pills	Beef liver, boiled spinach, black-eyed peas, asparagus, Brussels sprouts, romaine lettuce, avocado, cooked broccoli, mustard greens, green peas, kidney beans, peanuts, wheat germ, fortified breads, cereals, orange juice, flour, pasta, rice, and other grains
Iron	Difficulty thinking clearly or paying attention, sleepiness/ low energy, increased irritability, mood changes, headaches, trouble maintaining body temperature, decreased endurance, pale appearance, weakened immune system	Pills, liquid drops (possibly intravenous but this is rare) *Tip:* Calcium supplements may interfere with iron absorption. Take pills or eat calcium- and iron-dense foods at different times.	Animal Sources: Clams, oysters, liver (beef), sardines, beef, and chicken Non-animal sources: Breakfast cereals fortified with 100% of daily value for iron, blackstrap molasses, lentils, dark chocolate (45–69% cacao solids), cooked spinach, tofu (firm), kidney beans, chickpeas, cashews *Tip*: More iron is needed for vegetarians or vegans, as non-animal sources of iron are not as well absorbed as animal sources. Vegetarians and vegans need almost twice the amount of iron of those who consume meat. *Tip:* A source of vitamin C helps the body better absorb non-animal sources of iron. See below for good sources of vitamin C.
Protein	Loss of lean body mass, decreased energy	Oral supplements (e.g., high-energy nutrition drinks), protein powder	Beef, chicken, turkey, pork, fish, eggs, beans/legumes (e.g., lentils), nuts, nut butter (e.g., peanut butter, almond butter), seeds, milk, yogurt, cheese, tofu, quinoa, oats, peas, meat substitutes with $\geq$ 14 g of protein in your chosen serving size
Riboflavin (Vitamin B2)	Low energy, poor growth, dry skin /skin problems, hair loss, dry cracked lips or cracks at the corners of mouth, swollen magenta-colored tongue, itchy and/or red eyes, sore throat, anemia and cataracts	Pills	Liver, fortified breakfast cereals, oats, yogurt, dairy, meat, clams, mushrooms, almonds, chicken, salmon, eggs, quinoa *Tip:* A diet low in dairy and animal products is more likely to be deficient in riboflavin.

Table 7.1 (*cont.*)

Deficiency	Signs and symptoms	Possible treatments your doctor may prescribe	Foods rich in this nutrient (in order of nutrient density)
Vitamin A	Night blindness or inability to see when it is dim or dark; decreased immunity	Pills	Sweet potato, beef liver, fish oil, spinach, raw carrots, pumpkin pie or canned pumpkin, cantaloupe, red peppers (raw), mango, dried apricots, broccoli, milk fortified with vitamin A
Vitamin B12	Low energy, weakness, loss of appetite and/or weight, constipation, difficulty thinking clearly and/ or remembering, mood changes, mouth and tongue discomfort, tingling or numbness, feeling unsteady or having trouble walking	Pills, sublingual tablet injection	Liver (all types), fish, meat, poultry, eggs, milk, yogurt, cheese, nutritional yeast *Tip:* Vitamin B12 is found in animal products and not plant based foods
Vitamin C	Can cause easy bruising or bleeding, low appetite, bleeding and/or swollen gums, feeling unwell, pain in muscles and joints, weakness and mood changes	Pills, chews, lozenges, powder packets	Bell peppers, orange juice, oranges, grapefruit juice, kiwi, broccoli, strawberries, Brussels sprouts, grapefruit
Vitamin D	Bone pain, muscle weakness, skeletal deformities (in growing children and adolescents), low mood	Pills, sunshine	Very few foods have Vitamin D naturally, aside from fish liver oil and the flesh of fatty fish (tuna, salmon and mackerel). Fortification also adds vitamin D to milk, breakfast cereals, yogurt, and soy beverages *Tip*: Read the label to know if a cereal, dairy product or dairy substitute is fortified
Vitamin K	Bruising, excessive bleeding, decreased bone health	Pills	Leafy green vegetables, broccoli, roasted or fermented soybeans, soy or canola oil, pomegranate juice, grapes, cashews, olive oil
Zinc	Poor growth and development, loss of appetite, taste and smell changes, difficulty seeing at night, hair loss, diarrhea, weakened immune function	Pills, lozenges	Oysters, crab, beef, lobster, pork, baked beans, chicken, yogurt, cashews, chickpeas, cheese, oatmeal, milk, fortified cereals *Tip:* Zinc is easier to absorb in animal sources

Note: Table prepared by dietitian Laurie Manzo, RD.
Sources: American Society for Enteral and Parenteral and Enteral Nutrition (2017); Office of Dietary Supplements (US), Calcium, 2016; Office of Dietary Supplements (US), Folate, 2016; Office of Dietary Supplements (US), Iron, 2016; Office of Dietary Supplements (US), Riboflavin, 2016; Office of Dietary Supplements (US), Vitamin A, 2016; Office of Dietary Supplements (US), Vitamin B12, 2016; Office of Dietary Supplements (US), Vitamin C, 2016; Office of Dietary Supplements (US), Vitamin D, 2016; Office of Dietary Supplements (US), Vitamin K, 2016; Office of Dietary Supplements (US), Zinc, 2016.

First, the therapist can suggest that the patient vary his or her meals or snacks each day, even while relying on preferred foods. For example, in reviewing the self-monitoring records, the therapist may find that, while the patient tolerates a few different meals or snacks, the patient typically eats the same foods each day (e.g., cereal for breakfast each day; chicken nuggets and fries for lunch; and so on). In such cases, the therapist should suggest that the patient vary these meals and snacks each day, even while sticking with preferred foods (e.g., cereal for breakfast one morning, but donuts for breakfast the next morning; chicken nuggets and fries for lunch one afternoon, but pizza for lunch the following afternoon).

Second, the therapist can also encourage the reintroduction of previously eaten or very-low-frequency foods. For example, the patient may rely primarily on highly preferred foods (e.g., cereal, plain pasta, and ice cream), and yet eat the occasional low-frequency food (e.g., a banana) that he or she had not previously identified as preferred. If this is the case, the therapist should praise the consumption of this low-frequency food and suggest that the patient consume this food again in the coming week. This is particularly helpful if the low-frequency food comes from a category (e.g., fruits and vegetables) that is otherwise missing from the patient's regular diet or may serve to correct an existing nutrition deficiency. However, the therapist should refrain from suggesting that the patient consume this new food every day, as it may promote a food jag in which the patient becomes bored of this food and eliminates it entirely.

As an at-home practice task this week, in addition to continuing with self- or parent-monitoring and weight gain (if necessary), the therapist and patient (and parents, in family-supported CBT-AR) should agree on one to two changes the patient will make to continue to support increases in eating flexibility during the upcoming week. If the patient is underweight, the therapist should again ask the patient (or family) to ensure that the patient continues eating sufficient volume to support a weight gain of 1–2 lbs/week.

Stage 2, Session 2

The second session of Stage 2 will focus on reviewing the patient's current intake from the five basic food groups and identifying foods to learn about in Stage 3. After weighing the patient and reviewing the self- or parent-monitoring, regular eating, changes in eating

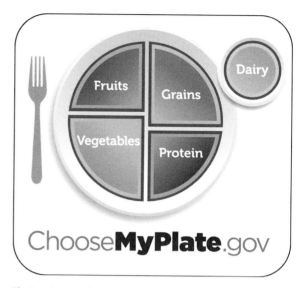

Fig 7.1 Patient education handout: 'United States Department of Agriculture MyPlate schematic'
Reprinted with permission from the USDA Center for Nutrition Policy and Promotion's ChooseMyPlate.gov Web site.

flexibility, and progress toward weight gain (if needed), the therapist will provide brief psychoeducation on the types of food to include in a healthy diet, review intake from the Primary Food Group Building Blocks, and prepare for the first (or only) maintaining mechanism to target in Stage 3.

Psychoeducation on types of food to include in a healthy diet. In 2011, the United States Department of Agriculture (USDA) released the MyPlate schematic (Fig 7.1) to help Americans plan a healthy diet. Interested readers can learn more about MyPlate at www.choosemyplate.gov. Briefly, the premise of MyPlate is that each meal should include items from the five basic food groups (i.e., fruits, vegetables, proteins, dairy, and grains) in the proportions shown on a hypothetical plate. The USDA recognizes that it may not be possible to get such varied representation at every single meal, but suggests that, on average, daily intake should reflect the proportions depicted on the plate. The therapist should share this handout with the patient (or family) and inquire about whether the patient's current list of preferred foods would allow him or her to achieve such a balance at most eating opportunities. In our experience, individuals with ARFID are rarely able to achieve such a variety at this stage in treatment. The therapist can then use Fig 7.1 to begin a conversation about food groups that might be over- or underrepresented in the patient's diet. To help the patient (or family) visualize the relationship between MyPlate and his or her current diet, the therapist should suggest that the patient draw a circle to create a pie chart in which the pie slices represent the current proportion of each food group in his or her diet. As described earlier, it is common for individuals with ARFID to regularly eat many grain and dairy foods but few or no proteins, fruits, or vegetables. The therapist may wish to provide examples of common patterns, but it is important to emphasize that it is the lack of variety in general (rather than the lack of a specific type of food) that defines ARFID.

Review intake from Primary Food Group Building Blocks. The therapist should then introduce Table 7.2, the Primary Food Group Building Blocks, which we adapted for CBT-AR from the USDA MyPlate food list. The therapist can explain that the purpose of providing such a comprehensive list is *not* to imply that the patient will eventually eat all (or even most!) of these foods. Instead, Table 7.2 highlights the wide variety of foods that *could* be incorporated into a healthy diet. Indeed, the patient may still be able to meet his or her nutritional needs in each group even if he or she has previously tried and disliked one or more foods from that group in the past. Another point to emphasize is that the list comprises individual, whole foods. Indeed, the foods on the list comprise the *building blocks* of more complex dishes. Some patients with ARFID dislike mixed foods (e.g., sandwiches, pasta with sauce), and in such cases it is easier to introduce the components of mixed dishes first as a bridge to prepared foods. Furthermore, the list does not include candy or other processed foods because these foods are often already highly preferred in ARFID. Some child-oriented approaches (Toomey et al., 2014) suggest introducing red licorice or lollipops as a way to chain to red peppers or apples, for example, but in our experience this is usually not necessary for older patients.

To review the Primary Food Group Building Blocks, the therapist should invite the patient to scan the list and identify foods that he or she is either 'consistently eating' (i.e., has eaten this food at least once in the past month and would readily eat if offered today), or 'willing to learning about' (i.e., would potentially take a small taste in Stage 3), by placing check marks in columns 2 and 3. For patients with fear of aversive consequences, foods that they used to consume prior to an aversive event but which they do not currently consume due to fear should usually be marked as 'willing to learn about' so that the therapist can consider adding them to the fear and avoidance hierarchy in Stage 3. (The checkboxes for the number of tastes will not be used until Stage 3.) Foods that the patient is neither consistently eating nor willing to learn about should be left blank. Foods are categorized as 'consistently eating' versus 'willing to learn about,' rather than 'likes' versus 'dislikes,' because the former terms are more descriptive, less emotionally charged, and allow for the possibility of movement across categories. Indeed, many foods that the patient is not currently eating will be those that he or she has never tried, or has not tried enough times to develop an informed preference. The patient can select 'willing to learn about' foods strategically to achieve treatment goals. For example, foods that are likely to help the patient correct a deficiency (e.g., B12-containing foods) or gain weight (i.e., high-energy foods) should certainly be checked off. Similarly, foods that are commonly served at school, work, or social events should also be included if their eventual inclusion in the patient's diet is likely to decrease psychosocial impairment. On the other hand, if the patient is not regularly exposed to a particular food and the family does not typically eat it (e.g., liver, starfruit), that food could be left blank because it is unlikely to be an important target for intervention. Table 7.2 also provides five blank rows within each food groups so that the patient can identify mixed or prepared foods that he or she is willing to learn about within that category. Our own patients, for example, have listed salad with dressing under vegetables, and pizza under dairy or grains.

In family-supported CBT-AR, it is important that the patient has the first opportunity to review the Primary Food Group Building Blocks. Only after the patient him- or herself selects foods that he or she is consistently eating and might be willing to learn about should the therapist invite the parents to add their own ideas. This gives the patient ownership over the process and enhances motivation for actually tasting the foods in Stage 3.

Prepare for first (or only) maintaining mechanism to target in Stage 3. For at-home practice tasks, the therapist should ask the patient (or family) to continue with self- or parent-monitoring, regular eating, and increasing eating flexibility. The therapist should also ask the patient to continue thinking about any foods that could be added to the 'willing to learn about' list in the Primary Food Group Building Blocks.

Table 7.2 Primary Food Group Building Blocks

The first column provides a list of common fruit, vegetable, protein, dairy, and grain foods. Use the second column to place an 'X' next to any foods that you are consistently eating (i.e., have eaten at least once in the past month and would readily eat if offered to you today). Use the third column to place an 'X' next to any foods that you are willing to learn about in CBT-AR. For foods that you are willing to learn about, place an 'X' in the fourth column for each taste you take during CBT-AR (either in session or at home). There are 10 boxes in the fourth column because research suggests that is the minimum number required to learn enough about a food to develop a clear preference.

	Consistently eating?	Willing to learn about?	Number of tastes since starting CBT-AR?

FRUITS

100% Fruit juice
- Apple juice
- Cranberry juice
- Grape juice
- Grapefruit juice
- Mango juice
- Orange juice
- Papaya juice
- Pineapple juice
- Pomegranate juice
- Prune juice

Berries
- Acai berries
- Blackberries
- Blueberries
- Cranberries
- Currants
- Goji berries
- Huckleberries
- Lingonberries (cowberries)
- Mulberries
- Raspberries
- Strawberries

Melons
- Cantaloupe
- Honeydew
- Horned melon (kiwano)
- Watermelon

Other fruits
- Apples
- Apricots
- Bananas
- Cherries
- Dates
- Figs
- Fruit cocktail
- Grapefruit
- Grapes

Table 7.2 (*cont.*)

	Consistently eating?	Willing to learn about?	Number of tastes since starting CBT-AR?
• Guava			
• Kiwi fruit			
• Lemons			
• Limes			
• Mangoes			
• Nectarines			
• Oranges			
• Papaya			
• Peaches			
• Pears			
• Persimmons			
• Pineapples			
• Plums			
• Pomegranate			
• Prunes			
• Raisins			
• Star fruit			
• Tangerines			

Other mixed or prepared foods with fruits?
1.
2.
3.
4.
5.

VEGETABLES

Dark-green vegetables
- Arugula (rocket)
- Bok choy
- Broccoli
- Broccoli rabe (rapini)
- Broccolini
- Collard greens
- Dark-green leafy lettuce
- Endive
- Escarole
- Kale
- Mesclun
- Mixed greens
- Mustard greens
- Romaine lettuce
- Spinach
- Swiss chard
- Turnip greens
- Watercress

Red and orange vegetables
- Acorn squash
- Bell peppers

Table 7.2 (cont.)

	Consistently eating?	Willing to learn about?	Number of tastes since starting CBT-AR?
• Butternut squash			
• Carrots			
• Hubbard squash			
• Pumpkin			
• Red chili peppers			
• Red peppers (sweet)			
• Sweet potatoes			
• Tomatoes			
• 100% vegetable juice			

Starchy vegetables
- Cassava
- Corn
- Green bananas
- Green lima beans
- Green peas
- Parsnips
- Plantains
- Potatoes, white
- Taro
- Water chestnuts
- Yams

Other vegetables
- Alfalfa sprouts
- Artichokes
- Asparagus
- Avocado
- Bamboo shoots
- Bean sprouts
- Beets
- Brussels sprouts
- Cabbage
- Cauliflower
- Celery
- Cucumbers
- Eggplant
- Garlic
- Green beans
- Green peppers
- Jicama
- Leeks
- Lettuce, iceberg
- Mung bean sprouts
- Mushrooms
- Okra
- Onions
- Pattypan squash
- Radicchio
- Radishes

Table 7.2 *(cont.)*

	Consistently eating?	Willing to learn about?	Number of tastes since starting CBT-AR?
• Red cabbage			
• Scallions			
• Snow peas			
• Tomatillos			
• Turnips			
• Wax beans			
• Yellow squash			
• Zucchini			
Other mixed or prepared foods with vegetables?			
1.			
2.			
3.			
4.			
5.			
PROTEIN FOODS			
Beans and peas			
• Bean burgers			
• Black beans			
• Black-eyed peas			
• Chickpeas (garbanzo beans)			
• Edamame (young soybeans)			
• Falafel (spiced, mashed chickpeas)			
• Hummus (chickpea spread)			
• Kidney beans			
• Lentils			
• Lima beans (mature)			
• Navy beans			
• Pinto beans			
• Soybeans			
• Split peas			
• White beans			
Eggs			
• Chicken eggs			
• Duck eggs			
Meat			
• Lean ground meats			
○ Beef			
○ Pork			
○ Sausage (beef, turkey)			
• Lean cuts			
○ Beef			
○ Ham			
○ Lamb			
○ Pork			

Table 7.2 (cont.)

	Consistently eating?	Willing to learn about?	Number of tastes since starting CBT-AR?
• Lean luncheon / deli meats			
○ Beef			
○ Chicken			
○ Ham			
○ Pork			
○ Turkey			
• Game meats			
○ Bison			
○ Rabbit			
○ Venison			
• Organ meats			
○ Giblet			
○ Liver			

Nuts and seeds
- Almonds
- Almond butter
- Cashews
- Chia seeds
- Hazelnuts (filberts)
- Mixed nuts
- Peanuts
- Peanut butter
- Pecans
- Pistachios
- Pumpkin seeds
- Sesame seeds
- Sunflower seeds
- Walnuts

Poultry
- Chicken
- Duck
- Goose
- Turkey

Seafood
- Canned fish
  - Anchovies
  - Sardines
  - Tuna
- Finfish
  - Catfish
  - Cod
  - Flounder
  - Haddock
  - Halibut
  - Herring
  - Mackerel
  - Pollock

Table 7.2 (*cont.*)

	Consistently eating?	Willing to learn about?	Number of tastes since starting CBT-AR?
o Porgy			
o Salmon			
o Sea bass			
o Snapper			
o Sushi			
o Swordfish			
o Tilapia			
o Trout			
o Tuna			
• Shellfish			
o Clams			
o Crab			
o Crayfish			
o Lobster			
o Mussels			
o Octopus			
o Oysters			
o Scallops			
o Shrimp			
o Squid (calamari)			

Soy products
- Tempeh
- Texturized vegetable protein (TVP)
- Tofu (made from soybeans)
- Veggie burgers

Other mixed or prepared foods with protein?
1.
2.
3.
4.
5.

DAIRY AND DAIRY SUBSTITUTES

Cheese
- Hard natural cheeses
  - Cheddar
  - Gouda
  - Mozzarella
  - Muenster
  - Parmesan
  - Provolone
  - Romano
  - Swiss
- Soft cheeses
  - Brie
  - Camembert
  - Cottage cheese

Table 7.2 (cont.)

	Consistently eating?	Willing to learn about?	Number of tastes since starting CBT-AR?
○ Feta			
○ Ricotta			
● Processed cheeses			
○ American			
○ Cheese spreads			

Milk
- **All fluid milk**
  - Fat-free (skim) milk
  - Flavored milks
  - Lactose-free milks
  - Low fat milk (1%)
  - Reduced fat milk (2%)
  - Whole milk
- **Milk-based desserts**
  - Frozen yogurt
  - Ice cream
  - Ice milk
  - Lassi
  - Pudding
  - Sherbet
  - Smoothies

Non-dairy calcium alternatives
- Almond milk
- Coconut milk
- Rice milk
- Soymilk

Yogurt
- All milk-based yogurt (fat-free, low fat, reduced fat, whole milk)
- Almond milk yogurt
- Coconut milk yogurt
- Soy yogurt

Other mixed or prepared foods with dairy or substitutes?
1.
2.
3.
4.
5.

GRAINS

Whole grains
- Amaranth
- Brown rice
- Buckwheat
- Bulgur (cracked wheat)
- Kamut

Table 7.2 (cont.)

	Consistently eating?	Willing to learn about?	Number of tastes since starting CBT-AR?
• Millet			
• Muesli			
• Oatmeal			
• Popcorn			
• Quinoa			
• Rolled oats			
• Sorghum			
• Spelt			
• Teff			
• Whole grain barley			
• Whole grain cornmeal			
• Whole grain sorghum			
• Whole rye			
• Whole wheat bread			
• Whole wheat cereal flakes			
• Whole wheat crackers			
• Whole wheat pasta			
• Whole wheat sandwich buns and rolls			
• Whole wheat tortillas			
• Wild rice			
Refined grains			
• Bagels			
• Biscuits			
• Breadcrumbs			
• Cakes			
• Challah bread			
• Cookies			
• Cornflakes			
• Corn tortillas			
• Cornbread			
• Couscous			
• Crackers, saltine			
• English muffins			
• Flour tortilla			
• French bread			
• Grits			
• Hominy			
• Matzo			
• Naan			
• Noodles			
• Pancakes			
• Pasta (spaghetti, macaroni)			
• Pie/pastry crusts			
• Pita bread			
• Pizza crust			
• Polenta			
• Pretzels			
• Ramen noodles			

Table 7.2 (*cont.*)

	Consistently eating?	Willing to learn about?	Number of tastes since starting CBT-AR?
• Rice cakes			
• Rice paper (spring roll wrappers)			
• Rice vermicelli			
• Waffles			
• White bread			
• White rice			
• White sandwich buns and rolls			
Other mixed or prepared foods with grains?			
1.			
2.			
3.			
4.			
5.			

Adapted from the USDA Center for Nutrition Policy and Promotion's ChooseMyPlate.gov Web site.

Finally, the therapist should presage the first module that will be addressed in Stage 3. For example, if the therapist wishes to begin with the Sensory Sensitivity module, the therapist should also ask the patient and/or family to bring in very small portions of five foods from the 'willing to learn about' list as an additional at-home practice task, for the first in-session exposure (see Stage 3 for further details). The foods need not have any unifying characteristics; they can be randomly selected from the Primary Food Group Building Blocks. In contrast, if Stage 3 will begin with the Fear of Aversive Consequences module, the therapist should ask the patient (or family) to begin generating a list of which fears the patient would like to tackle in Stage 3. Lastly, if Stage 3 will begin with the lack of interest module, the therapist should ask the patient (or family) to bring regular portions of five highly preferred foods to the next session. These should be foods the patient is already eating regularly or would eat readily even if they have not been presented lately (e.g., brownies, cakes), rather than 'willing to learn about' foods from the Building Blocks list.

Troubleshooting Stage 2

What if the patient is not continuing to gain weight? In the individual version of the treatment, the therapist should reemphasize the consequences of under-eating and underweight from Stage 1. In this case, it will be helpful to begin with the lack of interest in eating or food module in Stage 3 in order to promote appetite and willingness to tolerate larger volumes of food.

In the family-supported version of the treatment, the therapist should consider supporting the parents in implementing a reward schedule. Necessarily, appropriate rewards will differ across patients and could include, but are not limited to, money, toys, or additional screen time (e.g., television, mobile device). It is most helpful when rewards are immediate (rather than delayed) and used to reinforce behavior (rather than outcomes). For example, an underweight patient whose parents have agreed to give him or her a monetary reward should receive a small amount of money immediately after completing a large meal or consuming an extra supplement drink, rather than receiving a large amount of money in the distant future for achieving a target weight. Parents may find it helpful to stockpile small rewards (e.g., our patients have responded to toys, makeup) for immediate use rather than promising a trip to a favorite store at an unspecified time. Parents should start with a low demand for an immediate reward and slowly fade out the rewards as the desired behavior becomes more consistent. For example, an underweight adolescent may require extra screen time after each meal for the first few weeks but tolerate extra screen time at the end of the day for completing all of the day's meals and snacks later in treatment. Reward systems can be implemented from the beginning of treatment if the patient needs additional motivation to make changes, or they can be initiated midway through treatment if and when a patient stops responding to CBT-AR. Some patients and families are wary of rewards, often with the objection that the patient should not receive rewards for something he or she should already be doing (i.e., eating more or trying new foods). In such cases, the therapist should work to normalize the idea of rewards. Most of us receive rewards every day, including good grades for completing schoolwork and salary for working.

What if the patient does not select any foods he or she is 'willing to learn about'? Given the comprehensive nature of the Primary Food Group Building Blocks and the limited opportunities for exposure that characterize most individuals with ARFID, in our experience nearly all patients will be curious enough to check off at least a handful of novel foods. However, if the patient does not elect to learn about any new foods at all, the therapist should help the patient identify the pros and cons (in both the short and long term) of changing his or her eating. From there the patient can explore with the patient how learning about a new food may improve his or her life in specific ways. If the patient still states that he or she unwilling to make any additional changes, the therapist and patient (or family) should have an honest conversation about whether it makes sense for the patient to continue in CBT-AR at this time. He or she may have learned a great deal about ARFID and made some important changes to his or her eating schedule in Stage 1, but if he or she is unwilling to make any further change, it may be time to conclude treatment, with an open invitation for the patient to return if and when he or should would like to make further changes. This is of course assuming that the patient's nutritional compromise does not necessitate hospitalization or another medically necessary intervention, in which case the alternative treatment should be pursued.

Checklist for Moving on to Stage 3

By the end of Stage 2, the patient should have accomplished the following tasks.

- The patient is steadily gaining weight (e.g., ~1–2 lb/week for 3–4 weeks in a row)
- The patient has identified foods that could be added to correct any nutritional deficiencies
- If applicable, the patient has begun to reincorporate low-frequency foods, or to consume slight variations on preferred foods, in his or her weekly diet
- Therapist and patient (and family, if doing family-supported CBT-AR) have identified several foods from the Primary Food Group Building Blocks that the patient is willing to learn about in Stage 3

Because Stage 2 primarily involves treatment planning, it is not usually advisable to extend this stage if goals are not being met. Instead, if the patient is having difficulty with these tasks, the therapist should consider the primary maintaining mechanism that is acting as a barrier to change. This mechanism should be the first barrier to address in Stage 3.

Stage 3: Maintaining Mechanisms in Order of Priority

The purpose of Stage 3 (14–22 sessions) is to focus on the maintaining mechanisms of the patient's ARFID. Depending on the patient's individualized formulation, the therapist will focus on one, two, or all three primary ARFID maintaining mechanisms in Stage 3. *It is important to prioritize the maintaining mechanisms and tackle them sequentially, moving on to the next one only after the preceding one has been at least partially resolved.* It is much better to do one intervention well than to do many interventions poorly. The therapist should begin with the mechanism that is causing the most impairment for the patient and then move to the next mechanism if needed. In line with the CBT-AR philosophy of volume before variety, the therapist will typically begin with the mechanisms associated with limited volume, namely lack of interest in eating or food and fear of aversive consequences. The sensory sensitivity mechanism, which is associated with limited variety, will typically be last. In our experience, the patient will often see benefit across mechanisms if the primary mechanism is addressed. The length of Stage 3 varies from 14 to 22 sessions depending on the number and severity of the maintaining mechanisms. *Regardless of which mechanism is being addressed, the primary agent of change and trans-mechanistic centerpiece of Stage 3 is exposure.*

Continuing to Support Weight Gain in Stage 3 (underweight patients only)

For patients who are underweight, a primary focus of Stages 1–2 was initiating weight gain. Through the introduction of parent monitoring, the family meal, and adding at least 500 calories of preferred foods per day, the patient will hopefully have initiated a weight gain trajectory of approximately 1–2 lbs per week. During Stage 3, the therapist has the challenging task of continuing the important work of weight gain while simultaneously addressing primary ARFID

maintaining mechanisms, as well as returning control of eating back to the patient once weight maintenance has been established. Some maintaining mechanisms (e.g., lack of interest in eating or food) lend themselves well to supporting continued weight gain, as they focus on increasing hunger cues and tolerating greater volumes of food. Others (e.g., sensory sensitivity) may not support weight gain directly, as the types of foods that patients need to introduce in this module are typically lower in calories (e.g., vegetables, fruit) than the foods they already prefer (e.g., processed carbohydrates).

When patients are underweight, the therapist monitors continued progress toward weight gain at a rate of 1–2 lbs per week at the beginning of each Stage 3 session. If the patient is gaining as expected, the therapist should identify and reinforce any behaviors that led to success (e.g., increasing portions of preferred foods, maintaining parent monitoring) and then move onto the Stage 3 interventions planned for that particular session. However, if a patient is not gaining as expected, the therapist should instead address any barriers to continued weight gain (e.g., skipping meals, eating inadequate portions, reduced parental supervision) and work with the patient (and family, in family-supported CBT-AR) to set a concrete goal for the week. For example, for a patient in the sensory module who is not gaining weight, the therapist may suggest increasing the portion of a preferred food (e.g., ice cream) at evening snack while simultaneously continuing to practice tasting novel foods (see Sensory Sensitivity module). Similarly, a patient in the Fear of Aversive Consequences module could continue to work on at-home exposures to target fear of vomiting or choking while also adding a high-calorie supplement drink every day at breakfast. Only once the therapist and patient (or family) have agreed on a weight gain plan for the week should they move on to the Stage 3 interventions planned for that session. A good rule of thumb is that, when patients are gaining as expected, addressing weight gain should take no more than 10 minutes at the beginning of the session. However, when patients are not gaining weight, the therapist may need to split the session in half (i.e., spend 25 minutes on weight gain and 25 minutes on the planned Stage 3 task). Indeed, for patients who are very underweight, the therapist should expect that Stage 3 will take longer in part to account for the additional session time devoted to weight gain strategies.

In family-supported CBT-AR, once the patient has reached and begun to maintain his or her healthy weight range, the therapist should work with the parents to gradually return control over eating to the patient as appropriate to age and developmental stage. For example, many 10-year-olds eat dinner with their parents every night, whereas it would not be unusual for an 18-year-old to prepare his or her own food or eat meals with friends. Intermediate steps can include allowing the child to eat lunch at school independently, or allowing the child to select his or her own foods for a snack or meal pending parent approval.

Maintaining Mechanism #1: Sensory Sensitivity

Stage 3, Sensory Sensitivity Module, Session 1

In the first session of the Sensory Sensitivity module, the therapist should set the agenda, weigh the patient, and review the at-home practice tasks from the past week. In particular, the therapist should check whether the patient has been able to increase eating flexibility by rotating meals and snacks, reintroducing previously dropped foods, and/or changing the presentation of preferred foods. The therapist should also confirm that the patient (or family) has brought five foods from the 'willing to learn about' list in the Primary Food Group Building Blocks. Then the therapist should move on to providing psychoeducation and conducting the first in-session exposure.

Psychoeducation on necessity of repeated exposure to enhance liking for novel foods. According to decades of research, exposure is a highly effective way of increasing liking for novel foods, in both children (Birch & Marlin, 1982) and adults (Methven, Langreney, & Prescott, 2012; Pliner, Pelchat, &

Grabski, 1993). To introduce this concept, the therapist can share that people's preferences (for both food and other things) inevitably change over time, and mere exposure to stimuli (e.g., pictures, music, foods) can enhance liking. In a seminal study by Zajonc (1968), study participants were presented with nonsense words and symbols. Later, when participants were presented with the same nonsense stimuli and new nonsense stimuli, participants reported greater liking for the words and symbols they had seen before, versus the new ones presented by the experimenter. In other words, it was *mere exposure* to the words and symbols – rather than any inherently pleasing properties of them – that enhanced liking. The therapist can link this concept to the patient's own experience by asking if the patient has ever had the experience of disliking a song the first time it played on the radio, only for the same song to become a favorite later. For younger children, the therapist can ask if the patient still likes the same toys, video games, or movies that they liked when they were younger, or if their tastes have changed over time.

Next the therapist should explain that trying new foods requires certain strategies that can be learned and practiced. Collaboratively with the patient, the therapist should review the primary strategy for food exposure that he or she will learn in CBT-AR: The Five Steps (Fig 8.1). The Five Steps will lead the patient through a sensory exposure exercise that breaks down the process of eating into a series of concrete steps starting with sight, touch, smell, taste, and then texture. The patient will follow this procedure for all in-session food exposures, and may also wish to use it to facilitate at-home practice tastes. This structured sensory exploration is based on the 'Food Science' adaptation for older children of Toomey's (2014) pioneering SOS approach to helping youth with feeding difficulties expand the variety in their diets.

After reviewing the handout, the therapist should ask the patient how the Five Steps strategy is similar or different from how the patient has attempted to try novel foods in the past. In this discussion, the therapist should be sure to highlight three key points. First, the purpose of the exposures is to *learn about* a new food, not necessarily to like that particular food on the first, second, or even third try. It may take several tastes for a patient to accept a food, and after many tastes the patient may decide he or she still doesn't like it. That's OK! Everyone – even those without

Learning About New Foods: The Five Steps

Ask yourself these FIVE questions when approaching a new food!

Trying a new food can be overwhelming at first. The next time you encounter a new food, slow down and give yourself a few minutes to explore it as if you've never seen it before. Try to use NEUTRAL words without describing foods as good or bad.

The Five Steps

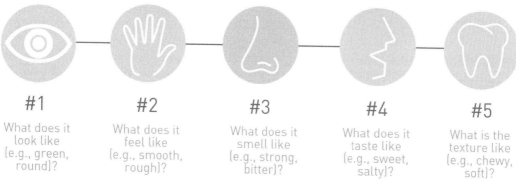

#1	#2	#3	#4	#5
What does it look like (e.g., green, round)?	What does it feel like (e.g., smooth, rough)?	What does it smell like (e.g., strong, bitter)?	What does it taste like (e.g., sweet, salty)?	What is the texture like (e.g., chewy, soft)?

Congratulations!

Remember, the more you practice, the more you learn. Even if you do not like a new food at first, that's okay. Research shows it can take 10 or more times to get comfortable with a new food. Plus, trying the same food multiple times will enhance your learning.

Thomas, J.J. and Eddy, K.T. (2018). *Cognitive-Behavioral Therapy for Avoidant/Restrictive Food Intake Disorder: Children, Adolescents, & Adults.* Cambridge: Cambridge University Press.

Fig 8.1 Patient education handout: 'Learning about new foods: The five steps'

ARFID – has likes and dislikes. In either case, just doing the Five Steps exercise will help the patient build new skills that can be applied to trying additional foods in the future. Second, the patient should always take the lead on selecting which foods to learn about. The therapist (or parents, in family-supported CBT-AR) can certainly make suggestions, but allowing the patient to select the foods him- or herself is an important pre-commitment strategy that will increase compliance with in-session tasting sessions. Third, although we recommend starting with exploration based on sight, touch, and smell, in order for the exercise to support the patient in changing his or her diet, the primary goal is to help the patient taste the food. Research suggests that no amount of looking at novel food will increase preference for that food; the food must actually be tasted (Birch, McPhee, Shoba, Pirok, & Steinberg, 1987). (This is why we suggest that the therapist stick to the Five Steps displayed in Fig 8.1 and do not design exposures to assist a patient in playing with, kissing, or licking novel foods. Although such interventions are unlikely to be harmful and are often recommended in speech and occupational therapy with young children, our view – particularly when working with older children, adolescents, and adults – is that finger painting with yogurt does not have the same therapeutic benefits as actually consuming it).

Conduct first in-session food exposure. To begin the first exposure, the therapist should ask the patient to select one of the five foods he or she has brought. The therapist should start with the first question, 'What does it look like?' and give the patient plenty of time to respond. Rather than offering his or her own observations, the therapist should reinforce and praise the patient for any neutral and nonjudgmental descriptions the patient offers. If the patient says anything positive or negative (e.g., 'This looks delicious,' or 'This looks disgusting'), the therapist should redirect the patient to remain neutral, and ask the patient to describe the food as he or she would to a blind person, an alien from outer space, or someone who has never seen that particular food (or anything like it) before. If the patient says that he or she 'doesn't know' how to respond, the therapist can offer one example descriptor and then ask the patient to identify more. The therapist can also remind the patient that there are no right or wrong answers, and encourage the patient to take all the time he or she needs to formulate a response. After the patient has

provided at least two or three adjectives, the therapist should move on to the next questions – 'What does it feel like?' and 'What does it smell like?' – and similarly guide the patient toward neutral descriptions.

Next, the therapist should ask, 'What does it taste like?' unapologetically and with the clear expectation that the patient will taste the food. If the patient expresses concern, the therapist should note that the actual taste itself can be very small. For young children, Williams and Seiverling (2016) have suggested that a taste the size of a grain of rice or a pea is sufficient for the first exposure. Similarly, Nicholls et al. (2001) have suggested that, for children and adolescents, half a teaspoon is adequate. In CBT-AR, we recommend that the therapist let the patient take the lead on deciding the initial bite size. For example, if the patient is doing an exposure with an apple, it is OK if the patient wants to take off the peel and eat only a bite from the inside. The patient need not eat the entire apple; in fact, there wouldn't be time, as there are many other foods to taste in the session. Between one and five bites are effective as an initial exposure to the novel food in session. The final question, 'What is the texture like?' can be used as a prompt to help the patient take the second bite, as a method of gathering sufficient information to answer the last question. After completing the Five Steps with the first food item, the therapist should repeat this procedure with the additional four items that the patient brought to session.

In family-supported CBT-AR, parents should learn the Five Steps in session alongside the patient and be given an opportunity to practice the skills by exposure to one or more of the foods in session. As parents will be key agents of change outside of the session, the therapist will want to ensure that the parents understand the purpose of the exposures and the Five Steps to allow them to assist their child in home-based practices. Parents can be asked to reflect, as well, on how different using the Five Steps may be from how they typically approach foods or encourage their child to approach foods. Parents commonly reflect that when they present their child with new foods, they express at least some investment in the child liking the food (e.g., 'Try it! You will really like this!'), which differs from the nonjudgmental approach of CBT-AR.

Assign at-home practice task. A common problem with the introduction of novel foods is that the patient may eat them in session (whether due to wanting to please the therapist or feelings of greater self-efficacy with the scaffolding of the therapy setting) but have difficulty consuming them independently between sessions. This is important to address because if the patient only has the opportunity to try the food in session, he or she will only very slowly be able to achieve the numerous presentations necessary for accepting the new food. This point cannot be emphasized enough and bears repeating: The patient must repeatedly taste a food to develop a preference for it. Thus between-session practice is absolutely crucial for the success of the treatment.

After completing the five exposures, the therapist should help the patient identify which of the foods tasted in the session he or she will continue learning about in the upcoming week. *An important principle of CBT-AR is that, whichever foods the patient selects to practice, the patient should practice at least one of these foods every day.* For example, if the patient was pleasantly surprised that he or she liked a particular food or found it to be more approachable than anticipated, that food should certainly be practiced at home. Early in Stage 3, the therapist can encourage the patient to incorporate tasted foods into meals or snacks, but the primary goal for at-home practice is to help the patient identify opportunities for small tastes throughout the week. For example, if an adult patient agrees to try peanuts four times before the next session, the therapist can suggest that the patient keep a jar of peanuts in his or desk at work, and set an alarm to remind him or her to eat one peanut at the same time each day. Similarly, if a child patient in family-supported CBT-AR would like to try apples three times in the upcoming week, the therapist can help the parents determine when the apples will be presented (e.g., after school) and how much the patient will eat (e.g., two or four bites). The patient should be sure to check off any completed tastes on the Primary Food Groups Building Blocks, to review with the therapist in the next session. Next, to help the patient identify the five foods that he or she will bring to the next session, the therapist and patient should consult the Primary Food Group Building Blocks. Any foods that the patient brought to today's session but did not taste could be repeated again at the next session. If the patient has difficulty identifying foods to bring in, the therapist might suggest that the patient bring in a food from a food group currently underrepresented in the patient's diet.

For many patients, the nonjudgmental learning framework of the Five Steps will be sufficient to motivate progress in tasting new foods. However, for some patients – particularly children in family-supported CBT-AR for whom avoidant or restrictive eating is egosyntonic – an operant conditioning system may be constructed to encourage further progress. For example, the patient may earn a point for each food he or she tastes during at-home practice, and later cash in the points for a particular reward. Very young children may prefer to use stickers rather than points. Although using praise or rewards to encourage food consumption is somewhat controversial (Rowell et al., 2015; Satter, 1987), contingency management is an evidence-based approach for pediatric feeding disorders (Sharp et al., 2010), and many published studies (e.g., Marshall et al., 2015) have successfully employed operant approaches to enhance dietary variety. In our experience, some degree of praise and encouragement is a necessary precondition for progress in the setting of low intrinsic motivation. Although we have found that operant conditioning is typically more relevant for child patients in family-supported CBT-AR, adult patients can also be encouraged to identify and self-administer their own rewards.

Stage 3, Sensory Sensitivity Module, Session 2

The therapist should begin the second session of the Sensory Sensitivity module by setting the agenda, weighing the patient, and reviewing the parent- or self-monitoring records. In addition, the therapist will review the patient's Primary Food Group Building Blocks to ensure that he or she has been practicing tasting new foods and checking them off on the handout. If the patient has practiced the foods as agreed on the prior week, the therapist should praise the patient and inquire whether the patient's attitude toward that particular food has changed (or not) as the result of at-home practice. Any increased comfort with a new food should be reinforced. If the patient did not perceive a change in attitude toward the novel food, the therapist should emphasize that the patient may require additional tastes to continue learning. Regardless, the therapist should confirm that the patient (or family) has brought five more foods from the patient's 'willing to learn about' list.

Conduct in-session food exposure. The therapist should then move on to the in-session exposure to the five foods that the patient brought in, using the Five Steps handout as a guide. If the patient is able to provide neutral descriptors more readily in the second session, the therapist should reinforce this progress by saying something like 'You're doing a really great job today,' or 'You're really getting the hang of this!' For example, the patient may no longer need to be prompted with the steps because he or she has begun to memorize them.

Distinguish between tasting and incorporating. After completing the in-session exposure, the therapist will review the handout 'Strategies for incorporating new foods at home' (Fig 8.2). CBT-AR makes a crucial distinction between tasting and incorporating. *Tasting* a novel food involves consuming a very small portion while going through the Five Steps. Tasting can take place between meals or at meal times, but the patient can continue to rely on preferred foods for calories and to satisfy hunger while learning about the novel food. In contrast, *incorporating* a novel food involves eating a larger portion of the novel food as part of an integrated meal or snack. When a patient incorporates a novel food, he or she starts relying on that food to provide calories and satisfy hunger, and begins eating this food on a regular basis. For example, *tasting* an apple would include eating just two small bites as an at-home practice in between afternoon snack and dinner. In contrast, *incorporating* an apple would involve eating a whole apple, along with peanut butter crackers, as an afternoon snack. Early in Stage 3 the therapist focuses primarily on tasting, but once a novel food has been tasted many times and the patient begins to feel more comfortable with that food, the therapist should quickly move to incorporation. Because the patient will have many opportunities to taste novel foods throughout the Stage 3 Sensory Sensitivity module, the patient will likely be incorporating foods tasted earlier in treatment while still tasting novel foods. Because the patient (rather than the therapist) determines which of the tasted foods will ultimately be incorporated, there is no expectation that all foods will reach the incorporation stage. For most patients with ARFID, incorporating one-half or even one-quarter of the foods tasted in treatment would represent a major improvement in dietary variety. It is particularly important to discuss the difference between tasting and incorporating with parents in family-supported CBT-AR. Parents may feel that progress with tasting is slow, and expect their child to be eating full meals composed of novel foods early in treatment. Given that the patient's selective eating has typically been

going on for years, this expectation is unrealistic. Instead, the therapist should encourage the parents to praise the patient's efforts at tasting a wide variety of foods and focus on incorporating only those foods on which the patient has chosen to focus.

For each strategy in Fig 8.2, the therapist should work with the patient to identify whether that particular strategy might help him or her approach a food from the 'willing to learn about' column of the Primary Food Groups Building Blocks. For example, a patient who currently eats meat and bread but not sandwiches may wish to try a fading technique (i.e., combining a large piece of bread with a small piece of meat, to start) to introduce a food for an in-session exposure or as an at-home practice task. Similarly, if the patient is not currently eating any fruit but has no difficulty with flavored liquids, the therapist could suggest that the patient using chaining by starting with apple juice (i.e., an antecedent manipulation that would introduce the novel flavor of a fruit without the unfamiliar texture) and subsequently moving on to apple sauce and then apples.

Assign at-home practice task. To conclude the second session of Stage 2, the therapist should confirm which of the tasted foods the patient will use for tasting and incorporation during in the upcoming week, and identify how and when these exposures will take place. The therapist should again emphasize the importance of tasting or incorporating a new food *every single day*. If the patient has been tasting very small amounts of novel food from the prior week (e.g., one cashew, one bite of apple), the therapist should encourage the patient to increase the portion size (e.g., four cashews, five bites of apple) this week. In other words, the wise therapist praises the patient for tasting novel foods but always has an eye toward incorporation as the ultimate goal. The patient should again identify five foods from the Primary Food Groups Building Blocks list to bring to the next session.

Stage 3, Sensory Sensitivity Module, Later Sessions

The remaining sessions of the Stage 3 Sensory Sensitivity module will follow the same basic structure as the first two. First the therapist will set the agenda, weigh the patient, and review the parent- or self-monitoring records and Primary Food Group Building Blocks to ensure that the patient and has been

Strategies for Incorporating New Foods at Home

*In CBT-AR, you first learn about new foods by <u>TASTING</u> small amounts of simple foods and practicing this at home

*As you continue to learn about more foods, you will work on mixing foods together and trying complex foods

*As you become more comfortable with these foods, it is time to <u>INCORPORATE</u> them into your meals and snacks

Here are some strategies for incorporating new foods into your meals and snacks at home

1 Fade it in

Start with a high proportion of a preferred food (e.g., applesauce) and add a small portion of a novel food (e.g., pieces of raw apple). Then gradually increase the proportion of the novel food while fading out the preferred food

 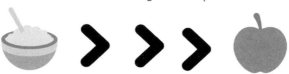

Fig 8.2 Patient education handout: 'Strategies for incorporating new foods at home'

2 Add some spice

Preferred condiments and spices can act as training wheels for trying new foods. For example, add cheese to your broccoli, ketchup to your meat, ranch dressing to your carrots, or garlic salt to vegetables

3 Chain to a goal

Use a preferred food to chain to a novel food. For example, if you currently prefer potato chips, try veggie chips. Before you know it, you might feel comfortable trying raw veggies!

4 Switch it up

If at first you don't succeed, try, try again -but change it up! Try different presentations of novel foods. Think cooked versus raw, salted versus unsalted, etc.

5 Deconstruct

If you have never tried a new food like pizza, try starting with one component of the food and then layering on individual components one-by-one. For example, try crust alone, then crust with cheese, then crust with cheese and sauce, and, finally, a slice of pizza!

Thomas, J.J. and Eddy, K.T. (2018). *Cognitive-Behavioral Therapy for Avoidant/Restrictive Food Intake Disorder. Children, Adolescents, & Adults.* Cambridge: Cambridge University Press.

Fig 8.2 *(cont.)*

tasting and incorporating new foods at home. Table 8.1 provides an example of the Primary Food Groups Building Blocks for a patient midway through the Sensory Sensitivity module of CBT-AR. Note that the patient has identified foods to learn about and begun recording the number of tastes of each novel food. If the therapy is going well, the patient should be accumulating more and more tastes from one session to the next. Of note, it is perfectly normal for the patient to taste some foods just once and decide not to continue learning about those foods as part of treatment, as illustrated in Table 8.1. As long as the patient selects a subset of foods to continue learning about, the treatment is on track to be successful.

Conduct in-session food exposure. After reviewing the at-home practice tasks, the therapist will guide the patient through the in-session exposure to the five foods the patient has brought to the session. Although the patient will start the exposures with simple foods from the Primary Food Groups Building Blocks, as CBT-AR progresses, the therapist should encourage the patient (or family) to bring in increasingly complex foods – for example, foods that can be eaten at main courses at a meal, foods that might be helpful socially, and foods that the patient's family routinely eats at home. It is perfectly fine to depart from the Building Blocks as the patient gains confidence in trying increasingly complex foods. The therapist should encourage the patient to add these new foods to the blank lines on the Building Blocks worksheet so that this becomes a working document that can be used for progress review in Stage 4.

In-session food exposures in these later sessions can also serve as an opportunity to practice portion-sized amounts of foods the patient is working to move from tasting to incorporating. While many patients are able to increase from tasting to incorporating on their own as homework, some will need these in-session exposures to practice portion-sized amounts before being able to do this independently.

Continue to emphasize importance of incorporating novel foods. For the remainder of Stage 3, it is important that the therapist continues to emphasize at-home tasting practice with novel foods while simultaneously beginning the important task of incorporating previously tasted foods into meals and snacks. Determining when a patient is ready to incorporate a novel food into meals and snacks can be challenging, but the following can serve as a helpful guide. The number of presentations required for a food to be

accepted varies across individuals. For healthy children, Birch and Marlin (1982) found 10 presentations sufficient. In contrast, Cooke and Webber (2015) recommend 15 tastes per vegetable for healthy children as part of their 'Tiny Tastes' program. Very little work has been done on individuals with frank ARFID, but our clinical experience suggests that such individuals may need even more presentations before they will readily accept a new food. For example, Williams and Foxx (2007) suggest 10–20 presentations for children with autism and developmental disabilities who also have feeding difficulties. Fitzpatrick et al. (2015) have suggested that, 'for truly novelty-averse children the number is often upwards of fifty presentations before a food is no longer experienced as novel' (p. 264). Although more research is needed, the bottom line is that a therapist should emphasize the paramount importance of repeated exposure. On the bright side, the number of exposures necessary for liking appears to decrease after initial foods are accepted (Williams, Paul, Pizzo, & Riegel, 2008). In one pediatric feeding clinic in which patients were exposed to several novel foods, the first food required 1–27 presentations to achieve acceptance, whereas the second 10 foods required 6–10, and the final 10 foods required only 1–7 presentations. This is consistent with our own clinical experience. The mechanism for this more rapid acceptance of later foods may be increased confidence in approaching new foods, increased threshold for just noticeable difference between foods, and/or decreased anxiety in novel eating situations. To that end, the therapist can reassure the patient that an initial investment in exposure is likely to pay exponential dividends as the patient graduates to trying more and more foods.

Assign at-home practice task. The therapist should conclude later sessions of Stage 3 by confirming that the patient (or family) will continue the self- or parent monitoring and identify five new foods to bring in the following week. Most importantly, the therapist should confirm which of the tasted foods the patient will use for tasting versus incorporation in the upcoming week, and ask the patient to either taste or incorporate a new food every day. Once the patient has recorded several tastes of a novel food on the Primary Food Group Building Blocks, the therapist should work with the patient (or family) to create a concrete plan for incorporating that particular food into preplanned meals and snacks

Table 8.1 Primary Food Group Building Blocks (worked example for ARFID with sensory sensitivity)

The first column provides a list of common fruit, vegetable, protein, dairy, and grain foods. Use the second column to place an 'X' next to any foods that you are consistently eating (i.e., have eaten at least once in the past month and would readily eat if offered to you today). Use the third column to place an 'X' next to any foods that you are willing to learn about in CBT-AR. For foods that you are willing to learn about, place an 'X' in the fourth column for each taste you take during CBT-AR (either in session or at home). There are 10 boxes in the fourth column because research suggests that is the minimum number required to learn enough about a food to develop a clear preference.

	Consistently eating?	Willing to learn about?	Number of tastes since starting CBT-AR?				
FRUITS							
100% Fruit juice							
• Apple juice	X						
• Cranberry juice							
• Grape juice							
• Grapefruit juice							
• Mango juice							
• Orange juice		X	X	X	X		
• Papaya juice							
• Pineapple juice							
• Pomegranate juice							
• Prune juice							
Berries							
• Acai berries							
• Blackberries							
• Blueberries							
• Cranberries							
• Currants	X	X					
• Goji berries							
• Huckleberries							
• Lingonberries (cowberries)							
• Mulberries							
• Raspberries	X	X					
• Strawberries	X	X					
Melons							
• Cantaloupe	X						
• Honeydew							
• Horned melon (kiwano)							
• Watermelon							
Other fruits							
• Apples							
• Apricots							
• Bananas	X	X	X	X	X	X	
• Cherries							
• Dates							
• Figs							
• Fruit cocktail							
• Grapefruit	X	X					

Table 8.1 (*cont.*)

	Consistently eating?	Willing to learn about?	Number of tastes since starting CBT-AR?
• Grapes			
• Guava			
• Kiwi fruit			
• Lemons			
• Limes			
• Mangoes		x	
• Nectarines		x	
• Oranges			
• Papaya			
• Peaches		x	x
• Pears			
• Persimmons			
• Pineapples			
• Plums			
• Pomegranate			
• Prunes			
• Raisins			
• Star fruit			
• Tangerines			
Other mixed or prepared foods with fruits?			
1. Apple pie		x	
2. Fruit smoothie		x	x x
3. Dried mangos		x	
4.			
5.			
VEGETABLES			
Dark-green vegetables			
• Arugula (rocket)			
• Bok choy			
• Broccoli		x	x
• Broccoli rabe (rapini)			
• Broccolini			
• Collard greens			
• Dark-green leafy lettuce			
• Endive			
• Escarole			
• Kale		x	
• Mesclun			
• Mixed greens			
• Mustard greens			
• Romaine lettuce		x	x x
• Spinach		x	x
• Swiss chard			
• Turnip greens			
• Watercress			

Table 8.1 (*cont.*)

	Consistently eating?	Willing to learn about?	Number of tastes since starting CBT-AR?	
Red and orange vegetables				
• Acorn squash				
• Bell peppers				
• Butternut squash				
• Carrots	X	X		
• Hubbard squash				
• Pumpkin				
• Red chili peppers				
• Red peppers (sweet)	X	X	X	
• Sweet potatoes				
• Tomatoes				
• 100% vegetable juice	X			
Starchy vegetables				
• Cassava				
• Corn				
• Green bananas				
• Green lima beans				
• Green peas				
• Parsnips				
• Plantains				
• Potatoes, white				
• Taro				
• Water chestnuts				
• Yams				
Other vegetables				
• Alfalfa sprouts				
• Artichokes				
• Asparagus	X	X		
• Avocado				
• Bamboo shoots				
• Bean sprouts				
• Beets				
• Brussels sprouts				
• Cabbage				
• Cauliflower				
• Celery				
• Cucumbers	X			
• Eggplant				
• Garlic				
• Green beans	X			
• Green peppers				
• Jicama				
• Leeks				
• Lettuce, iceberg	X	X	X	
• Mung bean sprouts				
• Mushrooms				
• Okra				
• Onions				

Table 8.1 (*cont.*)

	Consistently eating?	Willing to learn about?	Number of tastes since starting CBT-AR?
• Pattypan squash			
• Radicchio			
• Radishes		X	X
• Red cabbage			
• Scallions			
• Snow peas			
• Tomatillos			
• Turnips			
• Wax beans			
• Yellow squash			
• Zucchini			

Other mixed or prepared foods with vegetables?

1. Salad w dressing		X	
2.			
3.			
4.			
5.			

PROTEIN FOODS

Beans and peas

	Consistently eating?	Willing to learn about?	Number of tastes since starting CBT-AR?
• Bean burgers		X	
• Black beans			
• Black-eyed peas			
• Chickpeas (garbanzo beans)			
• Edamame (young soybeans)		X	X
• Falafel (spiced, mashed chickpeas)			
• Hummus (chickpea spread)		X	
• Kidney beans		X	
• Lentils			
• Lima beans (mature)			
• Navy beans			
• Pinto beans			
• Soybeans			
• Split peas			
• White beans			

Eggs

• Chicken eggs		X	
• Duck eggs			

Meat

• Lean ground meats			
○ Beef	X		
○ Pork			
○ Sausage (beef, turkey)			
• Lean cuts			
○ Beef	X		
○ Ham			

Table 8.1 (*cont.*)

	Consistently eating?	Willing to learn about?	Number of tastes since starting CBT-AR?
○ Lamb			
○ Pork			
● Lean luncheon / deli meats			
○ Beef			
○ Chicken			
○ Ham			
○ Pork			
○ Turkey		X	X X X
● Game meats			
○ Bison			
○ Rabbit			
○ Venison			
● Organ meats			
○ Giblet			
○ Liver			
Nuts and seeds			
● Almonds			
● Almond butter		X	X X
● Cashews		X	X
● Chia seeds			
● Hazelnuts (filberts)			
● Mixed nuts			
● Peanuts			
● Peanut butter			
● Pecans			
● Pistachios			
● Pumpkin seeds			
● Sesame seeds			
● Sunflower seeds			
● Walnuts			
Poultry			
● Chicken		X	
● Duck			
● Goose			
● Turkey			
Seafood			
● Canned fish			
○ Anchovies			
○ Sardines			
○ Tuna	X		
● Finfish			
○ Catfish			
○ Cod			
○ Flounder			
○ Haddock			
○ Halibut			
○ Herring			

Table 8.1 (*cont.*)

	Consistently eating?	Willing to learn about?	Number of tastes since starting CBT-AR?
○ Mackerel			
○ Pollock			
○ Porgy			
○ Salmon			
○ Sea bass			
○ Snapper			
○ Sushi			
○ Swordfish			
○ Tilapia			
○ Trout			
○ Tuna			
• Shellfish			
○ Clams			
○ Crab			
○ Crayfish			
○ Lobster			
○ Mussels			
○ Octopus			
○ Oysters			
○ Scallops			
○ Shrimp			
○ Squid (calamari)			
Soy products			
• Tempeh			
• Texturized vegetable protein (TVP)			
• Tofu (made from soybeans)	X		
• Veggie burgers	X		
Other mixed or prepared foods with protein?			
1. Chicken nuggets	X		X X X
2. Burger w/ bun	X		
3. Beef w/ sauce	X		
4.			
5.			
DAIRY AND DAIRY SUBSTITUTES			
Cheese			
• Hard natural cheeses			
○ Cheddar	X		
○ Gouda			
○ Mozzarella	X		
○ Muenster			
○ Parmesan			
○ Provolone			
○ Romano			
○ Swiss			
• Soft cheeses			
○ Brie			
○ Camembert			

Table 8.1 (*cont.*)

	Consistently eating?	Willing to learn about?	Number of tastes since starting CBT-AR?
o Cottage cheese			
o Feta			
o Ricotta			
• Processed cheeses			
o American			
o Cheese spreads		X	X
Milk			
• **All fluid milk**			
o Fat-free (skim) milk	X		
o Flavored milks	X		
o Lactose-free milks			
o Low fat milk (1%)	X		
o Reduced fat milk (2%)	X		
o Whole milk	X		
• **Milk-based desserts**			
o Frozen yogurt	X		
o Ice cream	X		
o Ice milk			
o Lassi			
o Pudding			
o Sherbet			
o Smoothies		X	
Non-dairy calcium alternatives			
• Almond milk			
• Coconut milk			
• Rice milk			
• Soymilk			
Yogurt			
• All milk-based yogurt (fat-free, low fat, reduced fat, whole milk)		X	X X X X
• Almond milk yogurt			
• Coconut milk yogurt			
• Soy yogurt			
Other mixed or prepared foods with dairy or substitutes?			
1. Cream cheese		X	
2. Mac & cheese		X	
3. Pizza		X	
4.			
5.			
GRAINS			
Whole grains			
• Amaranth			
• Brown rice			
• Buckwheat			
• Bulgur (cracked wheat)			
• Kamut			

Table 8.1 (cont.)

	Consistently eating?	Willing to learn about?	Number of tastes since starting CBT-AR?
● Millet			
● Muesli			
● Oatmeal	x		
● Popcorn			
● Quinoa			
● Rolled oats			
● Sorghum			
● Spelt			
● Teff			
● Whole grain barley			
● Whole grain cornmeal			
● Whole grain sorghum			
● Whole rye			
● Whole wheat bread		x	x x x x
● Whole wheat cereal flakes	x		
● Whole wheat crackers			
● Whole wheat pasta			
● Whole wheat sandwich buns and rolls	x		
● Whole wheat tortillas		x	
● Wild rice		x	
Refined grains			
● Bagels	x		
● Biscuits			
● Breadcrumbs			
● Cakes	x		
● Challah bread	x		
● Cookies	x		
● Cornflakes	x		
● Corn tortillas			
● Cornbread			
● Couscous			
● Crackers, saltine	x		
● English muffins			
● Flour tortilla			
● French bread			
● Grits			
● Hominy			
● Matzo			
● Naan			
● Noodles			
● Pancakes			
● Pasta (spaghetti, macaroni)		x	
● Pie/pastry crusts			
● Pita bread			
● Pizza crust			
● Polenta			
● Pretzels			
● Ramen noodles		x	

Table 8.1 (*cont.*)

	Consistently eating?	Willing to learn about?	Number of tastes since starting CBT-AR?
● Rice cakes			
● Rice paper (spring roll wrappers)			
● Rice vermicelli			
● Waffles			
● White bread			
● White rice		x	
● White sandwich buns and rolls			

Other mixed or prepared foods with grains?

1.
2.
3.
4.
5.

Adapted from the USDA Center for Nutrition Policy and Promotion's ChooseMyPlate.gov Web site.

(Williams and Seiverling, 2016). The ultimate goal of CBT-AR is to help patients with sensory sensitivity consume a greater variety of food on a day-to-day basis, rather that just become excellent food tasters. In other words, very early in this module, patients should be encouraged to move from tasting (i.e., taking small bites of a novel food either for the first time or as part of repeated practice) to incorporation (i.e., eating relatively larger portions of novel foods as part of meals and snacks). In our experience, this does not happen automatically, but instead requires forethought and planning. Thus, as soon as a patient has completed multiple tastes of the novel food – or a single taste if the patient has an initial positive experience with the food – the therapist should review the patient's self- or parent-monitoring records to determine where a normal-sized portion of that food could most easily be incorporated in the upcoming week. The therapist should refer the patient back to Fig 7.1 (the MyPlate schematic), and determine how this novel food might bring an existing meal or snack into closer compliance with this recommended scheme. For example, if the patient is currently eating cereal with milk for breakfast, and has recently completed five tastes of banana without difficulty, the therapist could encourage the patient to eat half a banana in addition to his or her morning cereal, thereby covering three food groups instead of just two and ensuring a more balanced meal. Similarly, if the patient is consistently eating macaroni and cheese for dinner, and has recently completed several tastes of broccoli, the therapist could set a goal for the patient to add broccoli to his or her macaroni and cheese at dinner so that the patient is covering three food groups (instead of just two) at his or her evening meal. The patient can also be encouraged to incorporate wholly novel meals (e.g., salad with a variety of vegetables) if desired, but the therapist should ensure that the goal is manageable so that the patient doesn't quickly lose his or her nerve and abandon the plan. For example, the patient and therapist can discuss supplementing the novel meal (e.g., salad) with a preferred food (e.g., bread roll) in case he or she does not feel able to consume the whole portion. Just as during the tasting phase, it is important for the therapist to assign repeated exposures to these new meals as at-home practice. Eating leafy green vegetables and meat at dinner just one time will not resolve an iron deficiency, whereas repeatedly consuming iron-rich meals over time will.

Prepare for next maintaining mechanism to target in Stage 3 (Final session of module only, if there are multiple maintaining mechanisms). If the therapist plans to move on to another module in Stage 3 before progressing to Stage 4, he or she should use the final session of the Sensory Sensitivity module to prepare for the next module. Specifically, if the therapist plans to do the Fear of Aversive Consequences module, he or she should ask the patient (or family) to begin thinking about fears he or she would like to tackle in that module. If the therapist plans to do the Lack of Interest module, the therapist should ask the patient (or family) to bring in five of the patient's highly preferred foods for the next in-session exposure.

Maintaining Mechanism #2: Fear of Aversive Consequences

Stage 3, Fear of Aversive Consequences Module, Session 1

The therapist will begin the first session of the Fear of Aversive Consequences module by setting the agenda, weighing the patient, and reviewing the self- or parent monitoring and at-home practice tasks. In particular, the therapist should review how the patient is doing with increasing eating flexibility and, if they have already completed another Stage 3 module, the at-home practice tasks associated with that particular module.

Psychoeducation about avoidance and exposure. The therapist will begin the first session of the Stage 3 Fear of Aversive Consequences module by reviewing the patient education handout 'How does avoidance increase anxiety over time?' (Fig 8.3). The therapist should explain that individuals with the fear of aversive consequences presentation of ARFID avoid specific food or eating situations that they worry are dangerous. This behavioral avoidance is functional in the shorter term because it gives the illusion of protecting the patient from future harm. However, the benefits of avoidance are short-lived, because avoidance limits any opportunities to disconfirm the patient's prediction that all such situations are dangerous. The therapist should present a competing hypothesis – namely, that exposure to the feared food or eating situation – is the optimal method of disconfirming catastrophic beliefs because it will demonstrate for the patient that the feared consequence is actually very unlikely to occur, or that if it does, the patient will be able to cope with it.

Co-create exposure hierarchy to guide future exposures. Once the patient (or family) expresses an understanding of avoidance and the rationale for

exposure, the next task is to help the patient create a fear and avoidance hierarchy. It is important to work collaboratively on this process to maintain patient engagement and ensure that the therapist assigns activities to the appropriate step in the hierarchy. Here we describe how to construct typical hierarchies for the aversive consequences of choking and vomiting, respectively.

Many patients presenting with fear of choking are eating very little at the time of clinical presentation. To construct the exposure hierarchy, the therapist may wish to categorize previously preferred foods from easiest to most challenging (Chorpita, Vitali, & Barlow, 1997; McNally, 1985; Nock, 2002). For example, the therapist and patient may decide to start with fluids (e.g., juice, milk), then soft, blended foods (e.g., ice cream, apple sauce), then hard, crunchy foods (e.g., cookies, crackers), and finally tough, chewy foods (e.g., beef, chicken). Because patients with fear of aversive consequences may be more intensely fearful about non-preferred foods (or food in general) than those with sensory sensitivities, in extreme cases, early steps on the hierarchy may need to comprise even easier first steps (e.g., sitting at a table in front of a plate, holding a spoon, picking up food with the spoon, and so on). The hierarchy may also need to include non-food situations that are related to the patient's feared aversive consequence, such as viewing photos or videos of individuals choking or vomiting. In order to build the hierarchy, the therapist will need to help the patient first develop a Subjective Units of Distress (SUDS) scale (Table 8.2). The therapist should explain that the SUDS scale ranges from 0 to 100, with 0 representing no distress whatsoever and 100 representing the highest distress imaginable. It is important to use the patient's own words to describe the distress construct. Some may describe it as frank fear or anxiety, whereas others may describe it as discomfort or uncertainty. For children, the therapist can present SUDS rating as a 'fear thermometer' (as in Kendall & Hedtke, 2006), ladder, or mountain to increase patient engagement and facilitate comprehension. For each step in the hierarchy, the therapist should ask the patient (assisted by the family, if necessary) where this step falls on their SUDS scale. Table 8.3 provides an example hierarchy for graded exposure for a patient with fear of choking.

Most patients presenting with fear of vomiting have begun restricting their intake in an attempt to

How Does Exposure Work to Reduce Fears about Eating?

Avoidance is only a temporary solution to anxiety

- The longer you avoid your anxiety, the more your anxiety grows and the less you feel you can cope with your fears

- You miss opportunities to test out predictions and learn your feared consequences are unlikely

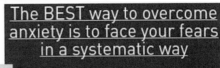

The BEST way to overcome anxiety is to face your fears in a systematic way

- Create a hierarchy of your fears from least anxiety-provoking to most anxiety-provoking, using a scale from 1-100 called subjective units of distress (SUDS)

- One at a time, face your fears, evaluate whether your feared outcomes come true, and watch what happens to your anxiety

-Over time, you will probably see your anxiety decrease and you will feel more confident in handling situations that used to be scary

Avoidance Increases Anxiety

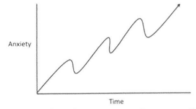

Your anxiety increases when you think about trying an avoided food and decreases when you decide not to. However, anxiety increases even more when you consider trying the food again, and decreases less when you decide not to. In other words - you get more scared and worried every time you avoid!

Exposure Decreases Anxiety

If you try a novel food, your anxiety will increase at first, but it will ultimately decrease as you keep practicing.

The best way to learn whether your predictions will really come true and that you can cope with fear is to eat foods that you fear!

Thomas, J.J. and Eddy, K.T. (2018). *Cognitive-Behavioral Therapy for Avoidant/Restrictive Food Intake Disorder: Children, Adolescents, & Adults*. Cambridge: Cambridge University Press.

Fig 8.3 Patient education handout: 'How does avoidance increase anxiety over time?'

Table 8.2 Hierarchy for food exposure in ARFID with fear of aversive consequences

Subjective units of distress/ temperature on fear thermometer	Food or eating situation to be tried
100	
90	
80	
70	
60	
50	
40	
30	
20	
10	
0	

Table 8.3 Hierarchy for food exposure in ARFID with fear of aversive consequences (worked example for choking)

Subjective units of distress/ temperature on fear thermometer	Food or eating situation to be tried
100	Pork chop (i.e., food that had been choked on)
90	
80	Steak
70	Chicken, celery
60	Berries with seeds
50	Rice, pasta noodles
40	Regular oatmeal
30	Chocolate chip cookies, blended oatmeal
20	Milkshake, yogurt
10	Electrolyte drink
0	Water

decrease the likelihood of vomiting. They may be avoiding food altogether, but in our clinical experience, they are more likely to be restricting their eating to a subset of 'safe foods' that they think are unlikely to cause nausea (e.g., bland foods, familiar foods, foods that they or their family have prepared). In other cases, they may be restricting the volume of food that they eat in order to avoid feeling overly full. Unfortunately, these restrictive eating behaviors can lead to further nausea, which may be misinterpreted as increasing the risk of vomiting and therefore drive further misdirected food restriction. In line with previous recommendations (e.g., Boschen, 2007; Hunter & Anthony, 2009), interventions for vomiting phobia can include exposure to feared nauseants/foods, video/audio of others vomiting, and interoceptive exposure to physical symptoms of anxiety or nausea without the feared outcome of throwing up (e.g., spinning in chair, running up/down stairs, reading in a moving vehicle, drinking a full-size milkshake). The therapist may also wish to pair eating with activities that will increase the likelihood that physical sensations will be experienced (e.g., eating a snack before riding in a car). The purpose of these exposures is for the patient to learn that uncomfortable physical sensations – particularly gastrointestinal sensations – are not necessarily a precursor to vomiting. In creating the hierarchy and running the session, the therapist should use the same general strategies described under fear of choking (see discussion earlier in this section). Of course, the hierarchy itself will be specific to vomiting. Table 8.4 provides a worked example.

Assign at-home practice task. After completing the exposure hierarchy, the therapist should conclude the session by asking the patient to continue self- or parent monitoring, regular eating, and increasing eating flexibility, and to consider whether any additional steps should be added to the exposure hierarchy. Then the therapist should help the patient (or family) select the first exposure to complete in the next session. Ideally, the first exposure will be to a food or an eating situation low on the hierarchy; steps higher in the hierarchy are likely to be too challenging for the first exposure. To that end, the therapist should also help the patient (or family) determine whether the patient needs to bring any items from home (e.g., a specific food) to the next session in order to complete the exposure task.

Stage 3, Fear of Aversive Consequences Module, Later Sessions

The remaining sessions of the Stage 3 Fear of Aversive Consequences module will follow the same basic structure. First the therapist will set the agenda, weigh the patient, and review the parent- or self-monitoring records to ensure that the patient is continuing with regular eating, increasing eating flexibility, and completing the at-home practice tasks. Next the therapist will guide the patient through in-session exposures that will facilitate progress up the exposure hierarchy and help the patient determine the appropriate exposure(s) to practice at home during the upcoming week.

Conduct in-session exposure. At the start of the first exposure and every exposure thereafter, the therapist should ask the patient to describe the feared consequence that he or she is concerned will occur as a result of the exposure. For example, the patient may predict that 'I will choke,' 'I will vomit,' 'I will have an allergic reaction,' or 'I will be so anxious that I will have a panic attack.' The therapist should then ask the patient to estimate the probability of the feared consequence, ranging from 0% to 100%. The therapist should then ask the patient to rate his or her starting SUDS (from 0 to 100). Next, the therapist should ask the patient to begin the exposure (e.g., eating the food that the patient is concerned will make him or her choke, vomit, or have an allergic reaction). The therapist should be careful to point out safety behaviors, such as chewing an excessive number of times or taking very small bites, and encourage the patient not to engage in these subtle avoidance behaviors. If the therapist observes an important safety behavior not previously represented on the hierarchy, the therapist may add overcorrecting behaviors to the hierarchy (e.g., swallowing after just one or two chews) for possible use in future exposures. It is also important that the therapist does not provide reassurance to the patient as the patient engages in the exposure. Rather than assuring the patient that he or she 'definitely will not choke' or 'probably will not vomit,' the therapist should remain neutral about the probability of the feared outcome. It is important that the patient him- or herself learn that the probability of an aversive consequence is unlikely from his or her own experience. The therapist should continue to take SUDS ratings periodically throughout the exposure. It is likely that the patient will experience a reduction in distress the longer he or she stays in the exposure

Table 8.4 Hierarchy for food exposure in ARFID with fear of aversive consequences (worked example for vomiting)

Subjective units of distress/ temperature on fear thermometer	Food or eating situation to be tried
100	Eating a whole portion of food that has led to vomiting in the past
90	Watching a video of vomiting (audio and sound); eating a bite of food after which patient has vomited in the past
80	Watching a soundless video or listening to an audio of someone vomiting
70	Showing a photo of vomiting; eating a small snack while riding in a car
60	Exposure to a feeling of fullness (e.g., drinking a large milkshake); eating a small snack before riding in a car
50	Pictures of people before and after vomiting
40	Pictures of people at toilets
30	Pictures of people looking and feeling sick
20	Showing cartoons of someone vomiting
10	Talking about vomiting (e.g., 'puke,' 'barf,' 'spew')
0	

situation without experiencing the feared consequence. However, it is OK if SUDS remain constant throughout the first exposure, or even go up before returning to the same baseline rating. In CBT-AR, habituation may occur *across* sessions rather than *within* sessions. Further, while habituation to anxiety occurs for many patients, new learning can occur even without habituation to anxiety.

After the exposure, the therapist should ask the patient to reestimate the probability of the feared consequence. For example, if the patient originally estimated that the likelihood of choking was 50%, but ultimately ate 10 bites of the target food without choking, the therapist should note that, under the patient's original prediction, the patient should have choked 5 times. The patient may then offer a lower probability (e.g., 25%) of choking.

Assign at-home practice task. As homework, the therapist should ask the patient to consume the foods or drinks consumed during the exposure session several times throughout the upcoming week to reinforce learning. For the remainder of Stage 3, it is important that the therapist continues to emphasize not only repeated practice of in-session exposures but ultimately the important task of incorporating previously feared foods into planned meals and snacks.

The last task is to select two to three new exposures to complete in the next session – ideally those higher up the hierarchy. This is important because, even if the exposure was successful in that the feared consequence did not occur and the patient's distress significantly decreased, the patient may simply create an amendment to his or her initial prediction ('I guess I'm not very likely to choke on oatmeal, but I'll definitely still choke on steak') that does not allow for generalization to other foods or eating experiences. The patient may find that, over time, once he or she has completed steps lower in the hierarchy without the feared consequence occurring, steps that used to be higher on the hierarchy will begin moving down, as they will be associated with less and less distress.

Prepare for next maintaining mechanism to target in Stage 3 (final session of module only, if there are multiple maintaining mechanisms). If the therapist plans to move on to another module in Stage 3 before progressing to Stage 4, he or she should use the final session of the Fear of Aversive Consequences module to prepare for the next module. Specifically, if the therapist plans to do the Sensory Sensitivity module, he or she should ask the patient (or family)

to bring in five foods the patient is willing to learn about from the Primary Food Groups Building Blocks. If the therapist plans to do the Lack of Interest module, the therapist should ask the patient (or family) to bring in five of the patient's highly preferred foods for the next in-session exposure.

Maintaining Mechanism #3: Apparent Lack of Interest in Eating or Food

Stage 3, Lack of Interest in Eating or Food Module, Session 1

The therapist will begin the first session of the Lack of Interest module by setting the agenda, weighing the patient, and reviewing the self- or parent monitoring and at-home practice tasks. In particular, the therapist should review how the patient is doing with increasing eating flexibility and, if they have already completed another Stage 3 module, the at-home practice tasks associated that module.

Psychoeducation on strategies for eating enough. The therapist will then begin the first session of the Stage 3 Lack of Interest module by reviewing the patient education handout entitled 'Strategies for Eating Enough' (Fig 8.4). The therapist should highlight and explain the importance of each strategy that will be presented in this module, including interoceptive exposures, self-monitoring of hunger and fullness cues, and remembering what the patient likes about his or her highly preferred foods.

Conduct interoceptive exposure. The therapist will then move on to introducing the concept of interoceptive exposure. For individuals with lack of interest in eating or food, the purpose of interoceptive exposure is to reduce nonacceptance of fullness cues and associated negative affect. Although tolerance to fullness may increase automatically as the patient increases his or her food intake in Stages 1–2, in our experience, further intervention is typically required in Stage 3 to fully address lack of interest as a maintaining mechanism. The primary difference between interoceptive exposure and the exposures we described to address the other two ARFID maintaining mechanisms is that in interoceptive exposure, the therapist encourages the patient to approach internal (i.e., physical bodily sensations) rather than external (e.g., novel foods, pictures of vomit) stimuli.

Strategies for Eating Enough

1. Reduce discomfort after eating

Interoceptive exposures

*Increasing your tolerance of full sensations can help you eat enough

*Types of exposures you can do with your therapist in session are: pushing your belly out, gulping water, and spinning in a chair
  -Try all three and then practice the hardest
  -Plan practices as homework (e.g., chug several full glasses of water before lunch each day)

2. Increase your hunger

Recognizing Hunger Cues

*Over time, eating too little confuses your hunger and fullness cues

*The best way to help increase your awareness of hunger cues is to keep track of how hungry you feel before you eat, and how full you feel afterward

*To begin shifting your hunger cues, you will need to start eating at a 3 or 4 (neither hungry nor full), rather than waiting for a 1 (extreme hunger). You will also need to keep eating until a 6 or a 7 (extreme fullness), rather than stopping at a 4 or 5 (neither hungry nor full)

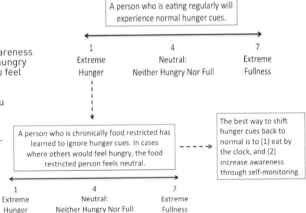

A person who is eating regularly will experience normal hunger cues.

| 1 | 4 | 7 |
| Extreme Hunger | Neutral: Neither Hungry Nor Full | Extreme Fullness |

A person who is chronically food restricted has learned to ignore hunger cues. In cases where others would feel hungry, the food restricted person feels neutral.

The best way to shift hunger cues back to normal is to (1) eat by the clock, and (2) increase awareness through self-monitoring.

| 1 | 4 | 7 |
| Extreme Hunger | Neutral: Neither Hungry Nor Full | Extreme Fullness |

3. Increase enjoyment of eating

Notice what you like about your preferred foods

*Remind yourself of foods you have eaten during happy occasions, such as eating birthday cake with your friends and family

*Pick 5 foods you prefer or used to really enjoy and closely describe them using "The Five Steps" handout

Thomas, J.J. and Eddy, K.T. (2018). *Cognitive-Behavioral Therapy for Avoidant/Restrictive Food Intake Disorder: Children, Adolescents, & Adults.* Cambridge: Cambridge University Press.

Fig 8.4 Patient education handout: 'Strategies for eating enough'

Table 8.5 Interoceptive exposure exercises for ARFID with apparent lack of interest in eating or food

Internal physical sensations that individuals with ARFID may find difficult to tolerate	Exposure exercises that will elicit these internal physical sensations
Bloating	Pushing belly out as far as possible for at least 30 seconds
Fullness	Gulping several glasses of water
Nausea	Spinning in a chair for at least 30 seconds

Boswell, Anderson, and Anderson (2015) have recently described a series of interoceptive exposures for classical eating disorders that we have adapted for ARFID and describe in detail in what follows (see Table 8.5).

The therapist should explain that the day's session is focused on giving the patient practice with different physical sensations – such bloating, fullness, or nausea – which may be contributing to the patient's lack of interest in eating or food. The therapist can explain that the exercises are designed to help the patient see these sensations are temporary, tolerable, and not associated with long-term negative consequences. With each exercise, the therapist will ask the patient (1) how similar the physical sensations are to the feelings the patient has (or is trying to avoid) when eating and (2) to rate the intensity of the sensation using the Subjective Units of Distress Scale (SUDS). If the therapist has not already explained SUDS (e.g., in the Fear of Aversive Consequences module), the therapist should explain that SUDS ranges from 0 to 100, with 0 representing no distress whatsoever and 100 representing the highest distress imaginable. In the context of interoceptive exposure, the SUDS rating should represent the intensity of the physical sensation, but because most patients with lack of interest associate fullness, bloating, or nausea with some degree of negative affect (e.g., anxiety), this negative affect will likely intensify the physical sensation and thus amplify the overall SUDS rating.

The therapist should then briefly demonstrate the first exercise (Table 8.5) before asking the patient to do it, then move on to demonstrate the second exercise before having the patient do it, and then finish by

demonstrating the third exercise and asking the patient to do it. Not only does demonstrating the exposures help ensure that patients will ultimately do them correctly; it also demonstrates that the therapist is willing to put him- or herself in the patient's shoes and is not afraid to look silly in the session. We have found that many of our young patients, while somewhat anxious about the prospect of experiencing fullness cues, rather enjoy the playful tone that the therapist sets by engaging in these demonstrations. First, to demonstrate the exposure for bloating, the therapist should sit tall in his or her chair facing the patient and push his or her belly out as far as possible for 30 seconds. Second, to demonstrate the exposure for fullness, the therapist should quickly gulp one very large glass or two to three small glasses of water in as few sips as possible. Third, to demonstrate the exposure for nausea, the therapist should spin around in a chair as fast as possible for 30 seconds.

After demonstrating each exercise and ensuring the patient understands what is expected, the therapist should invite the patient to do each exercise. For each exposure, the therapist should ask the patient to provide a starting SUDS rating. Once the patient begins the exposure, the therapist should ask the patient to indicate when he or she first experiences the anticipated sensation (i.e., bloating, fullness, or nausea). At that point the therapist should take a second SUDS rating. The therapist should then encourage the patient to continue the exposure for at least 30 more seconds (in the case of pushing out the belly or spinning in a chair) or another glass of water. Rather than providing reassurance that the uncomfortable feelings will go away, the therapist should encourage the patient to sit with the uncomfortable feelings – both physical and emotional – and notice whether they change in intensity during the exercise. After the patient completes each exercise, the therapist should ask questions to enhance processing (similar to Craske & Barlow, 2001). For example, after the patient pushes the belly out, the therapist could ask, 'How similar is this to when you've felt very bloated after eating?' After the patient gulps water, the therapist could ask, 'How similar is this to how you've felt after a recent meal when you felt very full?' Lastly, after the patient spins in a chair, the therapist could ask, 'How similar is this to when you've felt very nauseous after eating?' After drinking several glasses of water during the first interoceptive exposure session, one of our 13-year-old male patients said, 'If this is what being full feels like, then I've never been full before.'

At the conclusion of the interoceptive exposures, the therapist should praise the patient for his or her bravery and then ask the patient to practice the most distressing or relevant exposures several times throughout the next week as an at-home practice task. The therapist should also ask the patient to record SUDS ratings for these at-home practices because repeated interoceptive exposures to the uncomfortable physical sensations associated with eating are expected to lead to tolerance of eating larger volumes of food over time. For instance, the 13-year-old in the previous example went on to increase his eating volume substantially and gained 17 pounds during CBT-AR.

Assign extended self-monitoring with hunger and fullness ratings. Now that the patient has begun to approach the uncomfortable feelings of bloating, fullness, and nausea, the therapist should support the patient in enhancing the salience of hunger cues by bringing them into greater awareness (similar to Craighead's 2006 concept of appetite awareness). It is useful to do this intervention after completing the interoceptive exposures, because the patient will have experienced a greater intensity of fullness than he or she is used to experiencing, thus highlighting the potential extent of the 1–7 scale. Patients will have already been engaging in self- or parent monitoring, so the extended monitoring presented here will provide an opportunity to explore hunger and fullness sensations in greater detail. The therapist should explain that we all experience differing levels of hunger and fullness throughout the day, which can be described on a 7-point hunger and fullness scale going from 'extreme hunger' (a 1 on the 7-point scale) to 'extreme fullness' (a 7 on the 7-point scale) (Fig 8.4). The midpoint on this scale (a 4 on the 7-point scale) corresponds with 'neutral' (neither hungry nor full). To establish personalized anchors, the therapist should ask the patient to remember a time he or she felt extremely hungry (a 1 on the hunger and fullness scale) and another time he or she felt extremely full (a 7 on the hunger and fullness scale). (If the patient chronically eats very little, the therapist may have the patient use the gulping-water exercise from the interoceptive exposure as the anchor for a 7.)

The therapist can then go on to explain how the patient's own satiety anchors may have been inadvertently shifted due to chronic food restriction. Specifically, as depicted in Fig 8.4, when somebody is eating regularly throughout the day, that person will experience normal hunger cues. In contrast, a person who is chronically food restricted has learned to inadvertently ignore these cues. Over time, an individual's hunger and fullness scale is slowly shifted to the left. Ultimately, in cases where others would feel extreme hunger, the chronically food restricted person feels neutral (neither hungry nor full), which reduces their interest in food and/or eating. The best way to shift hunger cues back to normal is to eat by the clock (as described in Stage 1) and to increase awareness through self-monitoring hunger and fullness level before and after each meal and snack. Because these ratings can be somewhat cumbersome, the therapist should ask the patient to complete them for two days (rather than every day) over the upcoming week. Table 8.6 provides a blank self-monitoring record with additional hunger and fullness ratings, and Table 8.7 provides a worked example.

Five Steps for highly preferred foods. After completing the relevant interoceptive exposure(s), the final task is to use the Five Steps (Fig 8.1) to mindfully describe the properties of the five highly preferred foods that the patient has brought to the session. In our cognitive-behavioral model of ARFID with lack of interest in eating or food, we conceptualize low hedonic response to food as a potential biological risk factor for the disorder that is exacerbated and maintained by food avoidance. Like an individual with depression who has lost interest or pleasure in activities he or she used to enjoy, the patient with this presentation of ARFID has lost interest or pleasure in food – sometimes even food he or she used to enjoy. Therefore, similar to behavioral activation for depression, it will be important to help the patient bring into greater awareness the potentially rewarding properties of food. In preparation for this exercise, the therapist should encourage the patient to create a list of foods he or she currently enjoys or used to enjoy, particularly highly preferred foods (e.g., chocolate) or special foods associated with happy occasions (e.g., birthday cake). In our experience, even patients who find eating in general to be a chore can typically list a handful of foods – even if they do not eat them very often – that they find appealing.

Using the prompts provided in Fig 8.1, the therapist should ask the patient to mindfully describe the sensory properties of each of the five foods. (See

Table 8.6 Self-monitoring record with hunger and fullness ratings

Time	Food/drink consumed	Thoughts, feelings	Physical sensations (including 1–7 hunger/ fullness rating)

Table 8.7 Self-monitoring record with hunger and fullness ratings (worked example)

Time	Food/drink consumed	Thoughts, feelings	Physical sensations (including 1–7 hunger/fullness rating)
8:00 AM	1 chocolate donut glass of milk	Took her to her favorite donut place on the way to school	Starting: 3 Ending: 5
11:00 AM	small bag of tortilla chips apple juice box		Starting: 4 Ending: 6
12:30 PM	1 piece of cheese pizza handful of pretzels cup of water		Starting: 3 Ending: 6
3:00 PM	½ chocolate chip cookie		Starting: 3 Ending: 6
6:00 PM	½ bowl of mac & cheese glass of milk	I feel like we are always pressing her to eat more than she really can. Even though she was pretty hungry, she said she started to feel kind of sick after just ½ a bowl.	Starting: 2 Ending: 7
8:00 PM	1 bowl vanilla ice cream	Upon reflection, we probably could have given her a bit more here because she only ended at a 5.	Starting: 3 Ending: 5

Maintaining Mechanism #1: Sensory Sensitivity for full description of the technique.) The only distinction between using the Five Steps for sensory sensitivity and lack of interest in eating is that, when using the Five Steps for lack of interest in eating, the therapist should invite the patient to verbalize at least some positive aspects of his or her preferred foods. For example, the therapist can ask questions that may elicit a positive response, such as 'what do you like about your mom's brownies?' and 'what special events does this cake remind you of?' If the patient reports enjoying eating any of these foods in session, the therapist should suggest that he or she incorporate some of these favorite foods into his or her regular meals and snacks during the upcoming week.

Assign at-home practice task. The therapist should conclude the first session of the Stage 3 lack of interest in eating or food module by assigning the following at-home practice tasks: (1) ask that the patient continue with regular eating and increasing eating flexibility, (2) practice the most relevant interoceptive exposure(s) several times at home this week and make SUDS ratings, (3) confirm that the patient will add the hunger and fullness ratings to this week's self-monitoring on two days, and (4) identify five additional foods that the patient highly prefers or used to enjoy and bring them to the next session. These will ideally be foods that are highly palatable (e.g., cookies, pizza) and/or that the patient associates with fond memories (e.g., birthdays, family holidays). It is also okay if the patient prefers to bring in the same five foods he or she just tasted.

Stage 3, Lack of Interest in Eating or Food Module, Later Sessions

The therapist should begin the second and all subsequent sessions of the Stage 3 lack of interest in eating or food module by setting the agenda, weighing the patient, and reviewing the patient's self-monitoring records, which should include the extended hunger/fullness ratings for two days in the past week. Using the self-monitoring records, the therapist should help the patient identify times of day when he or she feels more hungry than others, and recommend increasing volume specifically at those times. For example, if the patient provides a hunger and fullness rating of 4 at breakfast time and 3 at lunchtime, the therapist could suggest keeping his or her breakfast portion the same but slightly increasing his or her portion size at lunch. Certainly, if the patient reports a 1 or 2 at dinnertime, the therapist should encourage a large portion increase at that meal. Overall, the therapist should discourage the patient from allowing him- or herself to get all the way to a 1, as the patient will have missed the opportunity to eat at a 3 or a 4. If the patient is routinely getting to a 1, an across-the-board increase in volume will be required. Furthermore, by persistently bringing hunger levels into greater awareness, the patient is likely to feel that these cues are becoming more salient, and that his or her hunger and fullness scale begins to shift back to normal. However, the patient must make consistent ratings to allow this critical shift to occur. As with learning any new skill, it is only through consistent practice that greater awareness and salience of hunger cues can be cultivated. Thus if the patient returns without completing the satiety ratings, the therapist should react with curiosity and help the patient identify barriers that can be overcome to facilitate regular satiety monitoring. However, in contrast to the self-monitoring of food intake (which is meant to last for the majority of treatment – from Stage 1 to Stage 3), if the patient is monitoring consistently, the therapist may only need to assign the hunger and satiety ratings for two to three weeks. The therapist should also check whether the patient has been practicing the interoceptive exposures at home and whether his or her associated SUDS ratings have decreased during this time.

Conduct further interoceptive exposure. The therapist should then move on to the interoceptive exposure portion of the session. Depending on which of the exposures the patient found most relevant at the last session, the therapist should ask the patient to do one, two, or all three of the interoceptive exposures. Just as in the prior session, the therapist should ask the patient to provide SUDS ratings before starting, again once the patient begins feeling the relevant sensation (i.e., bloating, fullness, or nausea), and again at the conclusion of the exposure. The therapist should encourage the patient to push further with each exposure than he or she did in the first session of the module. For example, if a patient held his or her belly out or spun in a chair for 30 seconds last time, the therapist should ask the patient to do so for 45 seconds this time. Similarly, if the patient drank three glasses of water last time, the therapist should encourage the patient to drink four or five glasses this time. Just as in the Fear of Aversive

Consequences module, the patient may find that reduction in SUDS occurs across (rather than within) exposure sessions.

Five Steps for highly preferred foods. Lastly, the therapist should ask the patient to use the Five Steps to explore the five highly preferred foods that he or she has brought to session. Again it is fine for the therapist to invite the patient to use positive language (rather than the neutral language required of the Sensory Sensitivity module) given that the purpose of this exercise is to help the patient remember what he or she likes about these highly preferred foods. Because the patient will have just completed an interoceptive exposure, it is often helpful to invite the patient to observe how quickly the feelings of bloating, fullness, or nausea dissipate. For example, the patient may have just rated his or her SUDS at a 75 after gulping water earlier in the session, but still have room for multiple tastes of preferred foods later in the session. The therapist may take this opportunity to point out that the patient is able to tolerate being more full than he or she previously thought possible.

Assign at-home practice task. For at-home practice tasks this week, the therapist should ask the patient to continue with self- or parent monitoring, regular eating, and increasing eating flexibility. The patient should also be asked to practice any relevant interoceptive exposure exercises. It can be particularly helpful to practice the interoceptive exposure exercises before eating (e.g., drinking four glasses of water before eating lunch). Lastly, the patient should be invited to bring five additional highly preferred foods (or the same highly preferred foods as he or she has previously brought in) to the next session, and to practice incorporating highly preferred foods into meals and snacks this week.

(Final session of module only, if there are multiple maintaining mechanisms). Prepare for next maintaining mechanism to target in Stage 3. If this is the final session of the Lack of Interest module and the therapist plans to move on to another Stage 3 module before beginning Stage 4, it will be important to tee this up by asking the patient (or family) to bring small portions of five items from the 'willing to learn about' list on the Primary Food Group Building Blocks (for the Sensory Sensitivity module) or asking the patient (or family) to begin thinking about fears he or she would like to tackle in Stage 3 (for the Fear of Aversive Consequences module).

Troubleshooting Stage 3

What if a patient with sensory sensitivity does not bring five foods to the session? The therapist should nonjudgmentally ask the patient what got in the way of bringing the agreed-on items. If the patient says that he or she forgot, the therapist can brainstorm ways of remembering to bring them next time. If the patient decided against trying the agreed-on items after all, the patient and therapist should collaboratively decide what to bring to the next session. Decreasing the task demands by selecting foods more similar to those that the patient already prefers may make compliance more likely. Most importantly, the patient should not be able to avoid the tasting session by not bringing food. Instead, after troubleshooting and making a plan for next time, the therapist should devise a plan for the patient to taste five foods anyway. For example, the therapist may wish to store some nonperishable items (e.g., nuts, pretzels) in his or her office for just such occasions, or, if possible, the therapist can take the patient to a nearby store to select items for tasting.

What if a patient with fear of aversive consequences actually experiences the aversive consequence (e.g., chokes, vomits, has an allergic reaction) during an exposure? An organic swallowing problem (e.g., dysphagia) should already have been ruled out in the pretreatment medical evaluation, and we therefore must stress that exposures should only be done with patients who are medically safe to swallow. In such cases, choking during an exposure would be unusual but not completely out of the realm of possibility. If the patient chokes, the therapist should explore with the patient whether his or her negative food predictions actually came true – in other words, the patient may have choked and felt momentarily terrified, but it was over in a few seconds and there was no lasting physical harm. Furthermore, the therapist should contrast this with the number of successful swallows the patient has already achieved during CBT-AR (e.g., 30), and ask the patient whether the occurrence of this single episode (e.g., 1 out of 30) matches up with their predicted likelihood of choking (i.e., 100%). If not, the evidence still does not support the catastrophic prediction.

Whether or not a patient has been previously diagnosed with a food allergy, we strongly recommend that the therapist have a plan to provide access to an epinephrine auto-injector if needed. A patient who shows any signs of anaphylaxis—such as skin rash, nausea, vomiting, difficulty breathing, or shock—within seconds or minutes of trying a new food, should be referred to the nearest emergency room and given epinephrine as directed (e.g., by the emergency room physician, in consultation with the patient's physician). One of the patients in our initial CBT-AR clinical trial tried a tree nut for the first time during Stage 3 and began experiencing nausea, a tingling sensation on his lips, and difficulty breathing. We referred him directly to the emergency room where a physician confirmed he had just experienced anaphylaxis and, later, an immunologist diagnosed him with a tree nut allergy. It is for this reason that we recommend that the therapist have a plan in place for dealing with an unexpected allergic reaction, particularly when the patient elects to try one of the top eight potentially allergenic foods: milk, eggs, fish, shellfish, tree nuts, peanuts, wheat, or soy.

What if the patient with fear of aversive consequences denies or minimizes anxiety? It is challenging to create a fear and avoidance hierarchy with a patient who exhibits avoidance yet does not endorse any fear. This is common among patients who may have lack of insight into their difficulties. Many of these patients are young, and some have autistic traits, both of which may contribute to their difficulty articulating feelings and predictions about feared consequences. Further, many of these individuals are boys who may not be socialized or reinforced for describing feelings and expressing vulnerabilities. In such cases, we recommend a behavioral rather than a cognitive approach. Using irreverence can be helpful (e.g., 'That's great! Then we can jump right in with exposures.'), as can using the patient's avoidance behaviors as a guide to how anxious he or she actually is.

Checklist for Moving on to Stage 4

By the end of Stage 3, the patient should have accomplished the following tasks. If the patient has made

good progress toward accomplishing these tasks but one or two specific objectives have not yet been fully met, extending Stage 3 may be useful. By contrast, if the patient has shown minimal improvement by the end of Stage 3, extending it is unlikely to be helpful.

- Patient is no longer underweight
- Patient is eating at regular intervals, typically three meals and two or three snacks per day, and has increased volume or variety (if needed) within meals and snacks
- While the patient may still be taking supplements to correct nutritional deficiencies, the patient is regularly incorporating foods that will help resolve these deficiencies
- Patient's primary ARFID maintaining mechanism (s) has been at least partially resolved, and the patient/family have an understanding of how to continue at-home strategies that will lead to a degree of resolution that eliminates clinical impairment

  ○ If sensory sensitivity was a primary focus, has the patient tried a large number of novel foods from my Primary Food Group Building Blocks and incorporated foods from the five food groups into their regular meals and snacks?

  ○ If fear of aversive consequences was a primary focus, has the patient practiced eating the specific food, or putting him- or herself in the specific eating situation, that he or she originally feared would cause vomiting, choking, pain, or another problematic outcome?

  ○ If lack of interest in eating or food was a primary focus, is the patient now consuming a sufficient volume and does he or she have a better sense of his or her internal hunger and fullness cues?

Chapter 9

Stage 4: Relapse Prevention

Stage 4 (two sessions) of CBT-AR comprises an assessment of progress and readiness to graduate from treatment (session 1) and the development of a personalized relapse prevention plan (session 2). In contrast to the sessions in Stages 1–3, which took place weekly, the sessions in Stage 4 should be spaced approximately two weeks apart to enable the patient more time to practice and consolidate gains. Specifically, we advise waiting two weeks after the final session of Stage 3 to start Stage 4, and another two weeks between sessions 1 and 2 of Stage 4.

Stage 4, Session 1

In the first session of Stage 4, after setting the agenda, weighing the patient, and reviewing the at-home practice tasks, the therapist should contrast the patient's baseline symptoms to his or her current functioning by revisiting the personalized formulation, Primary Food Group Building Blocks, and coverage from the MyPlate food groups now in comparison to prior to treatment, and discussing the patient's readiness to complete CBT-AR.

Revisit personalized formulation. The therapist should invite the patient to look back at his or her individualized formulation from Stage 2 and ask the patient what he or she thinks has changed since the formulation was originally created. For example, has the patient gained significant weight? Have nutrition deficiencies been resolved? Does he or she no longer avoid social situations due to food selectivity, and no longer avoid specific foods due to fears of vomiting or choking? In particular, the therapist should highlight how, due to the relationships among constructs in the formulation, targeting a single construct (e.g., food restriction and avoidance) has likely led to changes in other constructs (e.g., negative feelings and predictions about the consequences of eating, nutritional compromise, social avoidance) that were not specifically targeted. Finally, the therapist should praise the

patient for any progress and attribute any changes to the patient's (and family's) hard work.

Revisit Primary Food Group Building Blocks. Next, the therapist and patient should collaboratively review the patient's completed Primary Food Group Building Blocks. Together the therapist and patient should identify the novel foods that the patient has successfully tasted. The therapist should especially praise the patient for any foods that the patient has successfully incorporated into his or her diet. Note that this is likely to be only a subset of the foods tasted during treatment. This is fine as long as the patient is now eating multiple foods within each of the five food groups. To that end, the therapist should refer the patient back to the MyPlate schematic and ensure that the patient's recent meals have corresponded more closely to this model than they did before treatment.

Table 9.1 provides a worked example for a patient with sensory sensitivity who completed CBT-AR and was able to incorporate several new foods into his diet throughout the course of treatment. In addition to reviewing successes, the therapist should encourage the patient to look to the future by identifying any additional foods that he or she may be willing or excited to learn about independently now that CBT-AR is ending. The therapist should also take this opportunity to discuss with the patient whether any of the foods tasted during treatment but not incorporated into the patient's diet could ultimately be incorporated.

Discuss readiness to complete CBT-AR. Lastly, the therapist should have a candid discussion about the patient's readiness to complete CBT-AR. For patients who have not required frequent medical monitoring throughout treatment, the therapist should assist the patient in setting up an end-of-treatment medical evaluation to ascertain progress toward the resolution of any nutritional deficiencies and the maintenance of a healthy weight. Based on a discussion with the patient and feedback from the patient's

Table 9.1 Post-Treatment Primary Food Group Building Blocks (worked example for ARFID with sensory sensitivity)

The first column provides a list of common fruit, vegetable, protein, dairy, and grain foods. Use the second column to place an 'X' next to any foods that you are consistently eating (i.e., have eaten at least once in the past month and would readily eat if offered to you today). Use the third column to place an 'X' next to any foods that you are willing to learn about in CBT-AR. For foods that you are willing to learn about, place an 'X' in the fourth column for each taste you take during CBT-AR (either in session or at home). There are 10 boxes in the fourth column, because research suggests that is the minimum number required to learn enough about a food to develop a clear preference.

	Consistently eating?	Willing to learn about?	Number of tastes since starting CBT-AR?
FRUITS			
100% Fruit juice			
• Apple juice	X		
• Cranberry juice			
• Grape juice			
• Grapefruit juice			
• Mango juice			
• Orange juice		X	X X X X X X X X X X X
• Papaya juice			
• Pineapple juice			
• Pomegranate juice			
• Prune juice			
Berries			
• Acai berries			
• Blackberries			
• Blueberries			
• Cranberries			
• Currants	X	X	
• Goji berries			
• Huckleberries			
• Lingonberries (cowberries)			
• Mulberries			
• Raspberries	X		X X X X X X X X X X X
• Strawberries	X		X X X X X X
Melons			
• Cantaloupe	X		
• Honeydew			
• Horned melon (kiwano)			
• Watermelon			
Other fruits			
• Apples			
• Apricots			
• Bananas	X		X X X X X
• Cherries			
• Dates			
• Figs			
• Fruit cocktail			
• Grapefruit	X	X	
• Grapes			
• Guava			
• Kiwi fruit			

Table 9.1 (cont.)

	Consistently eating?	Willing to learn about?	Number of tastes since starting CBT-AR?
• Lemons			
• Limes			
• Mangoes		X	X X X X X X X X X X
• Nectarines		X	X X X X
• Oranges			
• Papaya			
• Peaches		X	X
• Pears			
• Persimmons			
• Pineapples			
• Plums			
• Pomegranate			
• Prunes			
• Raisins			
• Star fruit			
• Tangerines			

Other mixed or prepared foods with fruits?

	Consistently eating?	Willing to learn about?	Number of tastes since starting CBT-AR?
1. Apple pie		X	X X
2. Fruit smoothie		X	X X X X X X X X X X
3. Dried mangos		X	X X X X
4.			
5.			

VEGETABLES

Dark-green vegetables

	Consistently eating?	Willing to learn about?	Number of tastes since starting CBT-AR?
• Arugula (rocket)			
• Bok choy			
• Broccoli	X		X X X X X X X X X X
• Broccoli rabe (rapini)			
• Broccolini			
• Collard greens			
• Dark-green leafy lettuce			
• Endive			
• Escarole			
• Kale	X		X X X X X X X X X X
• Mesclun			
• Mixed greens			
• Mustard greens			
• Romaine lettuce	X		X X X X X X X X X X
• Spinach			
• Swiss chard			
• Turnip greens			
• Watercress			

Red and orange vegetables

	Consistently eating?	Willing to learn about?	Number of tastes since starting CBT-AR?
• Acorn squash			
• Bell peppers			
• Butternut squash			
• Carrots	X		X X X X X X X X X X
• Hubbard squash			

Table 9.1 (cont.)

	Consistently eating?	Willing to learn about?	Number of tastes since starting CBT-AR?									
• Pumpkin												
• Red chili peppers												
• Red peppers (sweet)		X	X	X	X	X	X	X	X	X	X	X
• Sweet potatoes												
• Tomatoes												
• 100% vegetable juice		X	X	X								
Starchy vegetables												
• Cassava												
• Corn												
• Green bananas												
• Green lima beans												
• Green peas												
• Parsnips												
• Plantains												
• Potatoes, white												
• Taro												
• Water chestnuts												
• Yams												
Other vegetables												
• Alfalfa sprouts												
• Artichokes												
• Asparagus		X	X									
• Avocado												
• Bamboo shoots												
• Bean sprouts												
• Beets												
• Brussels sprouts												
• Cabbage												
• Cauliflower												
• Celery												
• Cucumbers		X	X	X	X	X	X	X				
• Eggplant												
• Garlic												
• Green beans		X	X	X								
• Green peppers												
• Jicama												
• Leeks												
• Lettuce, iceberg		X	X	X	X	X	X	X	X	X	X	X
• Mung bean sprouts												
• Mushrooms												
• Okra												
• Onions												
• Pattypan squash												
• Radicchio												
• Radishes		X	X									
• Red cabbage												
• Scallions												
• Snow peas		X	X									
• Tomatillos												
• Turnips												

Table 9.1 (*cont.*)

	Consistently eating?	Willing to learn about?	Number of tastes since starting CBT-AR?
● Wax beans			
● Yellow squash			
● Zucchini			
Other mixed or prepared foods with vegetables?			
1. Salad w dressing	X		x x x x x x x x x x
2.			
3.			
4.			
5.			
PROTEIN FOODS			
Beans and peas			
● Bean burgers		X	
● Black beans			
● Black-eyed peas			
● Chickpeas (garbanzo beans)			
● Edamame (young soybeans)	X	X	
● Falafel (spiced, mashed chickpeas)			
● Hummus (chickpea spread)	X	x x x x	
● Kidney beans	X		
● Lentils			
● Lima beans (mature)			
● Navy beans			
● Pinto beans			
● Soybeans			
● Split peas			
● White beans			
Eggs			
● Chicken eggs	X		x x x x x x x x x x
● Duck eggs			
Meat			
● Lean ground meats			
○ Beef	X		
○ Pork			
○ Sausage (beef, turkey)			
● Lean cuts			
○ Beef	X		
○ Ham			
○ Lamb			
○ Pork			
● Lean luncheon / deli meats			
○ Beef			
○ Chicken			
○ Ham			
○ Pork			
○ Turkey	X		x x x x x x x x x x

Table 9.1 (*cont.*)

	Consistently eating?	Willing to learn about?	Number of tastes since starting CBT-AR?
• Game meats			
○ Bison			
○ Rabbit			
○ Venison			
• Organ meats			
○ Giblet			
○ Liver			
Nuts and seeds			
• Almonds	X	X	
• Almond butter	X	X X X X X X X X X X
• Cashews	X	X	
• Chia seeds			
• Hazelnuts (filberts)			
• Mixed nuts			
• Peanuts			
• Peanut butter			
• Pecans			
• Pistachios			
• Pumpkin seeds	X	X	
• Sesame seeds			
• Sunflower seeds			
• Walnuts			
Poultry			
• Chicken	X	X X X X X X X X X X
• Duck			
• Goose			
• Turkey			
Seafood			
• Canned fish			
○ Anchovies			
○ Sardines			
○ Tuna	X		
• Finfish			
○ Catfish			
○ Cod			
○ Flounder			
○ Haddock			
○ Halibut			
○ Herring			
○ Mackerel			
○ Pollock			
○ Porgy			
○ Salmon			
○ Sea bass			
○ Snapper			
○ Sushi			
○ Swordfish			

Table 9.1 (cont.)

	Consistently eating?	Willing to learn about?	Number of tastes since starting CBT-AR?
○ Tilapia			
○ Trout			
○ Tuna			
● Shellfish			
○ Clams			
○ Crab			
○ Crayfish			
○ Lobster			
○ Mussels			
○ Octopus			
○ Oysters			
○ Scallops			
○ Shrimp			
○ Squid (calamari)			
Soy products			
● Tempeh			
● Texturized vegetable protein (TVP)			
● Tofu (made from soybeans)	X		
● Veggie burgers	X		X X X X X X X X X X
Other mixed or prepared foods with protein?			
1. Chicken nuggets	X		X X X X X X X X X X
2. Burger w/ bun	X		X X X X X X X X X X
3. Beef w/ sauce	X		
4.			
5.			
DAIRY AND DAIRY SUBSTITUTES			
Cheese			
● Hard natural cheeses			
○ Cheddar	X		
○ Gouda			
○ Mozzarella	X		
○ Muenster			
○ Parmesan			
○ Provolone			
○ Romano			
○ Swiss			
● Soft cheeses			
○ Brie			
○ Camembert			
○ Cottage cheese			
○ Feta			
○ Ricotta			
● Processed cheeses			
○ American	X	X	
○ Cheese spreads	X	X	

Table 9.1 (cont.)

	Consistently eating?	Willing to learn about?	Number of tastes since starting CBT-AR?
Milk			
• **All fluid milk**			
○ Fat-free (skim) milk	X		
○ Flavored milks	X		
○ Lactose-free milks			
○ Low fat milk (1%)	X		
○ Reduced fat milk (2%)	X		
○ Whole milk	X		
• **Milk-based desserts**			
○ Frozen yogurt	X		
○ Ice cream	X		
○ Ice milk			
○ Lassi			
○ Pudding		X	X
○ Sherbet			
○ Smoothies		X	X X X X X X X X X X
Non-dairy calcium alternatives			
• Almond milk			
• Coconut milk			
• Rice milk			
• Soymilk			
Yogurt			
• All milk-based yogurt (fat-free, low fat, reduced fat, whole milk)		X	X X X X X X X X X X
• Almond milk yogurt			
• Coconut milk yogurt			
• Soy yogurt			
Other mixed or prepared foods with dairy or substitutes?			
1. Cream cheese		X	X X X X X X X X X X
2. Mac & cheese		X	X X X X X X X X X X
3. Pizza		X	X X X X X X X X X X
4.			
5.			
GRAINS			
Whole grains			
• Amaranth			
• Brown rice		X	X
• Buckwheat			
• Bulgur (cracked wheat)			
• Kamut			
• Millet			
• Muesli			
• Oatmeal	X		
• Popcorn			
• Quinoa		X	X

Table 9.1 (cont.)

	Consistently eating?	Willing to learn about?	Number of tastes since starting CBT-AR?
• Rolled oats			
• Sorghum			
• Spelt			
• Teff			
• Whole grain barley			
• Whole grain cornmeal			
• Whole grain sorghum			
• Whole rye			
• Whole wheat bread		X	X X X X
• Whole wheat cereal flakes	X		
• Whole wheat crackers			
• Whole wheat pasta			
• Whole wheat sandwich buns and rolls	X		
• Whole wheat tortillas		X	X X X X X X X X X X
• Wild rice		X	X X X X
Refined grains			
• Bagels	X		
• Biscuits			
• Breadcrumbs			
• Cakes	X		
• Challah bread	X		
• Cookies	X		
• Cornflakes	X		
• Corn tortillas			
• Cornbread			
• Couscous			
• Crackers, saltine	X		
• English muffins			
• Flour tortilla			
• French bread			
• Grits			
• Hominy			
• Matzo			
• Naan			
• Noodles			
• Pancakes		X	X
• Pasta (spaghetti, macaroni)		X	X X X X X X X X X X
• Pie/pastry crusts			
• Pita bread			
• Pizza crust			
• Polenta			
• Pretzels			
• Ramen noodles		X	X
• Rice cakes			
• Rice paper (spring roll wrappers)			
• Rice vermicelli			
• Waffles		X	X
• White bread			
• White rice		X	X X X X X X X X X X
• White sandwich buns and rolls			

Table 9.1 *(cont.)*

	Consistently eating?	Willing to learn about?	Number of tastes since starting CBT-AR?
Other mixed or prepared foods with grains?			
1.			
2.			
3.			
4.			
5.			

Adapted from the USDA Center for Nutrition Policy and Promotion's ChooseMyPlate.gov Web site.

physician or medical team, the therapist should consider the following benchmarks for determining the patient's readiness to discharge:

- Patient no longer meets criteria for ARFID and/or symptom severity has decreased
- Patient is able to eat several foods in each of the major food groups on a regular basis[1]
- Patient's growth (height and weight) has increased to that expected (e.g., patient is back on his or her pre-illness trajectory, patient is no longer underweight)
- Nutritional status is replete (i.e., deficiencies have been corrected, or are on their way to being corrected and have shown improvements, or patient is no longer exacerbating them with his or her diet)
- Patient no longer experiences clinically impairing psychosocial consequences of ARFID and has a plan for managing food-related social situations

However, it is important to note that individuals with ARFID should not be expected to eat all foods freely at the end of treatment, or have increased their weight to the 50th percentile if that was not their premorbid healthy trajectory. Instead, we agree with Fitzpatrick et al.'s (2015) assessment that 'it is unlikely that treatment will end when all eating concerns and rigidities

have been resolved' (p. 270). In other words, we expect that, through CBT-AR, individuals with ARFID will have progressed such that their eating no longer results in medical, nutritional, or psychosocial adverse outcomes. Further, we expect that, by now, the patient will have developed the skills to continue making progress over time. Importantly, individuals with ARFID may continue to need some degree of parent involvement and check-ins around eating even after CBT-AR has ended to support maintained treatment gains.

In the event that the patient does not meet all of these criteria, the patient and therapist should consider what additional support the patient may require to continue making forward progress after completing CBT-AR. As CBT-AR is a time-limited treatment, we do not recommend extending the treatment unless the therapist has a very specific rationale (i.e., a new maintaining mechanism has been identified; the patient has identified specific foods that he or she would very much like to taste or incorporate).

Discontinue self- or parent-monitoring records. The therapist need not assign any at-home practice tasks at this penultimate session. Specifically, the therapist should share with the patient (or family) that the self- or parent-monitoring records can now be discontinued. Patients (and families) are usually delighted to hear this. The therapist should emphasize that, upon graduation from the treatment, it will be the patient's or family's own responsibility to maintain accountability for maintaining adequate dietary volume and/or variety.

Stage 4, Session 2

In the final session of CBT-AR, the therapist will set the agenda and weigh the patient as usual. Although

---

[1] Some programs suggest that the patient should feel comfortable eating a certain number of foods – e.g., 5 foods from each food group (Williams & Foxx, 2007) or 10 proteins, 10 starches, and 10 fruits or vegetables (Toomey et al., 2014) before termination. In contrast, the CBT-AR clinician should stick to the time-limited approach and state his/her belief that the patient has now learned the skills to continue increasing both food variety and volume on his/her own.

Table 9.2 My personalized ARFID relapse prevention plan

Ways that my eating has improved since the start of treatment:

Possible future triggers for relapse:

Red flags that I might be starting to relapse:

CBT-AR techniques to continue or try on my own after treatment is completed:

Ways I'd like to continue to change my eating post-treatment:

Table 9.3 My personalized ARFID relapse prevention plan (worked example)

Ways that my eating has improved since the start of treatment:
- *I can eat all the foods I used to eat before I had the choking incident, but without a fear of choking*
- *Have added 25 new foods to my diet!*
- *I feel braver about trying new foods in social situations*

Possible future triggers for relapse:
- *Choking on my food again*
- *Going to college and having to choose food from the dining hall*

Red flags that I might be starting to relapse:
- *Going on a food jag where I eat the same food multiple times per day or week (e.g., brownies)*

CBT-AR techniques to continue or try on my own after treatment is completed:
- *Taking in new foods slowly and using the 5 steps*
- *I can stop at any point along the 5 steps; I can look/smell without eating, and I need to remind myself that that is still progress*
- *I only need to try a little bit of the new food*
- *Self-monitoring*

Ways I'd like to continue to change my eating post-treatment:
- *Continue to try foods on my 'Primary Food Groups Building Blocks, list*
- *Go on more food-related dates (e.g., out to dinner)*
- *Try to cook new recipes*

no at-home practice tasks were assigned in the penultimate session, the therapist should inquire about progress since the last session on the primary treatment goals including maintenance of a healthy weight or incorporation of new foods. The therapist will then move on to co-creating the relapse prevention plan and ending the treatment.

Co-create relapse prevention plan. Using Table 9.2 as a guide, the therapist should guide the patient (or family) in creating a relapse prevention plan. Specifically, it is important to review how the patient's eating has changed since the start of treatment. Next, the therapist should support the patient in anticipating triggers for food restriction and avoidance that may arise, particularly in the next six months – for example, major life changes such as moving to college, which may involve a change in available foods and a need for the patient to take greater accountability for maintaining treatment gains. The next step is to identify any red flags or old behaviors that may be indicative of relapse. The therapist should then assist the patient in identifying and reinforcing any CBT-AR techniques that were particularly helpful and brainstorming about when and how these could be implemented again in the future to support the patient in continuing to maintain a healthy weight and expand his or her diet. For example, the patient may choose to continue smartphone reminders for snack prompts. In the family-supported version, the parents should consider techniques they implemented that helped them support their child. For example, they may need to continue to present the child with new foods to support continued dietary expansion, and to continue to prompt the child to eat regularly. Lastly, it is important for the therapist to help the patient (or family) determine when and how to seek professional help in the future, if needed. Table 9.3 provides a worked example of one patient's relapse prevention plan.

End the treatment. After completing the relapse prevention plan, the therapist should end the final session on a positive note by giving the patient credit for his or her treatment successes and expressing optimism about continued progress after treatment has concluded. Many individuals continue to learn about new foods and develop new tastes for foods over their lifetimes, so the therapist can discuss the final session as a graduation to the process of lifelong learning outside the clinic.

Troubleshooting Stage 4

What if patient is reluctant to complete treatment? There are strong data from cognitive-behavioral therapy for other psychiatric disorders that, for many patients, symptoms continue to improve after treatment concludes. Although we are still collecting long-term outcome data on CBT-AR, we predict a similar trajectory. The therapist should share these data with the patient and express his or her confidence that, with the CBT-AR skills in hand, the patient can continue working on ARFID symptoms on his or her own. In other words, the patient has learned to be his or her own therapist. Of course, the therapist can also reassure the patient that the therapist will be available for booster sessions if necessary, particularly in the case of acute relapse.

CBT-AR Case Examples

Chapter 10

The following five case examples demonstrate CBT-AR in action. Although some details have been changed to protect patient confidentiality, the symptom presentations, clinical dilemmas, and CBT-AR interventions are real. Indeed, all five represent patients that we treated at the Massachusetts General Hospital Eating Disorders Clinical and Research Program as part of the initial development and evaluation of CBT-AR. Three we treated ourselves, and two are guest cases treated by our colleague and CBT-AR study therapist, Kendra R. Becker, Ph.D. As you will see, these patients came from diverse demographic backgrounds in terms of age, sex, and race/ethnicity, but all shared the commonality of an ARFID diagnosis. Some received family-supported treatment and others received individual treatment. Some benefited from a very straightforward application of CBT-AR whereas others required slight modifications that retained fidelity to the overall treatment principles. All experienced marked symptom improvement by the end of their treatment course and provided permission for their cases to be shared in this book for educational purposes.

Case Example #1: An 11-Year-Old Girl with Sensory Sensitivity (family-supported CBT-AR)

Presenting complaint. Emily was an 11-year-old Caucasian girl who presented to the MGH Eating Disorders Clinical and Research Program seeking treatment for ARFID. Her mother had seen a story on the local news about the disorder and felt the description matched the highly selective eating patterns she had long observed in her preteen daughter. Upon initial evaluation, Emily explained that, 'I eat a lot of the same foods, and it makes me feel bad about myself.' Mom shared that Emily had previously eaten a wide range of foods, but at 18 months old she began declining many of the items she had previously consumed. Inquiring about Emily's typical

daily intake revealed that her diet lacked variety and relied heavily on processed grains. Specifically, in the months prior to the evaluation, she reported eating saltine crackers for breakfast; cheese-flavored crackers for morning snack; plain pasta noodles for lunch; chicken nuggets and French fries for dinner; and popcorn for evening snack. She did not consistently eat any fruits, vegetables, or dairy foods, and her protein intake was limited to chicken nuggets. Emily described some psychosocial impairment as a consequence of her ARFID symptoms, including avoiding sleepovers, parties, and other social activities where her preferred foods were unlikely to be available; and being teased by family members about her selective eating, which would lead her to retire to her room in tears. Her parents also described that they were extremely limited in their ability to eat at restaurants or go on family vacations, where the availability of Emily's preferred foods would be uncertain, resulting in anxiety for Emily and conflict among family members.

Prior to initiating treatment, the therapist referred Emily for a medical evaluation with an adolescent medicine physician. At 5 feet 2 inches tall, Emily weighed 91.4 lbs (BMI = 16.7, 37th percentile for sex and age). She had not yet begun menstruating. Her blood work revealed a previously undiagnosed iron deficiency, even though Emily took a multivitamin daily to compensate for her limited diet. In addition, the physician expressed concern that Emily's calcium intake was insufficient, though her blood levels were in the normal range. When Emily shared with the physician that eating dairy foods typically caused her diarrhea, gas, or bloating, the physician evaluated her for, and ultimately provided a diagnosis of, lactose intolerance. The physician then recommended that in order to increase calcium intake, Emily consider drinking lactose-free milk, or taking a lactase enzyme supplement, prior to eating dairy products. At this visit, Emily also complained of constipation, which the physician attributed to Emily's low intake of dietary fiber.

Case Example #1: *(cont.)*

Apart from her ARFID, Emily was a bright, high-functioning young girl who earned straight As in school, had many close friends, and enjoyed many forms of dance. She shared that she was highly motivated to expand her dietary variety at this time because 'I really want to be healthy, go out to eat, and go to parties with my friends.' Because Emily was less than 16 years old, the therapist recommended family-supported CBT-AR. As Emily was not underweight, the therapist planned for approximately 20 sessions of treatment. Stage 3 would focus exclusively on the sensory sensitivity module with the primary treatment goal of introducing novel foods and expanding dietary variety.

Stage 1. Emily's father traveled frequently for work, but he was able to make time to attend both of the Stage 1 sessions along with Emily's mother. Both Emily and her parents were receptive to psychoeducation about ARFID, after which mom shared: 'That describes Emily to a T.' Because Emily was already eating three meals and two snacks per day upon presentation, no intervention was needed to support regular eating in session 1. In co-creating the individualized formulation, the therapist pointed out that although Emily's sensory sensitivity made her limited eating choices logical: her long-standing reliance on processed grains made dairy, protein, fruits, and vegetables feel increasingly novel and unapproachable. In particular, Emily appreciated how her avoidance of social activities limited her exposure to novel foods that her peers might model eating. She felt this was particularly true of pizza, a food her friends often ate at parties but which she herself found to difficult to consume. Armed with his new understanding of ARFID, at the end of session 2, Emily set a goal to reintroduce two previously dropped foods, including sugar snap peas at dinnertime and fruit smoothies at breakfast to supplement her saltine crackers.

Stage 2. For Stage 2 and for the majority of the remaining sessions, Emily attended sessions with her mother only, as her father was often traveling. However, because her father had attended both sessions in Stage 1, he was familiar with the CBT-AR tenets and treatment plan and was able to support Emily in her efforts to integrate new foods at home. Emily was successful in meeting her goal of incorporating smoothies at breakfast, which by session 4 had completely supplanted the saltines. In completing her Building Blocks worksheet, she identified several proteins, fruits, and vegetables to learn about in CBT-AR.

Because her adolescent medicine physician had been particularly concerned about Emily's low intake of iron and calcium, the therapist used the nutritional deficiencies handout to identify foods that Emily was willing learn about that were rich in iron (i.e., spinach, beef, chickpeas, and forms of chicken other than chicken nuggets) and calcium (i.e., lactose-free milk, yogurt, cheese). At the end of session 4, Emily identified five foods that she was willing to learn about in the next session (lettuce, grape juice, strawberries, peanut butter, and yogurt-covered raisins) and planned to bring small tasting portions of each.

Stage 3. The therapist had the luxury of focusing on a single maintaining mechanism for the entirety of Stage 3 – sensory sensitivity. The therapist began session 5 by sharing the CBT-AR technique of learning about new foods by asking Emily to look at, touch, smell, taste, and chew each of the five foods she had brought to session. Through this process Emily was surprised to find that she did not dislike any of the foods she had brought to session 5. In fact, she found that she was particularly fond of the yogurt-covered raisins, which she committed to adding to her morning snack three to four times during the upcoming week. She also declared that she was willing to continue learning about peanut butter and grape juice, and committed to taking small tastes of each – practicing with the Five Steps – at home prior to the next session. Of note, Emily said that she did not want to continue learning about the strawberries or lettuce, so the therapist left open the possibility that, though Emily might wish to learn about them in the future, she could decline to practice during the upcoming week with any foods she did not initially find appealing. Indeed, the therapist emphasized that she herself did not have a particular investment in Emily tasting or incorporating any specific food; rather, it was the range of foods across the five basic food groups that was important. Emily returned to session 6 having successfully incorporated the yogurt-covered raisins and having practiced with peanut butter. She had forgotten to practice the grape juice but had spontaneously tried steak, which had been on her list of iron-rich foods to try as part of treatment. The therapist made sure to praise Emily for her courage in trying the steak on her own outside of session, highlighting how using the strategies she was learning in CBT-AR were already changing how she approached new foods. The therapist also stressed the importance of only committing to practicing foods that Emily thought she would follow through with, and helped Emily and her mother

Case Example #1: *(cont.)*

brainstorm strategies for remembering to practice outside of session (e.g., putting a note in her smartphone, allowing her mother to prompt her). Emily continued to try new foods in each session and, as often occurs in Stage 3 of CBT-AR, began to feel increasingly comfortable trying novel foods outside of session as well. At session 6 she tried blueberries, corn, a soft pretzel, cucumbers, and non-breaded chicken breast. At session 7, she tried broccoli, mozzarella cheese, mashed potato, steak, and tomatoes. At session 8, she tried spinach, cashews, hummus, raspberries, and cantaloupe. Every time Emily practiced with a dairy food, her mother made sure that Emily took her lactase enzyme supplement to ensure a successful exposure.

By the time Emily had tried 15 novel foods in session and 3 novel foods (steak, salad, watermelon) spontaneously at home, the therapist returned to the MyPlate schematic and encouraged Emily to consider how she might incorporate the newly tasted foods into her routine meals and snacks. Between sessions 9–14, Emily continued to try fruits, vegetables, and proteins in session, but more importantly made great strides in incorporating these food groups into daily diet. For example, she began adding spinach to her noodles at lunchtime, and eating salad with steak at dinnertime. At snack time, she replaced her cheese-flavored crackers with fruits such as cantaloupe, kiwi, and watermelon. She became more adventurous in the foods she brought to session, trying mixed foods such as chicken tacos and pasta marinara with meatballs, rather than limiting herself to the individual whole foods highlighted in the Primary Food Group Building Blocks. The end of Stage 3 corresponded with the start of school, and Emily exclaimed with pride that she had increased her dietary variety so much that, 'This will be the first time I can buy lunch at school!' Her mother also commented that she had started helping Emily learn how to use a knife to cut tough food into small pieces, because previously Emily had eaten primarily finger foods or soft foods that could be cut easily with a fork. Emily also began visiting friends more often and eating the foods that were served at their homes. Emily was happy to report that she was now attending sleepovers and eating pizza and muffins with friends. Also of note, her family members had taken notice of her expanded variety and had stopped teasing her about her eating. By session 15, Emily and her mother felt she had made sufficient progress, so together with the therapist they made the decision to move on to

Stage 4 and end treatment 3 sessions early (i.e., at 17 sessions total) so that Emily would have more time to participant in school, dance, and other after-school activities.

Stage 4. In sessions 16 and 17, the therapist revisited the Primary Food Group Building Blocks to determine which foods Emily had successfully incorporated into her daily diet and which of those she had initially expressed interest in learning about remained to be tasted in the future. Emily identified that she had successfully incorporated 20 novel foods into her diet, including several fruits (cantaloupe, watermelon, blueberries, grapes, raisins), vegetables (broccoli, kale, romaine lettuce, spinach tomatoes, corn, potatoes, cucumbers), proteins (beef, grilled chicken, hamburger), dairy (lactose-free milk, yogurt, pizza), and grains (muffins). Importantly, due to the therapist's collaboration with the adolescent medicine physician and Emily's strategic selection of foods to learn about in Stage 3, Emily was now eating several iron- and calcium-rich foods on a consistent basis, and taking the appropriate steps to prevent symptoms of lactose intolerance. Rather than comprising primarily processed grains, Emily's meals more closely resembled the multiple food groups depicted in the MyPlate schematic. Of course, she continued to enjoy her initially preferred foods on occasion (e.g., eating chicken nuggets and French fries once per week, rather than every day). Looking to the future, Emily also identified several foods she would like to continue learning about posttreatment. The therapist highlighted how most people eat an even wider variety of foods as adults than they do as children and, to prevent relapse into ARFID, encouraged Emily to continue to use the skills she had learned in CBT-AR to embark on a process of life-long learning and dietary expansion. Emily set a goal to try one novel food per week for the next several months. In co-creating her relapse prevention plan in the final session, Emily and her mother identified several CBT-AR strategies – such as doing the five steps on her own when approaching novel foods, and allowing herself to take small bites when trying a novel food for the first time – that Emily had found helpful and wanted to continue implementing posttreatment.

Outcome and conclusion. After completing 17 sessions of CBT-AR, Emily was highly successful at increasing dietary variety, more than doubling the absolute number of foods that she ate on a consistent basis. Importantly, the new foods she added came from the food groups that had been relatively

Case Example #1: (*cont.*)

underrepresented in her diet at the beginning of treatment (i.e., fruits, vegetables, and proteins), including several foods that she selected to correct her nutrition deficiencies. Although Emily began by tasting novel foods in-session early in treatment, she quickly graduated to trying novel foods at home and incorporating them in larger portions into her routine meals and snacks. In the second half of the treatment, she began to report decreases in psychosocial impairment as her dietary variety increased. Her progress could also be observed on patient-reported outcome measures. For example, Emily decreased from the maximum score of 5 on the Food Fussiness subscale of the Adult Eating Behavior Questionnaire (indicating strong agreement with statements such as 'I often decide that I don't like a food, before tasting it') at session 1 to a score of 2.2 (indicating disagreement with that and similar statements) by session 17. Furthermore, at session 1 she endorsed the maximum score of 'very true' on a visual analogue scale evaluating her agreement with the statement 'I feel uncomfortable trying new foods,' but endorsed the same statement in the 'not at all true' range by session 17.

Emily's physical health improved during the course of treatment as well. By session 17, she no longer complained of constipation and her iron deficiency had resolved. Although Emily's height and weight had already been in the normative range pretreatment, over the course of 17 sessions, Emily grew 1.5 inches and gained 11.4 lbs. By the end of treatment, at 12 years old, Emily was 5 feet 3.5 inches tall and weighed 102.8 lbs. Her BMI of 17.9 put her at the 47th percentile for sex and age. By session 15, she had also begun menstruating. In contrast to patients with anorexia nervosa, Emily was very pleased with her growth in height and weight, and welcomed the appearance of her menses. At times she cheered and high-fived the therapist upon learning of her between-session weight gain. Emily's precipitous growth and physical maturation during CBT-AR highlight the difficulty in identifying at the pretreatment evaluation whether individuals who present with selective eating might benefit from increasing dietary volume as well as variety. Indeed, although weight gain was not a primary treatment goal and Emily did not complete the lack of interest in eating module of CBT-AR, it appeared that, with treatment, she was able to resume her own individualized growth and development trajectory.

In summary, Emily presents an example of a highly motivated young person with a relatively mild form of illness, a single ARFID maintaining mechanism, and no psychiatric comorbidities. All of these factors likely facilitated her rapid progress in CBT-AR. The following sections describe cases with more severe forms of ARFID, multiple ARFID maintaining mechanisms, additional psychiatric and medical comorbidities, and less linear treatment courses.

Case Example #2: A 13-Year-Old Boy with Sensory Sensitivity, Apparent Lack of Interest in Eating or Food, and Low Weight (family-supported CBT-AR) (Guest case by Kendra R. Becker, Ph.D.)

Presenting complaint. Rob was a 13-year-old boy who was urgently referred to the eating-disorder clinic by his adolescent medicine physician who suspected possible ARFID. At that time of his presentation, Rob weighed 90 pounds at a height of 5 feet 5.6 inches (BMI =14.7, < 1st percentile per age and sex-matched norms). Rob lived with his mother and two brothers (ages 11 and 16 years). His parents were divorced, but Rob saw his father regularly. Rob's mother described him as having gastroenterological problems since toddlerhood. She explained that Rob had always been a selective eater and had been followed by a pediatric gastroenterology specialist since he was eight years old for complaints about abdominal pain, poor appetite, diarrhea, and constipation. A review of his growth charts indicated that Rob's weight had generally been in the 5–10th percentile since age eight. At 12 years old, he jumped to above the 50th percentile when he was diagnosed with Crohn's disease and treated briefly with an oral steroid medication, which was discontinued once his symptoms resolved. Subsequently, Rob's mother reported that Rob began avoiding food and losing weight, such that his BMI fell to below the 1st percentile. Although Rob's pediatric gastroenterologist reported that, at the time of his eating disorder evaluation, Rob's Crohn's disease was well managed, Rob continued to have difficulty eating. His mother explained that he often refused to eat foods – even those he had requested – and spent meals shouting expletives at her and his brothers: 'Dinner is horrific in my house ... I know it's going to be a fight.'

Rob's pattern of eating was fairly erratic. He often skipped breakfast, skipped eating his lunch at school, had his lunch as an afternoon snack at home,

Case Example #2: *(cont.)*

skipped dinner on more than half of the days of the week, and ate a bowl of vanilla ice cream or a single-serving bag of tortilla chips as an evening snack. Rob's mother usually packed him a peanut butter sandwich, a low-calorie sports drink, and a bag of graham crackers for lunch, though the contents of his lunch bag often came home untouched. Two ground beef soft tacos with cheese were a typical dinner for Rob, if his mother could convince him to eat at all. While Rob could eat some foods in each of the five main food groups, including fruits (pears, bananas, apples strawberries, and raisins), vegetables (steamed green beans, corn, carrots, and fries), protein (pork tenderloin, steak, ground beef, chicken nuggets, peanut butter, and beef jerky), dairy (ice cream, cheese, whole milk, chocolate soymilk, and cheese), and grains (pasta, tortilla chips, wheat bread, pizza, crackers, and French toast), his variety within these groups was somewhat limited and he was not eating this range of foods regularly as evident by his typical daily eating pattern. In addition, Rob's mother reported that she encouraged Rob to drink one high-calorie nutritional supplement drink each day, as recommended by his adolescent medicine physician and gastroenterologist, to stabilize his weight.

Rob's eating behaviors were complicated by multiple psychiatric comorbidities. At three years old, Rob developed impairing hyperkinesis and impulsivity, had difficulty with rule-following and limit-testing, required frequent redirection, and began physically acting out. He was asked to leave two preschools for disruptive behaviors and poor performance. He continued to have behavioral and academic problems in kindergarten, and in first grade he was diagnosed with attention deficit/hyperactivity disorder. As he got older, he also developed anxiety and depressive symptoms including irritability and anhedonia. When he presented for ARFID treatment, Rob was failing every subject in school, was not involved in any extracurricular activities, and had few friends. His mother described his mood as chronically irritable, oppositional, and depressed. She gave examples of oppositional behavior such as door slamming, swearing, yelling, and swatting or pushing her. Although the family had sought treatment from three different therapists in the past, Rob's behavioral symptoms had persisted.

Rob's eating behaviors were consistent with *DSM-5* criteria for ARFID characterized by a severe lack of interest in eating and mild sensory sensitivity to the taste, texture, and smell of foods. Although his

mother was concerned that Rob was cautious about the amounts and types of foods he ate because he experienced pain with bowel movements or constipation, Rob denied any traumatic experiences with food leading to subsequent restriction. Thus the therapist ruled out fear of aversive consequences as an ARFID maintaining mechanism. He also denied body image concerns: 'I know I need to gain weight.' While Rob was generally disengaged and guarded during his initial evaluation, answering most questions by telling the therapist to ask his mother or stating, 'I don't know,' he did express concern that he was 'too skinny and weak' and said he would be willing to participate in treatment.

Stage 1. Given that Rob was 13 years old and needed to gain a substantial amount of weight, the therapist recommended family-supported CBT-AR. Because his parents were divorced, they did not feel they could participate productively together in-session. The therapist agreed that Rob would attend the majority of sessions with his mother, and that Rob's father would join only for critical sessions, such as the family meal. In order to reach a healthy weight, Rob's adolescent medicine physician recommended that he gain between 25 and 30 pounds, thus the therapist asked the family at the very first session to make changes to his eating. Rob appeared generally bored during the review of ARFID symptoms and CBT-AR, as he gave vague answers to questions and spent a large part of the session engaging with his smartphone or arguing with his mother. However, he agreed to replace his low-calorie sports drink (a preferred food) with a higher-calorie version, and his mother agreed to reintroduce fruit juices (a previously dropped food) that Rob used to enjoy.

Rob had not gained any weight by his second visit. The therapist discussed with Rob and his mother foods that he could eat to accomplish weight gain, and Rob stated that he wanted to have ice cream and eggnog. Although his mother initially expressed fear of Rob eating large amounts of 'unhealthy' foods, the therapist emphasized that weight gain was difficult and would be more easily accomplished with foods Rob was excited about eating. Rob's mother agreed to give Rob eggnog and whole milk daily before the next session. In addition, the therapist assisted Rob and his mother in establishing a monetary reward system to incentivize Rob to complete his meals and snacks. Specifically, Rob would earn one dollar for each day that he was successful in eating all of his meals.

Case Example #2: *(cont.)*

When constructing the individualized formulation, Rob mentioned that he was most concerned about his low mood rather than eating symptoms. The therapist discussed depression and irritability as possible consequences of malnutrition. The therapist explained that Rob likely had always been someone with a low appetite (i.e., biological vulnerability), making it hard for him to eat enough. Because he did not feel hungry often and needed less than others to feel full, he preferred to eat only the foods he really enjoyed. Over time, he was regularly eating only a limited range of foods, resulting in non-preferred foods tasting and smelling more unfamiliar and intense. Further, he got tired of eating the same foods over and over again – suggestive of sensory-specific satiety – and his interest in eating further declined. The therapist explained that Rob might have been more concerned about eating after experiencing Crohn's symptoms and, even if eating restriction were unconscious, it would nevertheless exacerbate his already low interest in eating. The therapist explained that complications of low weight included being more vulnerable to negative moods, feeling more tired, becoming socially isolated, and having more trouble concentrating.

Rob's weight began to increase toward the end of Stage 1 as his mom served him high-calorie but preferred foods including eggnog, whole milk, milkshakes, and pudding. With the help of the monetary rewards, he was more consistently eating breakfast, lunch at school, and at least two of three snacks that his clinician recommended. Further, Rob enjoyed a variety of ice cream flavors, which made the milkshakes less vulnerable to sensory-specific satiety. Already Rob was also willing to add some variety into his diet, reintroducing pears and clementines and replacing French fries with sweet potato fries.

Rob's father attended the final two sessions of Stage 1 including the family meal, during which Rob successfully ate an entire meatball sub, drank a full bottle of a high-calorie sports drink, and tasted two bites of kiwi (a new food). Rob wanted to stop eating approximately halfway though the meatball sub, but his parents successfully worked together to encourage Rob to eat the other half. They also discussed and devised ways to help Rob eat at both his mother's and father's homes, by introducing strategies such as limiting smartphone use at the table; making positive statements; providing extra monetary rewards; encouraging him to eat more quickly; and preparing and packing meals in advance.

Stage 2. In reviewing common nutritional deficiencies associated with ARFID, Rob's mother noted that Rob had been diagnosed with deficiencies in vitamin D, iron, and folate. The therapist reviewed foods on the Building Blocks worksheet that Rob could incorporate to address these deficiencies. Despite nutritional deficiencies, the therapist decided to begin Stage 3 by addressing Rob's lack of interest in eating. Rob still needed to gain more than 15 pounds and he was already starting to increase the variety in his diet mostly because he was eating more often and needed to eat different things to keep from being tired of his preferred items. By the end of Stage 2, Rob's mother had helped him reintroduce chicken nuggets, bacon, raw carrots, and cereal, and he had successfully tasted tortellini with a garden vegetable sauce. These changes to Rob's diet, along with adding whole milk (fortified with vitamin D), were already starting to address his nutritional deficiencies.

Stage 3. Rob was most engaged during the five sessions of the Lack of Interest module. He was excited to try interoceptive exposures targeting bloating, nausea, and feeling extremely full. He enjoyed spinning in a chair (targeting nausea) but had more difficulty with gulping water and pushing his stomach out. At first he was only able to drink one and a half glasses of water before feeling 'too full' and could only push out his stomach for 30 seconds before he voiced concern that he might vomit. During this module, Rob completed the bloating and fullness interoceptive exposures at the beginning of each session and he was instructed to practice these exposures at home at least three times a week. Also as part of every session in this module, Rob was asked to eat servings of his preferred foods using the Five Steps directly following interoceptive exposures. The therapist and Rob made a list of his favorite foods (i.e., bacon, cupcakes, potato chips, homemade chocolate chip cookies, chicken nuggets, candy, brownies), and his mother brought at least three of these to each session. The therapist emphasized how Rob reported he was overfull immediately after the interoceptive exposures, but was nonetheless able to find room in his stomach for his favorite foods shortly thereafter. By the end of this module, Rob was able to drink nine full glasses of water followed by pushing out his stomach for over three minutes, eat all of the preferred food items his mother brought to the session, and still go home and eat dinner. Further, his mother reported that, for the first time, Rob was asking for meals and snacks at home.

Case Example #2: *(cont.)*

Although Rob was more involved during these sessions of Stage 3, his attention and behavior sometimes caused challenges in addressing session material. For example, he was often very distractible, frequently asking unrelated questions, laying down in sessions with his eyes closed, ignoring his mother and the therapist, using his phone, providing cheeky responses, or purposely annoying his mother by poking her, talking over her, calling her names, or glaring at her. However, the therapist worked hard to ignore these undesirable behaviors, and instead plowed ahead with the agenda to demonstrate that such behaviors would not result in Rob escaping from therapy tasks. As a result, Rob always ate in-session and always completed exposures, and the therapist was able to model how to tolerate these outbursts without reinforcing them.

By session 11, Rob's weight had increased by 20 pounds and he and his mother noted that he was more willing to eat at meal times and was eating more calories at each eating opportunity. The therapist agreed that Rob was ready to move to the sensory sensitivity module. During this module, Rob's oppositionality persisted but sometimes manifested in less destructive ways. For example, at first he intentionally selected unusual foods – such as bok choy and goji berries – which he stated would be challenging for his mother to find at the grocery store. However, by allowing him the opportunity to try these foods, he became more willing to try the foods his mother wanted to him to attempt, such as avocado, spinach, and watermelon. Rob and his mother instituted a separate monetary reward system for practicing with new foods, and the therapist helped ensure that Rob was immediately reinforced for tasting new foods. Rob continued to be rewarded when he finished meals and snacks each day and was additionally rewarded another dollar every time he practiced or successfully incorporated a novel food (usually planned around dinner time). By the end of this module, Rob was able to eat a relatively wide range of foods from each food group and was successful in newly incorporating 16 foods across all five basic food groups, including English muffins, blueberries, roasted potatoes, pork chops, apples, bok choy, goji berries, kiwi, spinach, peppers, honeydew melon, lemons, cucumber, mango, pineapple, and celery with peanut butter.

Even with weight gain and improved dietary variety, Rob remained moody and occasionally disruptive in session, sometimes throwing food at his mother and swearing at her. He was also not improving socially and continued to fail his courses at school. Toward the end of Stage 3, he became argumentative at mealtimes again, sometimes refusing to finish. His mother became concerned about possible weight loss and reintroduced high-energy supplement drinks (without consulting the therapist), thereby inadvertently reducing the expectation that Rob needed to eat at the table and complete his meals. He told his mother in-session that, despite how hungry he was, he would rather starve than eat if she was 'nagging' him. Given that Rob had significantly expanded his diet, successfully gained weight, and demonstrated that he was able to eat on a regular schedule, the therapist and Rob's mother agreed that his remaining behaviors would be best treated in behavioral management therapy that could specifically target his depression, oppositionality, and attention deficit/hyperactivity disorder.

Stage 4. Rob finished CBT-AR after 18 sessions, with only one session in Stage 4. A large part of Rob's relapse prevention plan included transitioning to a new therapist who had expertise in oppositional behaviors and mood. The CBT-AR therapist validated Rob's mother's frustration with Rob's behaviors and her exhaustion at needing to continually monitor his eating. However, the therapist also reminded her that some short-term solutions, such as relying heavily on supplement drinks for nutrition and allowing Rob to skip meals, were unlikely to help him maintain his treatment gains. The therapist emphasized that replacing meals with supplement drinks lowered his dietary variety, could impact his appetite, and also reduced opportunities for engaging socially around food. Rob's mother expressed understanding and said she would work on discontinuing the drinks but was unsure how successful she would be.

Outcome and conclusions. By the end of treatment, Rob had gained 27 pounds and grown 2 inches. At a height of 5 feet 7.6 inches, he weighed 117 lbs (BMI = 18.0, 25th percentile; healthy weight range). He was still having difficulty at mealtimes, and still occasionally relying on supplement drinks, though his mother felt these difficulties were more due to his oppositionality than his ARFID. Furthermore, the majority of his food was now coming from oral intake rather than supplements. At the end of treatment, Rob was able to eat more than 10 foods in each of the five food groups and his nutritional deficiencies had resolved. Further, neither Rob nor his mother worried about abdominal pain or urgency

Case Example #2: (cont.)

after eating, and Rob's Crohn's symptoms remained in remission during CBT-AR.

Although Rob presented with both lack of interest in eating or food and sensory sensitivity characteristics, he needed to complete the Lack of Interest module first to help him gain weight. By eating regularly and using interoceptive exposures to increase his tolerance of fullness sensations, Rob reported feeling hungrier. As his appetite increased, Rob was more willing to eat previously dropped foods rather than consuming even more of the same preferred foods that he was quickly growing tired of eating. Reintroducing previously dropped foods increased Rob's dietary variety, which was important because it prevented Rob from under-eating due to sensory-specific satiety and provided early success with the introduction of novel foods that would be a focus of the Sensory Sensitivity module. For some patients, successfully targeting the first maintaining mechanism may lessen the severity of the second or third maintaining mechanisms, thereby increasing the efficiency of later modules in Stage 3.

Rob was a complex patient with several medical and psychological comorbidities in addition to his ARFID. However, previous attempts at therapy had demonstrated that he was not ready for behavioral management, possibly because his low weight and malnutrition were compromising his ability to engage in problem solving. Further, being under-nourished obscured the true severity of his attention deficit/hyperactivity disorder and mood symptoms. Thus, it seemed paramount that his health be improved first by helping him reach an appropriate weight and improving his dietary variety. However, specifically targeting ARFID symptoms was challenging, and the therapist often felt tempted to directly address other problem behaviors simultaneously. By ignoring outbursts in-session and redirecting Rob and his mother stay on track with relevant CBT-AR material and treatment goals, the therapist helped Rob successfully complete CBT-AR. These gains enabled Rob to transition to his new treatment in much better physical and mental health, where the therapist hoped he would make similar gains in other areas. In summary, CBT-AR can be appropriate for patients with significant psychiatric and medical comorbidities, as long as the therapist maintains a clear focus on the ARFID symptoms, appreciates the potential relationship between ARFID and co-occurring psychopathology, and does not allow CBT-AR to be derailed.

Case Example #3: A 16-Year-Old Girl with Sensory Sensitivity, Lack of Interest in Eating or Food, Comorbid Binge Eating, and Obesity (individual CBT-AR) (Guest case by Kendra R. Becker, Ph.D.)

Presenting complaint. Maya was a 16-year-old biracial girl (of Caucasian and African-American descent) who presented for treatment because she ate a limited diet, which was contributing to difficulties eating around others, low self-esteem, and doubts about attending college. She explained that she typically avoided eating at school, at restaurants, or with her family because she worried that her preferred foods would not be available or that others would negatively judge her food choices. 'I have a lot of anxiety around foods that I'm not comfortable eating, or not used to eating,' she explained. She and her mother reported that Maya's selective eating had remained unchanged since she was approximately two years old. Maya's diet at initial presentation consisted almost entirely of grains (pasta, cereal, bagels, crackers, granola bars, protein bars, oatmeal, bread, potato chips, corn chips) and dairy (cheese pizza, cheese quesadillas, macaroni and cheese, yogurt, milk, ice cream). Her diet did not include any proteins except peanut butter. Although she identified as a vegetarian, she did not eat any vegetables. She explained that she disliked certain textures common to fruits and vegetables: 'foods that you bite, but they stay firm.'

Another striking feature of Maya's clinical presentation was that she often waited long periods of time (up to seven hours) between eating episodes. At school, she rarely ate, due to embarrassment about her limited diet, difficulty planning lunches with preferred foods, and low appetite. Even at home, her mother stated that she often needed to prompt Maya to eat. In between periods of food restriction, Maya also reported twice-weekly episodes of binge eating: 'I start eating and I won't think about stopping.' She described a typical binge episode as comprising half a family-size bag of potato chips, a family-size bag of cheese-flavored crackers, and 1–2 servings of ice cream. She also endorsed associated features of binge eating including eating more rapidly than normal, eating when not hungry, eating until feeling uncomfortably full, eating to the point of disgust, and eating alone due to embarrassment.

In contrast to the prototypical patient with ARFID, Maya ranked weight and shape as the first and second most important aspects of her self-worth, respectively. 'I want to lose weight. There are times when I feel just awful about myself.' Maya was overweight upon initial evaluation (169.2 pounds at a

Case Example #3: (cont.)

height of 5 feet 4 inches; BMI = 28.8; 94th percentile) and she described several behavioral manifestations of body image disturbance, including body checking (mirror checking, comparing herself to others, looking at old photos, weighing herself multiple times per day) and avoidance (i.e., trying on several different outfits each morning, avoiding mirrors). Her global score of 4.9/6.0 on the Eating Disorder Examination-Questionnaire (EDE-Q) and 30/48 on the Clinical Impairment Assessment (CIA) indicated that she was experiencing clinically concerning levels of impairment related to disordered eating.

Maya met *DSM-5* criteria for ARFID of moderate severity characterized by mild sensory sensitivity to texture and taste of foods and moderate lack of interest in eating or food. However, Maya's reported weight and shape concerns were not encompassed by ARFID, and the frequency of binge eating she endorsed indicated that she also met *DSM-5* criteria for binge eating disorder (BED) of mild severity. Because *DSM-5* precludes the concurrent diagnoses of ARFID and BED, the evaluating clinician conferred a primary diagnosis of ARFID but acknowledged that Maya's binge eating would also need be addressed in treatment.

Although Maya was 16 and still living with her parents, she was insightful about the ways in which ARFID symptoms were disrupting her life and was motivated to increase her dietary variety. She was not underweight, meaning that she did not need the support of her family to monitor mealtimes and ensure she was receiving enough nutrition. Therefore, the therapist recommended 20 sessions of individual CBT-AR.

Stage 1. After discussing the ARFID diagnosis, Maya and her clinician worked together to construct an individualized model of how her symptoms developed as well as how they were maintained and how they impacted her mood and body image. Because Maya was attuned to small changes in texture, smells, tastes, and appearance of foods, it was likely that she experienced heightened sensory input from food (i.e., biological vulnerability). After a few instances of trying certain foods (e.g., apples, bananas) and experiencing their taste and textures as disgusting, she had learned to avoid similar foods. Because new food experiences were intense, she tended to choose familiar foods and became anxious about trying new foods for fear of not liking them and/or disappointing her parents. The more she avoided trying new foods, the harder it became to

consider eating something different, despite a growing desire to expand her diet. Although avoidance of trying new foods adeptly circumnavigated experiencing aversive tastes or textures, she became tired of eating the same foods and found less enjoyment in eating. Skipping meals was preferable to managing the inevitable anxiety about what to eat, or eating the same thing she had already eaten earlier that day. Over time, her eating schedule became less regular, making it difficult to notice hunger and satiety cues. She also began to notice that her friends were eating a larger variety of foods than she was, leading to embarrassment. As she was not experiencing hunger at regular times, it was easy to skip meals and snacks during the day. Avoiding eating with her friends at school and eating less often with her family allowed her to escape suggestions to try something new. Similarly, she avoided many social situations that involved food (e.g., dinners, celebrations). Isolation not only reduced opportunities for her to learn about different foods but also contributed to her worries about her friendships.

Although she did not feel hungry and had little interest in eating, her body needed calories. Consequently, after long periods of restriction, she would overeat her preferred foods. Increased consumption of high-calorie, high-fat, and high-sugar foods engendered fears of gaining weight, guilt around eating, and urges to compensate. Thus, the only foods she felt comfortable eating for sensitivity reasons became the same foods she feared would make her fat. Without the option of adding lower-calorie foods to her diet, she attempted to restrict her intake overall. However, by restricting more heavily, her binge eating frequency increased as did her body dissatisfaction and guilt and shame over eating behaviors.

The therapist asked Maya to begin self-monitoring at the first session, explaining that, in addition to tracking the types of foods she was eating, it was important to also record how often she was skipping meals because she was afraid of gaining weight, was not feeling hungry, or because her preferred foods were unavailable. After the first week of logging, it was clear that she was eating very little during the day (e.g., juice for breakfast and a granola bar for lunch) and overeating at night. Most commonly, she reported skipping meals because she 'just wasn't hungry.' She identified two episodes during which she felt out of control around her preferred foods, but also noted that she overate every night of the first week of treatment. The therapist returned to

Case Example #3: *(cont.)*

Maya's formulation, reviewing the increased risk of binge eating following periods of dietary restriction and how both binge eating and overeating elevated her worries of gaining weight and contributed to feelings of anxiety and low self-esteem.

Maya's self-monitoring demonstrated that her current eating schedule was far from three meals and two snacks, suggesting that establishing regular eating would require multiple smaller steps. The therapist provided psychoeducation about the role of appetite-regulating hormones in hunger and satiety to address Maya's reluctance in starting regular eating, specifically explaining the function of elevated ghrelin levels in stimulating hunger. Maya first agreed to add a mid-morning snack and throughout the next several sessions added lunch, breakfast, and an afternoon snack. As part of this planning, she discussed with the therapist which of her preferred foods she felt the least embarrassed to eat around others (e.g., granola bars, yogurt, protein bars, bagels), and how early to get up for breakfast.

After session 1, she tried different brands of apple and orange juice and elected to take a risk of choosing mixed berry juice instead of her preferred flavors. The therapist encouraged her to continue to increase her variety by rotating juices and cereals during the week. Though Maya was not low-weight, weekly weighing was used to further motivate for her for regular eating, because Maya noticed that her weight did not increase despite eating during the day.

Stage 2. As part of planning which foods Maya was interested in learning about in treatment, the therapist discussed symptoms associated with nutritional deficiencies. Maya's lab results did not indicate that she was deficient in any macro- or micronutrients. However, Maya noted that iron deficiency is associated with fatigue and difficulty concentrating, and realized that the only iron-rich food she ate was fortified breakfast cereals. Because Maya was a vegetarian, the therapist discussed other high-in-iron foods, and Maya identified those she wanted to taste in treatment (e.g., beans, tofu). Following this session, she also decided to reintroduce cashews, a previously dropped food, into her diet.

Maya wanted to be able to eat fruits and vegetables, thus it was not challenging for her to select foods that she wanted to learn about from the Primary Food Group Building Blocks. Given that Maya's main motivation for treatment was to expand her diet and that she was already working on developing a more regular eating schedule, the therapist decided to begin Stage 3 with the sensory sensitivity module and progress to the Lack of Interest module if necessary. Based on her formulation, the therapist also hoped that added dietary variety would help increase her appetite by reducing sensory-specific satiety.

Stage 3. As Maya's eating became more regular throughout Stage 3, the therapist tackled remaining binge episodes by focusing on eating enough at meals and snacks so that Maya felt hungry only at specified times. Maya quickly noted that she felt less guilty about eating her preferred foods when she was eating them in a planned way throughout the day versus feeling out of control around these foods at home. Further, regular eating was also effective in stopping her binge episodes. By session 8 she was no longer having weekly episodes.

For the first session of food tastings, Maya brought pistachios, a banana, an orange, a strawberry, and a peach. Using the Five Steps, Maya was able to try the pistachio nuts and the banana. Although there was only time to taste two of the five foods, Maya decided that she felt 'okay' with continuing to practice each during the upcoming week. At the end of this first tasting session, the therapist helped Maya consider how she could continue practicing with these foods at home, and Maya decided to use a fading technique by including the pistachios (a novel food) in yogurt (a preferred food) and to chase the banana (a novel food) with peanut butter (a preferred food). Maya stated that she was proud of herself for tasting new foods and was excited to keep tasting and tracking her progress over the next week.

The remainder of Stage 3 sessions continued similarly, with Maya successfully tasting strawberries, a peach, an avocado, an orange, a mango, spinach leaves, lettuce leaves, blueberries, a nectarine, a fruit salad, an apple, a grape, salad dressings, celery, red peppers, salad with caper dressing, candied walnuts, arugula, marinara sauce, broccoli, carrots, hummus, and onion and being willing to practice with most of the foods she tasted. When going through the Building Blocks worksheet to pick foods for the following week's tastings, Maya asked questions about the appearance, taste, and how to eat new foods (e.g., different ways to cook foods, differences between raw and cooked versions of foods, how to tell when certain foods were ripe). The therapist used session time to learn about these foods with Maya by looking up answers to her questions on the Internet.

Case Example #3: *(cont.)*

As treatment progressed, Maya noted that she was feeling more confident in trying new foods and was proud of herself for tasting and incorporating several foods that she had been wary of trying (e.g., oranges, grapes) due to difficult experiences in the past. Maya utilized several strategies to both help her taste foods and to help her tackle incorporating new foods. She often began tasting foods by taking small bites and chasing these with water. For many of the fruits, she quickly habituated to the taste, but had more difficulty feeling comfortable with different textures. In order to incorporate these fruits, she decided to add them to preferred foods. For example, she began eating oatmeal with bananas, yogurt with peaches, peanut butter with apples, and pasta with tomato sauce. For some vegetables like carrots and broccoli, she practiced with raspberry vinaigrette because she found that the dressing helped reduce the bitter taste. She also worked with her mother to think of ways to prepare certain vegetables that included preferred foods, such as broccoli with cheese.

Although Maya remained dedicated to her treatment goals and challenged herself both in and out of session to eat regularly, taste new foods, and expand her diet, difficulties following through on homework assignments were discussed at every session. Importantly, self-monitoring became much harder for Maya to maintain about halfway through treatment. Without logging, her eating became less regular, resulting in a recurrence of binge eating. The therapist reviewed the importance of logging in helping her see her progress in adding new foods, bringing awareness to her hunger levels, and reminding her to eat meals and snacks. To reinstate regular logging, Maya added alarms to her phone and kept a paper log on her refrigerator.

Finally, during Stage 3 it became clear that transitioning from tasting new foods to incorporating them into her diet was a significant challenge. The therapist began addressing this problem by discussing complex foods Maya would like to be able to eat around friends and family and reviewed the MyPlate schematic with Maya to see which food groups were still underrepresented in her meals and snacks. The therapist worked with Maya to plan which foods she could add, where to buy the foods, which day to purchase them, and how they would be prepared. However, these strategies did not result in increased incorporation. After continued trouble following through with plans made in session, Maya reported feeling uncomfortable incorporating new foods during meal times at home because she was afraid that she would disappoint her parents or they would be dissatisfied with the rate of her progress. The therapist suggested including Maya's mother in several sessions toward the end of Stage 3 to help Maya prepare and plan meals and snacks at home. The therapist also used these sessions to review Maya's treatment progress with her mother to help calibrate her parents' expectations about the speed of recovery and reduce any pressure Maya might have been feeling to like new foods immediately rather than simply learn about them. Maya and her mother worked together to consider strategies that could be more helpful and encouraging for Maya as she tried to incorporate new foods. Her mother agreed to leave out certain practice foods during breakfast and dinner and to pack these items as part of Maya's lunch. Maya also showed her mother the Five Steps, discussing the importance of adopting a nonjudgmental attitude toward tasting.

While Maya felt that it was helpful to have her mother assist with brainstorming solutions for incorporation and appreciated her mother's help in shopping for foods and planning meals, she also reported that including her mother so late in treatment seemed to communicate that she was failing to reach her goals. She explained that she felt disempowered, as if she could not progress on her own. It was clear that Maya had always been self-motivated for treatment and her progress in other areas was maintained because she felt as though she was 'winning' against ARFID. Further, because she was planning to matriculate at college in two months, it made sense for her to start considering her own solutions for incorporating foods without her mother's supervision. The therapist added three additional sessions to Stage 3 (making her total session number 23) and scheduled these sessions over the final two months of treatment. During this time, Maya picked a few foods she wanted to practice with friends while at restaurants and foods she felt ready now to include in her lunches (e.g., bananas, oranges, grapes) and for breakfast (scrambled eggs with red peppers, yogurt with strawberries). She reported increased success with using her friends as supports and was even able to spontaneously try foods during college visits and her after-school job (e.g., tofu, lentils, peas, green beans, dried cranberries, kale, plantain chips, and pears).

Stage 4. Maya identified regular eating as an intervention that would be helpful for her to

Case Example #3: *(cont.)*

maintain after treatment, as it helped balance her hunger and satiety cues and was the most successful strategy in preventing binge eating. She determined that difficulty maintaining regular eating would be an early sign that she was struggling with dietary restriction, weight and shape concerns, and a warning sign for binge eating. She decided to reinstate self-monitoring if she was going long periods of time without eating or was eating the same things every day. As part of these logs, she decided it would also be important to record if she was skipping meals for weight and shape reasons or because she was avoiding newer foods. She identified feeling guilty or embarrassed about her food preferences and thoughts that she 'should' like certain foods as unhelpful in maintaining her recovery. Strategies she listed to intervene early against these thoughts, feelings, and likely subsequent avoidant behaviors included reminding herself of all the things she tried and incorporated in treatment, the fading strategy, and reviewing the psychoeducation handouts in her workbook.

Outcome and conclusions. At the end of treatment, Maya no longer met criteria for either ARFID or BED. She felt more comfortable eating with her friends, at college, at work, and at home. Further, she was able to eat several foods in each of the five food groups and was continuing to work toward expanding her diet even further by tasting complex foods. She explained that it remained effortful to continue tasting foods and to add foods to her preferred items. However, after treatment, she was no longer ashamed or embarrassed by her eating and she felt confident that she could continue working on expanding her diet using the skills she had learned.

Maya's weight fluctuated throughout treatment. Her weight reached a high value of 182.2 pounds (BMI = 31.0; 96th percentile; obese) when she was having trouble eating regularly and reported several binge-eating episodes, but decreased steadily as she reinstituted regular eating. Her final weight was 158.8 pounds (BMI = 27; 89th percentile; overweight), when she was eating more variety and on a regular schedule. She noted that seeing that her weight did not increase with regular eating, but instead decreased, also helped her challenge her body image concerns. By the end of treatment, her scores on both the EDE-Q (1.7/6.0) and CIA (4/48) had fallen substantially from her pretreatment scores and were no longer in a clinical range.

For patients like Maya who present with co-occurring weight and shape concerns, the therapist may feel torn as to whether to focus on ARFID, more classical eating-disorder symptoms, or both. However, many of the early intervention strategies such as regular eating, monitoring, and weekly weighing are similar to interventions in CBT for other eating disorders. Maya's binge eating reduced substantially with these strategies. With regular eating, her hunger was better controlled and she felt empowered by her ability to resist binge eating. Without frequent binge-eating episodes, she did not feel as though she needed to restrict her intake for weight and shape reasons. As the binge-eating episodes decreased, she worried less about her weight and shape, continued to feel better about herself, and her weight stopped increasing. Thus, by addressing her ARFID symptoms, her other disordered eating symptoms improved without additional intervention. Similarly, Maya presented with a lack of interest in eating as well as sensory sensitivity. However, the early emphasis on regular eating and monitoring targeted this maintaining mechanism early, presumably by normalizing her hunger and satiety cues. Further, as she practiced with new foods and expanded her preferred items, her interest in eating increased because she was no longer bored of eating the few foods she preferred. Increased options for meals and snacks allowed her to experience hunger for different tastes. Thus it was not necessary to also complete the lack of interest module of CBT-AR. Maya's progress demonstrates that, for some patients, some maintaining mechanisms are so intertwined that by addressing one the other improves concurrently.

Case Example #4: A 20-Year-Old Man with Fear of Aversive Consequences, Apparent Lack of Interest in Eating or Food, and Low Weight (family-supported CBT-AR)

Presenting complaint. Luke was a 20-year-old Caucasian man who presented to the Eating Disorders Clinical and Research Program at MGH seeking treatment for suspected ARFID. He was referred for an evaluation by his pediatric gastroenterologist who was considering acute hospitalization for re-feeding due to his significantly low weight and severely restricted intake. At the time of the initial evaluation, Luke was 5 feet 7 inches tall and weighed 104 lbs (BMI = 16.3) and had limited his diet to just three

Case Example #4: *(cont.)*

foods – a specific type of white bread, a specific brand of hot dog, and two energy-dense supplement drinks per day. Luke's parents reported that Luke was born prematurely and had always been underweight, but that prior to high school he had no difficulty with food variety, eating all types of foods albeit in limited volume due to low appetite. In high school, Luke began having what he described as 'episodes' during which he would eat a food and then within 30–60 minutes develop an urgency to go to the bathroom where he eventually passed loose, painful stools, with subsequent discomfort for a few hours. After the first such episode he dropped the food he had been eating (clam chowder) from his diet. The next episode occurred after eating a similar soup, which he also subsequently cut out. After a number of episodes (e.g., pizza, pasta, tuna sandwich), he began eliminating large categories of foods that seemed similar those that had previously caused episodes (e.g., all dairy foods). Luke reported, 'I started assuming an episode would happen, and I asked myself, 'Is this food worth this level of discomfort and inconvenience?' And the answer was always no, so I didn't take the risk.' This gradual elimination process continued throughout high school, and worsened upon graduation when he no longer had a schedule or need to pack lunch for school.

Luke's painful gastrointestinal (GI) issues had been thoroughly worked up by a medical team who identified irritable bowel syndrome (IBS) but judged that his level of subsequent restriction was above and beyond that needed to manage his IBS. In addition to the physical health consequence of low weight, Luke's limited diet and restrictive eating had impacted his emotional well-being and overall functioning. Specifically, Luke had long-standing social anxiety and depression, for which he had been in mental health treatment since high school. While his anxiety and low mood were responsive to cognitive-behavioral therapy, previous attempts to address his eating in this context had not been successful. Since graduating from high school, Luke had been living at home and not going to school or working, but rather spending most of his time attending medical appointments. In the past two years since graduation, he had struggled with activities of daily living including showering and brushing his teeth, and his sleep/wake schedule was shifted such that he typically awoke at noon and went to bed between 2:00 and 3:00 AM.

In spite of these challenges, Luke impressed the therapist with his wry humor and intelligence, both of which suggested his ability to be resilient. Likewise, his parents reported that they would do anything to help, demonstrating their investment in their son and a strong commitment to help him be well. Given Luke's low weight and the fact that he still lived at home, the therapist recommended family-based CBT-AR. Luke's mother was not working outside the home, and Luke's father's work afforded him the flexibility allowing him to prioritize treatment, and thus both parents attended the majority of sessions throughout CBT-AR.

Stage 1. Both Luke and his parents were receptive to psychoeducation about ARFID and identified Luke's long-standing low appetite and narrowing range of accepted foods secondary to gastrointestinal 'episodes' as fueling his now problematic restrictive eating pattern. As Luke had previously completed a course of CBT for social anxiety, he was familiar with the principles of avoidance exacerbating anxiety and the recipe for graded exposure to promote habituation and corrective learning. He acknowledged that while becoming more careful about eating after his 'episodes' made sense initially, the avoidance was now impacting his health and might also be maintaining his anxiety and in turn even promoting the gastrointestinal distress that he was intending to prevent. Further, his eating pattern was carefully planned to mitigate feared 'episodes' such that he would start the day at 1:00 PM with a few slices of bread before having an energy-dense supplement drink in the early afternoon, one hot dog in the late evening, and more bread and a second supplement drink throughout the night.

Luke's father took responsibility for tracking Luke's eating during treatment. As a first change to increase caloric intake while still relying on preferred foods, the therapist asked Luke to increase from two to four energy-dense supplement drinks per day to begin to promote weight gain.

Although Luke generally denied motivation to get well ('I don't care. I'm lazy!'), he successfully increased to four energy-dense supplement drinks per day and began steadily gaining 1–2 lbs/week. In addition to adding the drinks, he agreed to increase from one to two hot dogs daily. He had much more difficulty shifting his schedule and so the therapist's suggestion to promote regular eating was initially a prescription of eating every 3–4 hours from wake to sleep, albeit on a delayed schedule (e.g., first eating episode at 1 PM, last eating episode closer to midnight).

Case Example #4: (cont.)

Because he was not having clear meals or snacks and was eating/drinking only three to four times per day, the target of three meals and two to three snacks was discussed as a longer-term goal and the initial focus of regular eating was strictly on timing. As Luke endorsed low appetite, the therapist focused on this regular eating time schedule to promote emergence of hunger signals at predictable intervals.

The family meal was planned for mid-afternoon, and Luke elected to bring his preferred foods (i.e., bread, hot dogs, and his energy-dense supplement drink). As he would eat only at home (due to his fear that he may have an 'episode' and need to be in proximity to his bathroom), any in-session eating and drinking was anticipated to be an anxiety exposure for him. He was able to eat some bread and have his drink but then stopped, reporting that he was too full to begin his hot dog. The therapist used this as an opportunity to coach the parents around helping Luke have another bite. His father said, 'I'm not going to try to convince him; he'll either do it or not,' and his mom nodded in agreement. They shared that the advice they had been given by professionals was to back off, although they acknowledged that it wasn't working. The therapist framed this in-session eating as an opportunity for everyone to do something differently – for parents to offer direct support and for Luke to practice tolerating anxiety and fullness by eating more. Both parents shifted their stance, and Luke's father revised his message to say, 'I would love it if you took a bite of your hot dog.' They validated Luke's efforts and his perception of feeling full, and as a family came up with the tool of offering an immediate incentive for Luke's additional bite. Thus, with encouragement and with the tool of using an immediate reward, Luke was able to eat in-session, tolerating the anxiety of eating outside the home and then pushing himself to have a bite of hot dog even though he was feeling full.

Stage 2. In the second stage of CBT-AR, Luke continued to work on weight gain via daily intake of a larger volume of preferred foods (bread, hot dogs) and four energy-dense supplement drinks. The family worked together to develop a monetary reward system whereby Luke's achievement of these daily targets earned him a daily allowance. For Luke, this reward system was critical to cinching his engagement in treatment because whereas he denied any inherent motivation to change, he did express passion about many of his hobbies and interests, for which he needed money.

In preparation for Stage 3, Luke completed the Primary Food Group Building Blocks but shared his impression that the exercise felt like 'a waste of time.' By contrast to the prototypical ARFID patient presenting with limited dietary variety, Luke denied any sensory sensitivity and stated, '[My restriction] has never been because I don't like food. I do like food, I just don't like pain. I know certain things will lead to an episode and it's not worth it.' However, the therapist remained persistent, and used this opportunity to help Luke determine which foods from the Building Blocks he used to enjoy but was now avoiding due to fear of gastrointestinal upset, so that these foods could be leveraged for exposures in Stage 3.

Stage 3. Luke's weight continued to increase steadily, and in Stage 3 the therapist began with the Fear of Aversive Consequences module. While Luke also presented with low appetite, his fear of aversive consequences was so severe that the therapist made the decision to start there and then move to the Lack of Interest in Eating or Food module if necessary. Luke had a firm understanding of the rationale for a fear and avoidance hierarchy, and experience in working through such a hierarchy from his previous experiences in psychotherapy. Except dairy and fried foods, which he reported avoiding because they exacerbated his IBS and was thus unwilling to include in his hierarchy, Luke identified foods from several of the food groups, ranking them by how likely it was that he believed they would upset his stomach and cause an episode. The hierarchy was treated as a working document that was regularly re-reviewed in-session. Notably, although the traditional frame for use of a fear and avoidance hierarchy is to give patients an opportunity to test a prediction (and learn that their feared outcome did not occur, or if it did occur was survivable), Luke viewed the likelihood of foods at the highest rungs on his hierarchy leading to gastrointestinal episodes as certainties rather than predictions. He was willing to practice eating foods from his hierarchy in-session but expressed that he was unwilling to try a food for the first time outside of his home (e.g., one that he had not practiced at least one time in the days leading up to our session). Although Luke's unwillingness to try a food for the first time in session was a roadblock, the therapist worked with him and his family to identify specific ways (type of food, timing, setting) that he could try foods from his hierarchy out of session. Early in Stage 3, Luke was willing to reintroduce some of his old preferred foods (popcorn, candy bar, saltine crackers) and experienced

Case Example #4: *(cont.)*

that while his stomach had been 'a bit off,' he enjoyed the foods and was willing to keep practicing those both in and out of session. By the second session of Stage 3, his parents noted that his mood was brighter and that he had made other positive changes including eating with a friend and brushing his teeth, the latter of which he had not done in years.

All Stage 3 sessions involved review of Luke's weight trajectory, parent-monitoring records, and homework; in-session exposures to one or more foods from his hierarchy; troubleshooting around obstacles to expansion of the variety and volume of his diet during the week; and assignment of practices for the week ahead. Given Luke's severe low weight, increasing food volume and regularity of eating (i.e., progression from one meal plus two to three snacks to two meals plus three to four snacks) continued to be a part of each session throughout most of Stage 3. Most sessions were very similar in structure and content with a dual focus of (1) continued reinforcement for increasing volume of energy-dense foods to promote weight gain and (2) in-session practice with newly reintroduced foods to promote variety and approximation of the MyPlate schematic in meals and snacks.

During the in-session exposures, the therapist would ask Luke and his family to unpack the foods they had brought in (typically one or two foods he had reintroduced for the first time during the week) and ask Luke to rate his subjective units of distress (SUDS) before, during, and after eating to give the family an opportunity to quantify his anxiety habituation. Notably, Luke would typically deny or minimize anxiety about eating in-session, reporting instead, 'I'm not worried this will hurt my stomach. I ate it this week; it's fine.' Although this challenged the exposure exercise, it was the therapist's impression that the routine of practicing eating and the expectation that Luke would be eating a newly introduced food in-session gave the structure to facilitate and expedite his progress in diversifying his intake. Furthermore, given Luke's extreme degree of food avoidance pretreatment, the therapist inferred that Luke might have lacked insight into his high levels of underlying anxiety.

His weight continued to increase steadily at a rate of 1–2 lbs/week and he had reached 124.4 lbs (BMI = 19.5) by session 18 when his family went away for a planned three-week vacation. The family had not been away from home in years due to Luke's eating difficulties, and their willingness to take this trip was a reflection of Luke's progress. Indeed while on his trip, Luke had a number of breakthroughs, routinely eating a new preferred meal (hamburger) out at restaurants, and even trying foods from a number of new food categories (seafood, vegetables). It was clear that Luke was proud of his accomplishments and using them as motivation to continue to push forward. On his trip, he noted that he had had an episode, but rather than stopping eating, as he might have done in the past, he noted, 'with the cramps, I was basically like this can't conceivably get worse, so I might as well try something else,' and he used it as an opportunity to reintroduce other foods. After the family's trip, Luke's progress continued and he steadily gained weight and expanded the range of accepted foods.

By session 24, Luke's weight had reached 130.2 lbs (BMI = 20.4, within the target range of 130–135 lbs), and the therapist began to focus the work on challenging him to shift his eating schedule in order to allow him to start eating earlier in the day, and thus begin to open the door for more regular meals. By session 30, he had moved successfully to four snacks per day but was still having great difficulty moving to two meals, and was still relying on four energy-dense supplement drinks. By session 32, he had reached 136.2 lbs (BMI = 21.3) and began to work to reduce his reliance on the supplement drinks. In the first week he moved from four to three drinks, and in the second week he reduced to two drinks, with the prescription that he instead supplement with food in the form of a second or third meal. To promote these changes his parents worked with him around daily incentives to reinforce behaviors of more frequent meals and increased food variety, which we reviewed at each session.

At session 33, Luke's grandfather became ill and his father needed to spend more time away from home caring for his elderly parents. As his grandmother was also unwell, the stress that having both of Luke's father's older adult parents requiring monitoring, transportation to and from their own treatments, and ultimately transition to assisted living was impactful toward the end of Stage 3. During a 10-week window of time (spanning sessions 33–38), Luke and his family needed to balance the competing demands of caring for Luke's grandparents, which was time-intensive and emotional for everyone. Luke's weight fluctuated from the high of 136.2 lbs to the low of 127.8 during this window of time, and he had more difficulty motivating himself to

Case Example #4: *(cont.)*

maintain the positive changes he had made in treatment (e.g., returning to having fewer snacks and less diversity in his diet). The therapist used this window as an opportunity to reinforce to the parents just how important their roles were in supporting Luke and in keeping him accountable for maintaining and continuing to move forward. With the therapist's guidance, they identified and reinstated tools that had been useful early on, including returning to three energy-dense supplement drinks per day for a week, and having parents increase the incentives for his behaviors. These strategies were helpful, as was the reminder to the parents that they were instrumental in helping Luke effect change.

Throughout Stage 3, Luke made increasing progress toward diversifying his diet. Because Luke generally reported liking the foods he was eating, in addition to asking about his anxiety, the therapist would ask about his experience of foods he was eating in-session, encouraging him to pay attention to some of the pleasurable aspects of eating. During the course of treatment, he moved from not eating outside of the home to requesting to go out to eat and enjoying planning for meals at restaurants.

Stage 4. By session 39, Luke's weight had returned to 131.2 lbs, and he was regularly eating two meals and four snacks per day, plus one to two energy-dense supplement drinks. As Luke and his family prepared to discharge from treatment, the focus was on review of progress, identification of skills and tools used in treatment that had been most instrumental in promoting change for him, and delineation of ongoing and next steps for him and his family to take to encourage further improvements.

Outcome and conclusions. Luke reached a healthy weight range and at the end of treatment he no longer met diagnostic criteria for ARFID. He gained 30 lbs over the 40 sessions of treatment and broadened his diet, expanding from two foods (bread and hot dogs) to include several foods from four food categories (minus dairy, which he was unwilling to try due to his IBS), and demonstrating a renewed comfort in enjoying meals out of the house (e.g., at restaurants). Notably, he continued to eat two meals per day plus three to four snacks, and was having one or two energy-dense supplement drinks per day. He and his family felt that he had made substantial progress and that they were equipped with the tools to help him continue to move forward in broadening his diet on their own. His father stated, 'He's gone from having the

episodes rule his life to really pushing through it, and coping with it.' Both parents echoed that life for Luke was now fuller: going out to eat was now a regular occasion, they would comfortably spend time together over meals, and he was able to be more free with eating flexibly and eating a wider range of all food types.

In addition to the strides he made in conquering his ARFID, there were global changes in his functioning. He and his parents reported a huge improvement in his mood and willingness to engage socially during treatment, which may have been secondary to nutritional rehabilitation but also to his gains in confidence. He began engaging in household responsibilities and took ownership over the development of a hobby room in his home, all of which he would not have had the strength or energy for prior to treatment. He also became more attentive to self-care activities, including going to the dentist and brushing his teeth and hair. While he had graduated from high school, he had not worked since graduation and had also not pursued college due to his psychopathology, and in the last month of treatment he applied for and got a job.

In sum, Luke presented with a severe form of ARFID characterized by significant low weight and food restriction coupled with complicating psychiatric and medical comorbidities. His family was highly motivated to support him and hopeful that CBT-AR would be helpful to him, as all other attempts at targeting his food restriction and low weight had been unsuccessful. The treatment capitalized on both their investment and sense that this treatment was their last option short of hospitalization and tube-feeding.

The therapist worked to meet the family where they were both on treatment presentation and during the course of the therapy. For example, this meant adjusting expectations: Luke's long-standing daily schedule was a roadblock that was not moveable in treatment, but which was worked around by having meals and snacks later in the day; while Luke had not achieved three meals regularly or sufficiency without any energy-dense supplement drinks, his progress forward was enormous and he and his family deserved kudos for their work.

The therapist elected to target the most pressing problems (i.e., his low weight, reliance on two to three foods) and mechanism (i.e., fear of aversive consequences) first rather than addressing all problems simultaneously (i.e., the therapist never presented the Lack of Interest module). This approach

Case Example #4: (cont.)

was parsimonious, as Luke's self-reported hunger and tolerance for fullness (and capacity to consume more volume) increased naturally as he moved forward in treatment, and he had reported his enjoyment of food to be intact from the outset of treatment.

Of note, the therapy proceeded over 40 planned sessions due to Luke's very low weight (and need to gain 25–30 lbs) and extreme presentation (i.e., regular consumption of just two to three foods). He reached his target weight by session 24. Although his continued achievements beyond session 24 were not incremental, Luke's weight progress informed our team's thinking that 30 sessions, rather than 40, may be all that is needed even for the more unwell patients. Indeed, despite Luke's psychiatric and medical complexity, he made an excellent response to a fairly simple intervention (CBT-AR), which had positive ripple effects on other important domains of functioning including mood, self-care, social activities, and employment.

Case Example #5: A 32-Year-Old Man with Sensory Sensitivity (individual CBT-AR)

Presenting complaint. Thomas was a 32-year-old Caucasian man who presented to the Eating Disorders Clinical and Research Program at MGH seeking treatment for suspected ARFID. He had found the clinic online and self-referred with long-standing picky eating and associated difficulties. He stated, 'I've been a peculiar eater my whole life and I'd like to work on it now. It's a good time to do it.' He shared that he and his wife were starting to talk about having children and he wanted to be more comfortable eating before they moved forward in order to be able to be a healthy role model for his child. At the time of the initial evaluation, Thomas weighed 195 lbs at a height of 6 feet (BMI = 26.4, barely into the overweight range). He was eating the same foods at multiple meals per day. He had limited his diet to one protein (chicken), three starchy vegetables (potatoes, sweet potatoes, and corn on the cob), one fruit (banana), a few grains (e.g., sandwich bread, sweets), and the occasional dairy food (e.g., milk). While he had sporadically tried other fruits and vegetables in childhood, he had not had them since; he noted that he could also eat cereal with milk but had fallen out of the habit of eating this in the past

few years. A typical day would include chicken tenders and sweet potato tots for both breakfast and dinner, a peanut butter sandwich for lunch, and banana or candy throughout the day. Thomas reported that while his pattern of limited dietary variety was long-standing, he had successfully made some modest changes over time – for example, integrating sweet potatoes (bridged to from white potatoes) and a full range of chicken preparations (i.e., moving from popcorn fried chicken to grilled chicken).

Thomas reported that he had been born premature and had frequent ear infections (10–15 per year) during childhood resulting in the need for bilateral surgery to repair his tympanic membrane in adolescence, but had grown as expected with no other major health issues. He shared that, per his mother's report, he had been an 'okay' eater as a baby, but that 'as soon as I was able to make a choice, I said 'no!'' He was the youngest of four boys who all had varying degrees of picky eating tendencies, but his were the most profound. He remembered that his brothers would tease him and 'force' food on him, which shamed him and made him even less inclined to try new foods. He had grown up playing sports and was a strong hockey player with a core group of friends on his team and in his neighborhood, which bolstered his self-esteem. While his parents had encouraged him to expand his diet in early childhood, he recalled that they stopped doing so by late elementary school and he did not feel there was any expectation from his family or long-time friends that his eating would change over time.

However, after completing college and moving into a big city for work, he met and married his wife and had a renewed sense of how different his eating was from others'. In his 20s, he met briefly with a psychiatrist where the focus was on managing his anxiety, but his eating went unaddressed. Nearly a decade later, Thomas was pursuing treatment once more, having heard about ARFID and recognizing himself in the symptoms. While Thomas's general selective eating pattern was lifelong, he was self-motivated to change, which boded well for engagement and favorable outcomes. Given that Thomas was not underweight, the therapist offered 20 sessions of individual CBT-AR.

Stage 1. Thomas was very receptive to psychoeducation about ARFID and felt that the sensory sensitivity rationale for selective eating really resonated for him. In particular, he described long-standing texture aversions that would elicit in him a strong

Case Example #5: *(cont.)*

disgust reaction. For example, he noted that he liked the smell of pizza and really wanted to enjoy it but could not get over the 'gooey' texture combination of cheese and tomato sauce on bread and had never tried this food. In addition to having strong reactions to certain textures, he disliked the idea of mixed or combined foods. He denied any food traumas and similarly denied low appetite, instead reporting that he 'look[ed] forward to eating things he enjoy[ed] with a good appetite.' By way of example, he shared that he enjoyed candy and at times needed to hold himself back from excess snacking on candies in the office during lulls at work.

Thomas and the therapist worked to co-create a formulation of his ARFID, which centered on his predictions that he would dislike new foods, and in turn his reliance on strictly preferred foods that he felt confident that he would like. The therapist explained how Thomas's restrictive eating pattern followed logically from his predictions about novel or mixed foods, and how his consequent avoidance of social eating situations limited his opportunities to practice and gain familiarity with these foods. While Thomas had very occasionally tried some of his non-preferred foods in childhood under duress, he had never had the repeated exposures that could aid in habituation to some of the properties of foods to which he was having the strongest sensory reactions. Notably, Thomas's weight was stable and he denied any experience of sensory-specific satiety, instead noting that he could easily eat adequate portions of preferred foods. Thomas's narrow food preferences had significant social implications: he shared that he and his wife did not eat meals together; he ate lunch at his desk rather than in the common room; and he avoided going out to eat with friends or colleagues due to his prediction that his preferred foods would be unavailable or that explaining his food preferences would be embarrassing.

Thomas was already eating regularly, having three meals and two snacks per day, and he began using an app on his phone as a logging tool. While he was generally eating at the same times daily during the workweek, he found that the weekends could be more variable due to his recreational sports commitments.

Even in the first few weeks of treatment, Thomas made changes in his eating. He was enthusiastic about reintroducing breakfast cereal with milk in the morning (in place of the chicken tenders and sweet potato) and successfully made this change

between sessions 1 and 1. In the second and third week, Thomas also managed to reintroduce some infrequently eaten foods, such as hot dogs, and he worked to change the presentation of his chicken at lunch and dinner to increase flexibility as well. In addition to telling his wife about his therapy, Thomas elected to share his treatment plan with some close family and friends from home, who were very supportive, and this disclosure set the stage for involving them in meals out during the course of treatment.

Stage 2. As a part of his pretreatment evaluation, Thomas had met with a primary care physician who identified deficiencies in vitamin C and zinc. These deficiencies reflected the absence of fruits, vegetables, or dairy in his diet and potentially contributed to low energy and fatigue at work. Notably, Thomas reported that he had recurrent problems with canker sores, which made it hard for him to have citrus fruits, even though he thought that he would like these. His evaluating physician had prescribed a multivitamin to treat his vitamin deficiencies, and so he already had that on board and was eager to learn how to correct his deficiencies with food.

He was familiar with the MyPlate schematic and very much wanted to increase consumption of fruits, vegetables, dairy, and other proteins in order to approximate it. In reviewing the Primary Food Group Building Blocks handout with the therapist, Thomas identified a number of foods from each of the food categories that he was willing to learn about. Together they made a plan for him to bring in five foods for the first session of Stage 3.

Stage 3. Stage 3 focused exclusively on sensory sensitivity as the maintaining mechanism of Thomas's ARFID. Thomas took the lead in selecting five (and sometimes more) foods to each session, which he then tried using the Five Steps. In the first session of Stage 3, Thomas brought in three kinds of cheese, carrots, sliced deli chicken (novel presentation of a preferred food), blueberries, and blueberry juice. The therapist coached him through using the Five Steps, and he was receptive to reminders to use nonjudgmental language. In this first tasting, Thomas found himself to be pleasantly surprised by the taste of blueberries and felt this was a food he wanted to work on incorporating in his diet during the course of the next week. He had strong reactions to the texture of the cheese and the deli meat, and the therapist pointed out that some of what he was reacting to was their novelty, which would be reduced with repeated practices; he agreed to continue to work on the deli meat as this was another food that he

Case Example #5: *(cont.)*

wanted to be able to incorporate in his diet. After this initial tasting session, Thomas and his therapist identified concrete ideas for daily practices in the coming week to increase his comfort with these new foods. Before the next session, he managed to have blueberries daily and had found that he started to enjoy them and looked forward to them as a midmorning snack.

In the next tasting session, Thomas brought in the deli chicken again, strawberries, spinach leaves, and cooked vegetables (broccoli, carrots, and cauliflower). He found that the fruits were easier for him than he had anticipated and he liked their sweet taste and was not bothered by their texture. Because he had anticipated vegetables to be much harder, he had the idea to use a garlic salt powder as a condiment to increase the palatability of the cooked vegetables. Again, Thomas surprised himself by finding that the cooked vegetables were less intense in flavor than he had feared they would be, and when flavored with the garlic salt, he found he was able to try several bites of all three of the vegetables. For Thomas, the spinach leaves were low in flavor, and he came up with the idea of adding a mild flavored seasoning to them, as the idea of the texture of any salad dressing was not appealing to him. Thomas elected to practice all of these foods during the next week at home and he even moved to having the evening meal with his wife, and using that as an opportunity to get some support from her around practicing some of the foods he was learning about in sessions.

Over the next 13 sessions, Thomas brought in foods from the Primary Food Groups Building Blocks, and the therapist guided him in walking through the Five Steps for each. His primary focus was on in-session practices with fruits and vegetables, but as he gained traction with these and began incorporating them into his diet outside of sessions, we also continued to work in session on other foods that would serve him in being able to go out to dinner, as well as the more challenging mixed-texture foods.

At home, in addition to practicing and then incorporating many of the foods he had worked on in-session, Thomas also took the initiative to work toward tasting some of the foods he wanted to include in his diet long term. Thomas reported that he liked the smell of steak and felt that this was a food he may be able to incorporate. Thomas had decided to work on grilling steak at home, as a meal he would be able to take in with his wife. Over the

next few months, he experimented with different cuts of meat and with different marinades, learning more about his preferences and ultimately increasing his comfort level with being able to eat steak. By the end of stage 3, Thomas was enjoying steak as a meal, which he was able to eat both at home and out at restaurants.

Thomas used some of the strategies for incorporating new foods at home, including chaining. He had become comfortable eating chicken kebab at a Middle Eastern restaurant and decided to try a falafel sandwich there, as the spices would be similar and he felt comfortable with fried food. He found that he didn't like the taste of the falafel after the first few tries, but felt proud that he had tried it. Given his desire to be able to eat pizza ('It's a perfect kid food, and I even like the smell of it!'), he worked to bridge toward pizza from foods he was comfortable with. He already felt comfortable with garlic bread and was willing to add parmesan shavings and then a very thin slice of cheese warmed up, which was a challenge, but one that got easier for him after repeated practice.

Near the end of Stage 3, Thomas experienced the serious medical illness in a close family member. Thomas's need to care for his relative understandably interrupted treatment by making it more difficult to schedule sessions due to competing commitments; it also made it harder for Thomas to prioritize his repeated practices, and he found himself reverting to eating 'comfort' foods. In addition to working in-session to practice tastings and review his progress toward incorporating new foods, time in these sessions was spent acknowledging and empathizing with this emotional situation and then reinforcing some of the strategies he had learned in order to maintain his treatment gains, presaging the end of treatment work that would take place in Stage 4.

Stage 4. In the final two sessions, the therapist reviewed Thomas's Building Blocks to identify the wide range of foods he had successfully tasted and now incorporated into his diet. He had managed to fully incorporate several fruits (e.g., blueberries, pineapple, grapes, strawberries), vegetables (e.g., broccoli, cauliflower, carrots, spinach, lettuce), and proteins (steak, burgers, nuts), and to begin to make progress toward some of the more complex mixed foods, like pizza. Thomas identified pizza as a food that he was still willing to continue learning about in the future. When reviewing the MyPlate schematic, Thomas reflected that his meals now often closely resembled the image. He stated, 'It's like night and

Case Example #5: *(cont.)*

day comparing how I was doing before treatment with [how I am doing] now.'

The therapist reviewed his ARFID symptoms at initial treatment presentation and reflected on his progress, noting that he no longer met criteria for ARFID at the end of treatment. He had his labs rechecked, and his deficiencies in vitamin C and zinc had resolved. Together, the therapist and Thomas co-created a relapse prevention plan, highlighting the strategies from CBT-AR that had been most helpful in effecting change for him. They identified stress – at work and in family – as being triggers that increased his vulnerability lapse into his old eating patterns. For Thomas, ensuring that foods from all five of the food groups were available and ready for eating (at home and at work) increased his likelihood of success. In addition, regular meals with his wife, and planning for special occasions out with friends, also made him more likely to maintain his newly incorporated foods.

Outcome and conclusions. After 20 sessions of CBT-AR, Thomas was successfully eating foods from all five of the food groups at the end of treatment and no longer met diagnostic criteria for ARFID. He shared that over the last two months of treatment he had had the opportunity to get together with family and friends from home. He remarked that they had noticed his substantial changes in eating habits and were genuinely excited for him and intrigued by the process. He reflected that ingredients in his success included his motivation to change, the set-aside time each week (and ultimately each day) to work on his ARFID, the nonjudgmental regard for his eating pattern, and the repeated exposures to new foods, all of them being instrumental in his progress. Moreover, his spontaneous tasting and willingness to continue to practice different preparations of foods he hadn't liked on the initial tasting both presaged his positive prognosis. In summary, Thomas presented with a chronic moderate form of ARFID characterized by sensory sensitivity and nutritional deficiencies secondary to his restrictive eating pattern. He made an excellent response to CBT-AR. His case illustrates how adult patients with ARFID who seek treatment independently (e.g., without pressure from family members) often possess an internal motivation that can be an asset to treatment progress.

Chapter 11

Conclusion and Future Directions

What's in a name? The formal naming of ARFID validated the experience of individuals of all ages aggrieved by a range of clinically significant food avoidance or restriction behaviors who had previously been overlooked. Inclusion of ARFID in *DSM-5* has catalyzed clinical research into the phenomenology and clinical management of this heterogeneous illness. Although the formal diagnosis is new, the problem set is not, and both patients and professionals in the field of eating and feeding disorders have eagerly adopted its use.

Our decision to develop CBT-AR was borne out of necessity: patients and families of those with ARFID were presenting to our Eating Disorders Clinical and Research Program at Massachusetts General Hospital, desperate for help. In the five years since its recognition, research into ARFID has proliferated, and clinical and research groups around the world are learning more about this prevalent and heterogeneous disorder every day. Using our depth of experience in the empirically supported treatment of eating and anxiety disorders, and immersing ourselves in the feeding disorders literature, we began to put together an intervention to meet the needs of the patient population seeking care. After careful thought about what may be maintaining the disorder, we designed a treatment using techniques we know work for specific symptoms. Over nearly four years of testing and refinement, this treatment has evolved into CBT-AR.

CBT-AR is new, and we continue to actively refine and improve it. Our initial data – including both the case examples in this book as well as data from our open trial of 20 patients – are promising. Most patients who receive CBT-AR improve by expanding food variety and volume. They grow taller, gain weight, begin puberty, reduce dependency on nutritional supplement drinks, resolve nutritional deficiencies, and reduce psychosocial impairment. Many individuals fully recover, no longer meeting criteria for ARFID at the end of treatment. These preliminary findings underscore the power of a structured, short-term intervention in effecting substantial change, even in an illness that has often been experienced as lifelong.

One young patient summed up this experience well. After completing 20 sessions of CBT-AR in which he had moved from having zero to five accepted vegetables, 12-year-old Steve reflected, 'If someone had said to me six months ago, 'You're going to love Caesar salad soon!' I would have said they were crazy. But now, I really just love it. I thought I was someone who flat out hated vegetables, but I guess that's not the whole story.' His mom echoed that, as a result of treatment, Steve had experienced a major shift not only in his willingness to try new foods but also in becoming less rigid and more open to new experiences in general.

The pilot data are promising, and the next step in CBT-AR refinement is a randomized controlled clinical trial to compare CBT-AR to a credible control condition. While no other published manualized outpatient protocol exists for individuals with ARFID ages 10 years and up, they may be forthcoming given the growing focus on ARFID in the eating disorders field. Furthermore, routine care in outpatient medical feeding or eating disorders clinics, nutrition services, or occupational therapy programs may represent candidate controls.

Subsequently, we envision dismantling studies to identify which components of CBT-AR are necessary or sufficient to bring about change. During the development process, we have worked to streamline CBT-AR, cutting out any extraneous components to make this treatment maximally effective and parsimonious. For example, in earlier versions of the treatment we asked patients to identify pros and cons of their ARFID to promote engagement and enhance motivation to change. While this was helpful for some, we ultimately found that it was unnecessary and that instead, the time in session was better spent focusing on making early changes. Indeed we noticed that successful patients were making changes to their eating during treatment even before we specifically ask them to do so. Based on the advantage conferred by early change, we now ask everyone to make changes to their eating from the first treatment session. In addition, we also are developing a mobile application that patients can use to track eating tastes and progress toward incorporation. We plan to test the incremental value of this e-tool in CBT-AR, with the expectation that the ease of an app may increase homework compliance and even expedite change.

CBT-AR is designed to be for most – but it is not for all. Indeed, while most people do well, some people continue to struggle with avoidant and restrictive eating at the end of treatment. We as a field need more research on the optimal treatments for individuals who do not respond to, or who are not appropriate for, outpatient treatments. For example, in CBT-AR, we assume patients are eating or drinking calories at the beginning of treatment; for those who are being tube-fed, we recommend tube weaning first. The transition between tube feeding and CBT-AR warrants investigation. On the other hand, while CBT-AR delivered in its individual or family-based formats will be necessary for many, self-help and/or parent guidance CBT-AR may be sufficient for the milder forms of ARFID eating. A self-help and parent guidance version of CBT-AR is planned to increase clinical reach and will require testing. Finally, our joint expertise is in individuals who are ages 10 years and older. Whether CBT-AR can be translated for use with younger patients – e.g., through reliance primarily on parent guidance – may be important to study given the high rates of avoidant and restrictive eating in younger children.

Among the many unknowns about ARFID at this point is understanding of its pathophysiology – and likely multiple pathophysiologies. Our research team hypothesizes that neurobiological factors (e.g., neural appetite, reward, fear, and sensory circuits) underlie the presentations of sensory sensitivity, anxiety, and low appetite, and that these exist on dimensions, continuous with normality. In an NIH-funded R01 study ongoing at the time of publication, we are testing the relevance of these proposed biological bases to ARFID and their ability to predict longitudinal illness course. Furthermore, our CBT-AR model postulates that these biological bases represent a premorbid risk factor for avoidant or restrictive eating that may become reinforced by the avoidant or restrictive eating pattern itself. We are actively testing whether any of these neurobiological factors predict treatment outcomes and are changeable as a function of treatment. Furthermore, while behavior genetics studies suggest that food preferences and body weight run in families, ARFID studies using family, twin, and molecular genetics methodologies are desperately needed. We also do not yet know whether chronic food restriction or the repeated consumption of preferred foods may give rise to epigenetic effects or changes in the gut mircobiome that serve to maintain the disorder. All of these represent exciting new directions for future research.

As we move forward, we plan to use our growing pool of biological and behavioral data to identify targets for treatment engagement, consistent with the experimental therapeutics guidelines set forth by the NIH. It is our hope that you will find this CBT-AR manual helpful in your clinical care and study of ARFID and that you will partner with us in caring for this important underserved patient population.

Appendix 1: CBT-AR Competence Ratings

Instructions: Use this scale to rate competent delivery of CBT-AR for any given session. For each competence item below, rate the extent to which the therapist completed it on the following scale:

1 = Not at all 2 = Somewhat 3 = Moderately
4 = Mostly 5 = Completely NA = not applicable

Question	Rating
1. Therapist conversational communication style	1–5
• Therapist behaves in a respectful, collaborative manner	
2. Positive outlook	1–5
• Therapist expresses a hopeful viewpoint regarding the likely success of treatment	
3. Keeping focused	1–5
• Therapist listens empathically and reflectively to patient's concerns and appropriately redirects patient to keep focused on ARFID symptoms and related beliefs	
• Therapist discourages and avoids irrelevant conversation about the patient (except when needed to establish rapport or put the patient at ease)	
4. Family involvement	1–5 or NA
• Therapist involves the family as appropriate to the decision tree	
○ Individual CBT-AR: Patient and therapist meet alone for most of the session unless visit has been designated for involvement of family member. For younger adolescents, parents may join for 10–15 minutes at the end of the session.	
○ Family-supported CBT-AR: One or both parents are present for all sessions	
5. Therapist knowledge	1–5
• Therapist speaks knowledgeably about ARFID and its treatment	
6. Therapist empathy	1–5
• Therapist acknowledges patient's difficulties and frustrations	
• Therapist does not attribute patient's selective eating or undereating to being 'stubborn' or 'willful'	
7. Therapist flexibility	1–5
• Therapist appropriately chooses treatment modules or strategies that are appropriate to the one, two, or three ARFID maintaining mechanisms most relevant to the patient	
8. Reinforcing	1–5
• Therapist reinforces patient's hard work and progress	
• Therapist reinforces patient's change talk	

(cont.)

Question	Rating
9. Addressing sensory sensitivity (if applicable) • Therapist cues patient to experience each food through the 5 questions • Therapist encourages patient to engage in neutral and nonjudgmental descriptions • Therapist emphasizes that the goal is to 'learn about' new foods rather than to like them immediately	1–5 or NA
10. Addressing fear of aversive consequences (if applicable) • Therapist devises exposures relevant to the patient's specific fears • Therapist designs manageable experiments/exposures (not too anxiety provoking) • Therapist encourages repeated at-home practice	1–5 or NA
11. Addressing lack of interest in eating or food (if applicable) • Therapist encourages self-awareness of hunger and fullness cues • Therapist devises interoceptive exposures as appropriate	1–5 or NA
12. Avoiding common pitfalls • Therapist does not set the unrealistic expectation that the patient will immediately enjoy a new food (e.g., 'Try this! You'll love it!') • Therapist does not set the unrealistic expectation that the feared consequence has 0% chance of occurring (e.g., 'There's no way you'll choke on this food')	1–5
13. Attributing progress to patient • Therapist attributes progress to patient's efforts. Therapist does not take credit for improvement.	1–5

14. Assigning at-home practice tasks
• Therapist assigns homework that is relevant to the target symptoms and to CBT methods designed to address them
• When patients have difficulty completing homework:
  ○ Therapist inquires about reasons for non-completion
  ○ Therapist asks for estimate of likelihood of completion and only assigns if it is high
	1–5 or NA

15. *Overall competence rating*	1–5

Appendix 2: CBT-AR Adherence: Session-by-Session Ratings

CBT-AR Adherence: Stage 1

Session 1

Instructions: Use this scale to rate adherence to instructions in the treatment manual. For each adherence item below, rate the extent to which the therapist completed it using the following scale:

1 = Not at all 2 = Very Little 3 = Little 4 = Somewhat 5 = Moderately 6 = Mostly 7 = Completely

NOTE: Use bulleted items as a general guideline for what the therapist should have done in the session. However, as those are very detailed, your rating should capture only what is marked in bold font.

Question	Rating
1. Introductions (optional if therapist already knows patient and/or family)	1–7
Did the therapist. . .	
• Introduce him- or herself and greet the patient (and each family member) individually?	
2. Set agenda	1–7
Did the therapist. . .	
• Verbally set the agenda jointly with the patient?	
3. Weigh patient	1–7
Did the therapist. . .	
• Weigh the patient and share the patient's weight?	
4. Provide psychoeducation on ARFID in general	1–7
Did the therapist. . .	
• Review patient education handout: What is ARFID?	
5. Provide psychoeducation on all maintaining mechanisms relevant for the patient?	Rate 1–7 for each relevant handout
Did the therapist review one, two, or all three of the following:	
• Patient education handout: What happens when you eat a limited variety of food?	
• Patient education handout: What happens when you become more careful about your eating after a negative experience with food?	
• Patient education handout: What happens when you eat a limited volume of food?	
6. Provide psychoeducation on CBT-AR	1–7
Did the therapist. . .	
• Review patient education handout: How is ARFID treated?	

(cont.)

Question	Rating
7. Patient-generated agenda items	1–7
Did the therapist...	
• Respectfully address patient-generated agenda items or defer them to the next session, without allowing non-ARFID-related topics to dominate the session?	
8. Assign at-home practice tasks	1–7
Did the therapist...	

• Assign self- or parent-monitoring of food intake?
• Request that the patient make the first change in either:
  ○ Volume (if underweight) by increasing intake of preferred foods by 500 calories/day?
  ○ Variety (if not underweight) by making a small change in food presentation, reintroducing a previously eaten food, eliminating a minor safety behavior, or rotating meals?	

9. Did the therapist use any of the following non-CBT techniques?	Please rate how many minutes the therapist focused on non-CBT techniques
• Allow patient to discuss non-agenda items for the majority of the session (i.e., >25 of 50 minutes) • Encourage the patient to explore dynamic conflicts that could have given rise to his/her ARFID • Play with food for the majority of the session • Encourage parents to 'leave the child alone' or 'not apply pressure' to increase volume or variety (family-supported cases only)	
10. Overall Adherence Rating	1–7

*If the therapist did not use cognitive-behavioral strategies for ARFID for the majority of the session or suggested any non-CBT strategies (e.g., allowed patient to discuss non-agenda items for the majority of the session, encouraged the patient to explore dynamic conflicts that could have given rise to his/her ARFID, played with food for most of the session, encouraged parents to 'leave the child alone' or 'not apply pressure' to increase volume or variety), the overall rating should reflect this with an overall adherence score ≤ 5).

CBT-AR Adherence: Stage 1

Session 2

Instructions: Use this scale to rate adherence to instructions in the treatment manual. For each adherence item below, rate the extent to which the therapist completed it using the following scale:

1 = Not at all 2 = Very Little 3 = Little 4 = Somewhat 5 = Moderately 6 = Mostly 7 = Completely

NOTE: Use bulleted items as a general guideline for what the therapist should have done in the session. However, as those are very detailed, your rating should capture only what is marked in bold font.

Question	Rating
1. Set agenda *Did the therapist...* • Verbally set the agenda jointly with the patient?	1–7
2. Weigh patient *Did the therapist...* • Weigh the patient and share the patient's weight?	1–7
3. Review at-home practice tasks *Did the therapist...* • Review in detail the patient's self-monitoring record (in individual CBT-AR) or parent-monitoring (in family-supported CBT-AR)? • Confirm that the patient completed the first change to volume or variety and review the outcome?	1–7
4. Create individualized formulation *Did the therapist...* • Use the patient's or family's own words to co-create an individualized formulation of the patient's ARFID symptoms? • Highlight how it is now the food avoidance itself that maintains the ARFID cycle?	1–7
5. Prescribe a schedule of regular eating relying on preferred foods *Did the therapist...* • Ask the patient to eat 3 meals and 2–3 snacks per day? • Discuss how closely the patient's current pattern of eating approximates this schedule and identify specific changes that the patient should implement in the upcoming week?	1–7
6. Discuss critical importance of gaining weight (underweight patients only) *Did the therapist...* • Review the handout 'Why do I need to gain weight and how do I do it?'	1–7
7. Plan therapeutic meal (underweight patients only) *Did the therapist...* • Plan the therapeutic meal by requesting that the patient (or parents) bring a meal to the next session that is composed of preferred foods and of sufficient volume to facilitate weight gain? • Request that the patient (or parents) bring one item to the next session that would increase the patient's eating flexibility (e.g., a different presentation of a preferred food, or a previously preferred food that was recently dropped)?	1–7

(cont.)

Question	Rating
8. Patient-generated agenda items	1–7

Did the therapist...

- Respectfully address patient-generated agenda items, without allowing non-ARFID-related topics to dominate the session?

	Rating
9. Assign at-home practice tasks	1–7

Did the therapist...

- Assign regular eating, in addition to continuing self- or parent-monitoring, as this week's at-home practice task?
- Request that the patient make the continued changes in either:
  - Volume (if underweight) by increasing intake of preferred foods by 500 calories/day?
  - Variety (if not underweight) by making a small change in food presentation, reintroducing a previously eaten food, eliminating a minor safety behavior, or rotating meals?

	Rating
10. Did the therapist use any of the following non-CBT techniques?	Please rate how many minutes the therapist focused on non-CBT techniques

- Allow patient to discuss non-agenda items for the majority of the session (i.e., >25 of 50 minutes)
- Encourage the patient to explore dynamic conflicts that could have given rise to his/her ARFID
- Play with food for the majority of the session
- Encourage parents to 'leave the child alone' or 'not apply pressure' to increase volume or variety (family-supported cases only)

	Rating
11. Overall Adherence Rating	1–7

*If the therapist did not use cognitive-behavioral strategies for ARFID for the majority of the session or suggested any non-CBT strategies (e.g., allowed patient to discuss non-agenda items for the majority of the session, encouraged the patient to explore dynamic conflicts that could have given rise to his/her ARFID, played with food for most of the session, encouraged parents to 'leave the child alone' or 'not apply pressure' to increase volume or variety), the overall rating should reflect this with an overall adherence score ≤ 5).

CBT-AR Adherence: Stage 1

Session 3 (underweight patients only)

Instructions: Use this scale to rate adherence to instructions in the treatment manual. For each adherence item below, rate the extent to which the therapist completed it using the following scale:

1 = Not at all 2 = Very Little 3 = Little 4 = Somewhat 5 = Moderately 6 = Mostly 7 = Completely

NOTE: Use bulleted items as a general guideline for what the therapist should have done in the session. However, as those are very detailed, your rating should capture only what is marked in bold font.

Question	Rating
1. Set agenda	1–7
Did the therapist...	
• Verbally set the agenda jointly with the patient?	
2. Weigh patient	1–7
Did the therapist...	
• Weigh the patient and share the patient's weight?	
3. Review at-home practice tasks	1–7
Did the therapist...	
• Review the self- or parent-monitoring and regular eating?	
• Review the patient or family's progress with increasing the patient's daily food intake by at least 500 calories per day?	
4. Increase volume with the therapeutic meal	1–7
Did the therapist...	
• Invite the patient (and/or parents) to eat the meal they had brought?	
• Make very specific requests of the patient to increase calorie consumption (e.g., 'Here, have another bite of pizza') and to praise any successes ('Great work almost finishing your mashed potatoes!')? Or encourage the parents to do this?	
• Successfully support patient to eat one more bite than the patient was intending to eat? Or encourage the parents to do this?	
5. Increase variety with one bite of novel presentation	1–7
Did the therapist...	
• Support the patient in eating at least one bite of a novel presentation of a preferred food? Or coach the parents to do this?	
6. Patient-generated agenda items	1–7
Did the therapist...	
• Respectfully address patient-generated agenda items, without allowing non-ARFID-related topics to dominate the session?	
7. Assign at-home practice task	1–7
Did the therapist...	
• Ask that the patient continue with self- or parent-monitoring and regular eating as this week's at-home practice task?	
• Ask the patient to continue eating sufficient calories (i.e., keeping calories the same if patient has gained weight, increasing further if patient has not gained)? Or ask the parents to support their child in doing this?	

(cont.)

Question	Rating
8. Did the therapist use any of the following non-CBT techniques? • Allow patient to discuss non-agenda items for the majority of the session (i.e., >25 of 50 minutes) • Encourage the patient to explore dynamic conflicts that could have given rise to his/her ARFID • Play with food for the majority of the session • Encourage parents to 'leave the child alone' or 'not apply pressure' to increase volume or variety (family-supported cases only)	Please rate how many minutes the therapist focused on non-CBT techniques
9. Overall Adherence Rating	1–7

If the therapist did not use cognitive-behavioral strategies for ARFID for the majority of the session or suggested any non-CBT strategies (e.g., allowed patient to discuss non-agenda items for the majority of the session, encouraged the patient to explore dynamic conflicts that could have given rise to his/her ARFID, played with food for most of the session, encouraged parents to 'leave the child alone' or 'not apply pressure' to increase volume or variety), the overall rating should reflect this with an overall adherence score ≤ 5).

CBT-AR Adherence: Stage 1

Session 4 (underweight patients only)

Instructions: Use this scale to rate adherence to instructions in the treatment manual. For each adherence item below, rate the extent to which the therapist completed it using the following scale:

1 = Not at all 2 = Very Little 3 = Little 4 = Somewhat 5 = Moderately 6 = Mostly 7 = Completely

NOTE: Use bulleted items as a general guideline for what the therapist should have done in the session. However, as those are very detailed, your rating should capture only what is marked in bold font.

Question	Rating
1. Set agenda *Did the therapist...* • Verbally set the agenda jointly with the patient?	1–7
2. Weigh patient *Did the therapist...* • Weigh the patient and share the patient's weight?	1–7
3. Review at-home practice tasks *Did the therapist...* • Review how the patient is doing with regular eating, and identify further changes that can be made? • Review the patient's or family's progress with increasing the patient's daily food intake by at least 500 calories per day?	1–7
4. Continue to focus on weight gain *Did the therapist...* • Brainstorm with the patient (and family) about how to continue increasing the energy density of meals and snacks by focusing on preferred foods?	1–7
5. Continue to focus on increasing eating flexibility (optional) *Did the therapist...* • If the patient has successfully begun to gain weight, encourage the patient to continue to increase eating flexibility while relying on energy-dense preferred foods by (1) varying meals and snacks each day, even while sticking with preferred foods, and/or (2) slightly changing the presentation of preferred foods?	1–7
6. Patient-generated agenda items *Did the therapist...* • Respectfully address patient-generated agenda items, without allowing non-ARFID-related topics to dominate the session?	1–7
7. Assign at-home practice task *Did the therapist...* • Ask that the patient continue with self- or parent-monitoring, regular eating, and increasing eating flexibility as this week's at-home practice tasks? • Ask the patient to continue eating sufficient calories (i.e., keeping calories the same if patient has gained weight, increasing further if patient has not gained)? Or ask the parents to support their child in doing this? • If the patient has successfully begun gaining weight, ask the patient to work on increasing eating flexibility?	1–7

(cont.)

Question	Rating
8. Did the therapist use any of the following non-CBT techniques? • Allow patient to discuss non-agenda items for the majority of the session (i.e., >25 of 50 minutes) • Encourage the patient to explore dynamic conflicts that could have given rise to his/her ARFID • Play with food for the majority of the session • Encourage parents to 'leave the child alone' or 'not apply pressure' to increase volume or variety (family-supported cases only)	Please rate how many minutes the therapist focused on non-CBT techniques
9. Overall Adherence Rating	1–7

*If the therapist did not use cognitive-behavioral strategies for ARFID for the majority of the session or suggested any non-CBT strategies (e.g., allowed patient to discuss non-agenda items for the majority of the session, encouraged the patient to explore dynamic conflicts that could have given rise to his/her ARFID, played with food for most of the session, encouraged parents to 'leave the child alone' or 'not apply pressure' to increase volume or variety), the overall rating should reflect this with an overall adherence score ≤ 5).

CBT-AR Adherence: Stage 2

Session 1

Instructions: Use this scale to rate adherence to instructions in the treatment manual. For each adherence item below, rate the extent to which the therapist completed it using the following scale:

1 = Not at all 2 = Very Little 3 = Little 4 = Somewhat 5 = Moderately 6 = Mostly 7 = Completely

NOTE: Use bulleted items as a general guideline for what the therapist should have done in the session. However, as those are very detailed, your rating should capture only what is marked in bold font.

Question	Rating
1. Set agenda	1–7
Did the therapist...	
• Verbally set the agenda jointly with the patient?	
2. Weigh patient	1–7
Did the therapist...	
• Weigh the patient and share the patient's weight?	
3. Review at-home practice tasks	1–7
Did the therapist...	
• Review the self- or parent-monitoring, regular eating, and progress on increasing eating flexibility?	
• (underweight patients only) Review the patient's progress with increasing daily food intake by at least 500 calories per day?	
4. Continue to focus on weight gain (underweight patients only)	1–7
Did the therapist...	
• Brainstorm with the patient (and family) about how to continue increasing the energy density of meals and snacks by focusing on preferred foods?	
5. Psychoeducation on nutrition deficiencies	1–7
Did the therapist...	
• Review patient education handout: Common nutrition deficiencies associated with ARFID?	
• Inquire about any deficiencies with which the patient has been diagnosed, or any symptoms of potential deficiencies that the patient has experienced?	
6. Continue to increase eating flexibility	1–7
Did the therapist...	
• Encourage the patient to continue to increase eating flexibility by (1) varying meals and snacks each day, even while sticking with preferred foods, and/or (2) reintroducing previously eaten or very low-frequency foods – particularly those foods that might correct any nutrition deficiencies that the patient already has or for which he or she is potentially at risk based on current diet?	
7. Patient-generated agenda items	1–7
Did the therapist...	
• Respectfully address patient-generated agenda items, without allowing non-ARFID-related topics to dominate the session?	

(cont.)

Question	Rating
8. Assign at-home practice task *Did the therapist...* • Ask that the patient continue with self- or parent-monitoring, regular eating, and increasing eating flexibility as this week's at-home practice tasks? • Ask the family to support the patient in eating sufficient calories (i.e., keeping calories the same if patient has gained weight, increasing further if patient has not gained)?	1–7
9. Did the therapist use any of the following non-CBT techniques? • Allow patient to discuss non-agenda items for the majority of the session (i.e., >25 of 50 minutes) • Encourage the patient to explore dynamic conflicts that could have given rise to his/her ARFID • Play with food for the majority of the session • Encourage parents to 'leave the child alone' or 'not apply pressure' to increase volume or variety (family-supported cases only)	Please rate how many minutes the therapist focused on non-CBT techniques
10. Overall Adherence Rating *If the therapist did not use cognitive-behavioral strategies for ARFID for the majority of the session or suggested any non-CBT strategies (e.g., allowed patient to discuss non-agenda items for the majority of the session, encouraged the patient to explore dynamic conflicts that could have given rise to his/her ARFID, played with food for most of the session, encouraged parents to 'leave the child alone' or 'not apply pressure' to increase volume or variety), the overall rating should reflect this with an overall adherence score ≤ 5).*	1–7

CBT-AR Adherence: Stage 2

Session 2

Instructions: Use this scale to rate adherence to instructions in the treatment manual. For each adherence item below, rate the extent to which the therapist completed it using the following scale:

1 = Not at all 2 = Very Little 3 = Little 4 = Somewhat 5 = Moderately 6 = Mostly 7 = Completely

NOTE: Use bulleted items as a general guideline for what the therapist should have done in the session. However, as those are very detailed, your rating should capture only what is marked in bold font.

Question	Rating
1. Set agenda	1–7
Did the therapist...	
• Verbally set the agenda jointly with the patient?	
2. Weigh patient	1–7
Did the therapist...	
• Weigh the patient and share the patient's weight?	
3. Review at-home practice tasks	1–7
Did the therapist...	
• Review the self- or parent-monitoring, regular eating, and progress on increasing eating flexibility?	
• (underweight patients only) Review the patient's progress with increasing daily food intake by at least 500 calories per day?	
4. Psychoeducation on types of food to include in a healthy diet	1–7
Did the therapist...	
• Review patient education handout: Choose my plate?	
• Discuss foods that may be under- or overrepresented in the patient's diet?	
5. Review intake from Primary Food Group Building Blocks	1–7
Did the therapist...	
• Review the Primary Food Group Building Blocks handout	
• Invite the patient to identify foods he or she is (1) consistently eating and (2) willing to learn about?	
• Ensure that the patient considers checking off or writing in the 'willing to learn about' column specific foods that could correct the patient's existing nutritional deficiencies and/or decrease psychosocial impairment?	
6. Prepare for first (or only) maintaining mechanism to target in Stage 3	1–7
Did the therapist do one of the following:	
• Ask the patient (or family) to bring small portions of 5 items from the 'willing to learn about' column of the Primary Food Group Building Blocks for the first in-session exposure? *(Sensory Sensitivity module only)*	
• Ask the patient (or family) to begin thinking about fears he or she would like to tackle in Stage 3? *(Fear of Aversive Consequences module only)*	
• Ask the patient (or family) to bring in 5 highly preferred foods for the first in-session exposure? *(Lack of Interest module only)*	

(cont.)

Question	Rating
7. Patient-generated agenda items *Did the therapist...* • Respectfully address patient-generated agenda items, without allowing non-ARFID-related topics to dominate the session?	1–7
8. Assign at-home practice task *Did the therapist...* • Ask that the patient continue with self- or parent-monitoring, regular eating, and increasing eating flexibility as this week's at-home practice tasks? • Ask the family to support the patient in eating sufficient calories (i.e., keeping calories the same if patient has gained weight, increasing further if patient has not gained)? • Ask that the patient continue to think about any foods that should be added to the 'willing to learn about' list (or bring in 5 items from the list, if starting Stage 3 with sensory sensitivity module)?	1–7
9. Did the therapist use any of the following non-CBT techniques? • Allow patient to discuss non-agenda items for the majority of the session (i.e., >25 of 50 minutes) • Encourage the patient to explore dynamic conflicts that could have given rise to his/her ARFID • Play with food for the majority of the session • Encourage parents to 'leave the child alone' or 'not apply pressure' to increase volume or variety (family-supported cases only)	Please rate how many minutes the therapist focused on non-CBT techniques
10. Overall Adherence Rating **If the therapist did not use cognitive-behavioral strategies for ARFID for the majority of the session or suggested any non-CBT strategies (e.g., allowed patient to discuss non-agenda items for the majority of the session, encouraged the patient to explore dynamic conflicts that could have given rise to his/her ARFID, played with food for most of the session, encouraged parents to 'leave the child alone' or 'not apply pressure' to increase volume or variety), the overall rating should reflect this with an overall adherence score ≤ 5).*	1–7

CBT-AR Adherence: Stage 3

Sensory Sensitivity Module, Session 1

Instructions: Use this scale to rate adherence to instructions in the treatment manual. For each adherence item below, rate the extent to which the therapist completed it using the following scale:

1 = Not at all 2 = Very Little 3 = Little 4 = Somewhat 5 = Moderately 6 = Mostly 7 = Completely

NOTE: Use bulleted items as a general guideline for what the therapist should have done in the session. However, as those are very detailed, your rating should capture only what is marked in bold font.

Question	Rating
1. Set agenda	1–7
Did the therapist...	
• Verbally set the agenda jointly with the patient?	
2. Weigh patient	1–7
Did the therapist...	
• Weigh the patient and share the patient's weight?	
• (*Underweight patients only*) Reinforce changes that have led to successful weight gain, or, if the patient hasn't gained, work with the patient (or family) to create a concrete weight gain plan for the week?	
3. Review at-home practice tasks	1–7
Did the therapist...	
• Review how the patient is doing with regular eating and increasing eating flexibility, and identify further changes that can be made?	
• Confirm that the patient has brought in 5 foods from his or her 'willing to learn about' list?	
4. Psychoeducation on necessity of repeated exposure to enhance liking for novel foods	1–7
Did the therapist...	
• Describe the 'mere exposure' effect, using examples relevant from the patient's own life (food or non-food)?	
• Review the patient education handout: Learning about New Foods: The Five Steps?	
5. Conduct first in-session food exposure	1–7
Did the therapist...	
• Guide the patient through the Five Steps for each of the 5 foods he or she brought to session?	
• Ask the patient to check these items off on the Primary Food Group Building Blocks?	
• Identify opportunities for repeated exposure with at least some of these foods in the upcoming week?	
6. Patient-generated agenda items	1–7
Did the therapist...	
• Respectfully address patient-generated agenda items, without allowing non-ARFID-related topics to dominate the session?	

(cont.)

Question	Rating
7. Assign at-home practice task	1–7
Did the therapist...	
• Ask that the patient continue with self- or parent-monitoring, regular eating, and increasing eating flexibility as this week's at-home practice tasks?	
• Confirm which of the tasted foods the patient will use for at-home practice tasting in the upcoming week, and ask the patient to do a tasting every day?	
• Identify 5 foods from the Primary Food Groups Building Blocks list that the patient will bring to the next session?	
8. Did the therapist use any of the following non-CBT techniques?	Please rate how many minutes the therapist focused on non-CBT techniques
• Allow patient to discuss non-agenda items for the majority of the session (i.e., >25 of 50 minutes)	
• Encourage the patient to explore dynamic conflicts that could have given rise to his/her ARFID	
• Play with food for the majority of the session	
• Encourage parents to 'leave the child alone' or 'not apply pressure' to increase volume or variety (family-supported cases only)	
9. Overall Adherence Rating	1–7
*If the therapist did not use cognitive-behavioral strategies for ARFID for the majority of the session or suggested any non-CBT strategies (e.g., allowed patient to discuss non-agenda items for the majority of the session, encouraged the patient to explore dynamic conflicts that could have given rise to his/her ARFID, played with food for most of the session, encouraged parents to 'leave the child alone' or 'not apply pressure' to increase volume or variety), the overall rating should reflect this with an overall adherence score ≤ 5).	

CBT-AR Adherence: Stage 3

Sensory Sensitivity Module, Session 2

Instructions: Use this scale to rate adherence to instructions in the treatment manual. For each adherence item below, rate the extent to which the therapist completed it using the following scale:

1 = Not at all 2 = Very Little 3 = Little 4 = Somewhat 5 = Moderately 6 = Mostly 7 = Completely

NOTE: Use bulleted items as a general guideline for what the therapist should have done in the session. However, as those are very detailed, your rating should capture only what is marked in bold font.

Question	Rating
1. Set agenda *Did the therapist...* • Verbally set the agenda jointly with the patient?	1–7
2. Weigh patient *Did the therapist...* • Weigh the patient and share the patient's weight? • *(Underweight patients only)* Reinforce changes that have led to successful weight gain, or, if the patient hasn't gained, work with the patient (or family) to create a concrete weight gain plan for the week?	1–7
3. Review at-home practice tasks *Did the therapist...* • Review the patient's self- or parent-monitoring to ensure that novel foods are being repeatedly tasted? • Confirm that the patient has given him/herself credit for tasting by checking off number of tastes (e.g., in the workbook)? • Confirm that the patient has brought in 5 foods from his or her 'willing to learn about' list?	1–7
4. Conduct in-session food exposure *Did the therapist...* • Guide the patient through the Five Steps for each of the 5 foods he or she brought to session? • Identify opportunities for repeated exposure with at least some of these foods in the upcoming week?	1–7
5. Distinguish between tasting and incorporating *Did the therapist...* • Review the patient education handout: Strategies for Incorporating New Foods at Home? • Work with the patient (or parents) to identify some techniques from the handout 'Strategies for Incorporating New Foods at Home' that could help the patient incorporate a novel food from his or her 'willing to learn about' list?	1–7
6. Patient-generated agenda items *Did the therapist...* • Respectfully address patient-generated agenda items, without allowing non-ARFID-related topics to dominate the session?	1–7

(cont.)

Question	Rating
7. Assign at-home practice task	1–7

Did the therapist. . .

- Ask that the patient continue with self- or parent-monitoring, regular eating, and increasing eating flexibility as this week's at-home practice tasks?
- Confirm which of the tasted foods the patient will use for tasting versus incorporation in the upcoming week, and ask the patient to either taste or incorporate a new food every day?
- Identify 5 foods from the Primary Food Groups Building Blocks list that the patient will bring to the next session?

Question	Rating
8. Did the therapist use any of the following non-CBT techniques?	Please rate how many minutes the therapist focused on non-CBT techniques

- Allow patient to discuss non-agenda items for the majority of the session (i.e., >25 of 50 minutes)
- Encourage the patient to explore dynamic conflicts that could have given rise to his/her ARFID
- Play with food for the majority of the session
- Encourage parents to 'leave the child alone' or 'not apply pressure' to increase volume or variety (family-supported cases only)

Question	Rating
9. Overall Adherence Rating	1–7

*If the therapist did not use cognitive-behavioral strategies for ARFID for the majority of the session or suggested any non-CBT strategies (e.g., allowed patient to discuss non-agenda items for the majority of the session, encouraged the patient to explore dynamic conflicts that could have given rise to his/her ARFID, played with food for most of the session, encouraged parents to 'leave the child alone' or 'not apply pressure' to increase volume or variety), the overall rating should reflect this with an overall adherence score $\leq$ 5).

CBT-AR Adherence: Stage 3

Sensory Sensitivity Module, Later Sessions

Instructions: Use this scale to rate adherence to instructions in the treatment manual. For each adherence item below, rate the extent to which the therapist completed it using the following scale:

1 = Not at all 2 = Very Little 3 = Little 4 = Somewhat 5 = Moderately 6 = Mostly 7 = Completely

NOTE: Use bulleted items as a general guideline for what the therapist should have done in the session. However, as those are very detailed, your rating should capture only what is marked in bold font.

Question	Rating
1. Set agenda	1–7
Did the therapist...	
• Verbally set the agenda jointly with the patient?	
2. Weigh patient	1–7
Did the therapist...	
• Weigh the patient and share the patient's weight?	
• *(Underweight patients only)* Reinforce changes that have led to successful weight gain, or, if the patient hasn't gained, work with the patient (or family) to create a concrete weight gain plan for the week?	
3. Review at-home practice tasks	1–7
Did the therapist...	
• Review the patient's self- or parent-monitoring to ensure that novel foods are being repeatedly tasted and/or incorporated into planned meals and snacks?	
• Confirm that the patient has given him/herself credit for tasting by checking off number of tastes (e.g., in the workbook)?	
• Confirm that the patient has brought in 5 foods from his or her 'willing to learn about' list?	
4. Conduct in-session food exposure	1–7
Did the therapist...	
• Guide the patient through the Five Steps for each of the 5 foods he or she brought to session?	
• Confirm that the patient has given him/herself credit for tasting by checking off number of tastes in the workbook?	
• Identify opportunities for repeated exposure with at least some of these foods in the upcoming week?	
5. Continue to emphasize importance of incorporating novel foods	1–7
Did the therapist...	
• Help the patient identify foods that the patient has tasted multiple times now with minimal difficulty that could be incorporated this week into meals or snacks?	
• Use the My Plate concept to guide the addition of novel foods into existing meals and snacks or the inclusion of novel meals and snacks?	
6. Patient-generated agenda items	1–7
Did the therapist...	
• Respectfully address patient-generated agenda items, without allowing non-ARFID-related topics to dominate the session?	

(cont.)

Question	Rating
7. Assign at-home practice task	1–7

Did the therapist. . .

- Ask that the patient continue with self- or parent-monitoring?
- Confirm which of the tasted foods the patient will use for tasting versus incorporation in the upcoming week, ask the patient to either taste or incorporate a new food every day?
- Identify 5 foods that the patient will bring to the next session and encourage the patient (or parents) to bring in complex or mixed foods comprised of multiple Primary Food Group Building Block items? *(Except final session of Stage 3)*

Question	Rating
8. *(Final session of module only, if there are multiple maintaining mechanisms)* Prepare for next maintaining mechanism to target in Stage 3	1–7

Did the therapist do one of the following. . .

- Ask the patient (or family) to begin thinking about fears he or she would like to tackle in Stage 3? *(Fear of Aversive Consequences module only)*
- Ask the patient (or family) to bring in 5 highly preferred foods for the first in-session exposure? *(Lack of Interest module only)*

Question	Rating
9. Did the therapist use any of the following non-CBT techniques?	Please rate how many minutes the therapist focused on non-CBT techniques

- Allow patient to discuss non-agenda items for the majority of the session (i.e., >25 of 50 minutes)
- Encourage the patient to explore dynamic conflicts that could have given rise to his/her ARFID
- Play with food for the majority of the session
- Encourage parents to 'leave the child alone' or 'not apply pressure' to increase volume or variety (family-supported cases only)

Question	Rating
10. *Overall Adherence Rating*	1–7

If the therapist did not use cognitive-behavioral strategies for ARFID for the majority of the session or suggested any non-CBT strategies (e.g., allowed patient to discuss non-agenda items for the majority of the session, encouraged the patient to explore dynamic conflicts that could have given rise to his/her ARFID, played with food for most of the session, encouraged parents to 'leave the child alone' or 'not apply pressure' to increase volume or variety), the overall rating should reflect this with an overall adherence score ≤ 5).

CBT-AR Adherence: Stage 3

Fear of Aversive Consequences Module, Session 1

Instructions: Use this scale to rate adherence to instructions in the treatment manual. For each adherence item below, rate the extent to which the therapist completed it using the following scale:

1 = Not at all 2 = Very Little 3 = Little 4 = Somewhat 5 = Moderately 6 = Mostly 7 = Completely

NOTE: Use bulleted items as a general guideline for what the therapist should have done in the session. However, as those are very detailed, your rating should capture only what is marked in bold font.

Question	Rating
1. Set agenda	1–7
Did the therapist...	
• Verbally set the agenda jointly with the patient?	
2. Weigh patient	1–7
Did the therapist...	
• Weigh the patient and share the patient's weight?	
• (Underweight patients only) Reinforce changes that have led to successful weight gain, or, if the patient hasn't gained, work with the patient (or family) to create a concrete weight gain plan for the week?	
3. Review at-home practice tasks	1–7
Did the therapist...	
• Review how the patient is doing with regular eating and increasing eating flexibility, and identify further changes that can be made?	
4. Psychoeducation on avoidance and exposure	1–7
Did the therapist...	
• Review patient education handout: How Does Avoidance Increase Anxiety Over Time?	
5. Co-create exposure hierarchy to guide future exposures	1–7
Did the therapist...	
• Explain the concept of subjective units of distress/fear thermometer?	
• Work together with the patient to co-create the exposure hierarchy and add items that are most relevant to his/her trauma?	
6. Patient-generated agenda items	1–7
Did the therapist...	
• Respectfully address patient-generated agenda items, without allowing non-ARFID-related topics to dominate the session?	
7. Assign at-home practice task	1–7
Did the therapist...	
• Ask that the patient continue with self- or parent-monitoring, regular eating, and increasing eating flexibility as this week's at-home practice tasks?	
• Ask that the patient consider whether any additional steps should be added to the exposure hierarchy?	
• Ask that the patient bring any food items to the next session that may necessary for conducting the in-session exposure?	

(cont.)

Question	Rating
8. Did the therapist use any of the following non-CBT techniques? • Allow patient to discuss non-agenda items for the majority of the session (i.e., >25 of 50 minutes) • Encourage the patient to explore dynamic conflicts that could have given rise to his/her ARFID • Play with food for the majority of the session • Encourage parents to 'leave the child alone' or 'not apply pressure' to increase volume or variety (family-supported cases only)	Please rate how many minutes the therapist focused on non-CBT techniques
9. Overall Adherence Rating	1–7

*If the therapist did not use cognitive-behavioral strategies for ARFID for the majority of the session or suggested any non-CBT strategies (e.g., allowed patient to discuss non-agenda items for the majority of the session, encouraged the patient to explore dynamic conflicts that could have given rise to his/her ARFID, played with food for most of the session, encouraged parents to 'leave the child alone' or 'not apply pressure' to increase volume or variety), the overall rating should reflect this with an overall adherence score ≤ 5).

CBT-AR Adherence: Stage 3

Fear of Aversive Consequences Module, Later Sessions

Instructions: Use this scale to rate adherence to instructions in the treatment manual. For each adherence item below, rate the extent to which the therapist completed it using the following scale:

1 = Not at all 2 = Very Little 3 = Little 4 = Somewhat 5 = Moderately 6 = Mostly 7 = Completely

NOTE: Use bulleted items as a general guideline for what the therapist should have done in the session. However, as those are very detailed, your rating should capture only what is marked in bold font.

Question	Rating
1. Set agenda	1–7
Did the therapist...	
• Verbally set the agenda jointly with the patient?	
2. Weigh patient	1–7
Did the therapist...	
• Weigh the patient and share the patient's weight?	
• *(Underweight patients only)* Reinforce changes that have led to successful weight gain, or, if the patient hasn't gained, work with the patient (or family) to create a concrete weight gain plan for the week?	
3. Review at-home practice tasks	1–7
Did the therapist...	
• Review how the patient is doing with regular eating and increasing eating flexibility, and identify further changes that can be made?	
• Ask if the patient he or she has anything to add to the exposure hierarchy and/or review at-home practice exposures?	
4. Conduct in-session food exposure	1–7
Did the therapist...	
• Ask the patient to estimate the probability of the feared consequence, ranging from 0% to 100%?	
• Ask the patient for a starting SUDS rating?	
• Identify safety behaviors and ask the patient to refrain from using them?	
• Ask the patient for an ending SUDS rating?	
• Ask the patient to re-estimate the probability of the feared consequence, ranging from 0% to 100%?	
5. Patient-generated agenda items	1–7
Did the therapist...	
• Respectfully address patient-generated agenda items, without allowing non-ARFID-related topics to dominate the session?	
6. Assign at-home practice task	1–7
Did the therapist...	
• Ask that the patient continue with self- or parent-monitoring, regular eating, and increasing eating flexibility as this week's at-home practice tasks?	
• Review any at-home exposures that the patient will do this week?	
• Ask that the patient bring any food items to the next session that may necessary for conducting the in-session exposure?	

(cont.)

Question	Rating
7. *(Final session of module only, if there are multiple maintaining mechanisms)* **Prepare for next maintaining mechanism to target in Stage 3** *Did the therapist do one of the following...* • Ask the patient (or family) to bring in 5 foods the patient is willing to learn about from the Primary Food Groups Building Blocks? *(Sensory Sensitivity module only)* • Ask the patient (or family) to bring in 5 highly preferred foods for the first in-session exposure? *(Lack of Interest module only)*	
8. Did the therapist use any of the following non-CBT techniques? • Allow patient to discuss non-agenda items for the majority of the session (i.e., >25 of 50 minutes) • Encourage the patient to explore dynamic conflicts that could have given rise to his/her ARFID • Play with food for the majority of the session • Encourage parents to 'leave the child alone' or 'not apply pressure' to increase volume or variety (family-supported cases only)	Please rate how many minutes the therapist focused on non-CBT techniques
9. *Overall Adherence Rating*	1–7

If the therapist did not use cognitive-behavioral strategies for ARFID for the majority of the session or suggested any non-CBT strategies (e.g., allowed patient to discuss non-agenda items for the majority of the session, encouraged the patient to explore dynamic conflicts that could have given rise to his/her ARFID, played with food for most of the session, encouraged parents to 'leave the child alone' or 'not apply pressure' to increase volume or variety), the overall rating should reflect this with an overall adherence score ≤ 5).

161

CBT-AR Adherence: Stage 3

Lack of Interest Module, Session 1

Instructions: Use this scale to rate adherence to instructions in the treatment manual. For each adherence item below, rate the extent to which the therapist completed it using the following scale:

1 = Not at all 2 = Very Little 3 = Little 4 = Somewhat 5 = Moderately 6 = Mostly 7 = Completely

NOTE: Use bulleted items as a general guideline for what the therapist should have done in the session. However, as those are very detailed, your rating should capture only what is marked in bold font.

Question	Rating
1. Set agenda	1–7
Did the therapist...	
• Verbally set the agenda jointly with the patient?	
2. Weigh patient	1–7
Did the therapist...	
• Weigh the patient and share the patient's weight?	
• *(Underweight patients only)* Reinforce changes that have led to successful weight gain, or, if the patient hasn't gained, work with the patient (or family) to create a concrete weight gain plan for the week?	
3. Review at-home practice tasks	1–7
Did the therapist...	
• Review how the patient is doing with regular eating and increasing eating flexibility, and identify further changes that can be made?	
4. Psychoeducation on strategies for eating enough	1–7
Did the therapist...	
• Review the patient education handout: Strategies for Eating Enough?	
5. Conduct interoceptive exposure	1–7
Did the therapist...	
• Explain the concept of subjective units of distress/fear thermometer?	
• Demonstrate each of the interoceptive exposures (i.e., pushing belly out, gulping water, spinning in a chair) for the patient?	
• Have the patient engage in each exposure and provide SUDS ratings?	
• Coach the patient to sit with rather than avoid anxious or uncomfortable feelings and to notice any reduction of SUDS ratings during exposures?	
6. Assign extended self-monitoring with hunger and fullness ratings	1–7
Did the therapist...	
• Assign self-monitoring with hunger and fullness ratings?	
7. Five Steps for highly preferred foods	1–7
Did the therapist...	
• Introduce the Five Steps handout and invite the patient to describe 5 highly preferred foods that the patient has brought to session?	

(cont.)

Question	Rating
8. Patient-generated agenda items	1–7

Did the therapist. . .

- Respectfully address patient-generated agenda items, without allowing non-ARFID-related topics to dominate the session?

| **9. Assign at-home practice task** | 1–7 |

Did the therapist. . .

- Ask that the patient continue with regular eating and increasing eating flexibility as this week's at-home practice tasks?
- Ask the patient to continue practicing any of the interoceptive exposures that elicited discomfort similar to what the patient experiences when eating?
- Confirm that the patient will add the hunger and fullness ratings to this week's self-monitoring?
- Help the patient identify 5 foods that the patient prefers or used to enjoy and will bring to the next session?

| **10. Did the therapist use any of the following non-CBT techniques?** | Please rate how many minutes the therapist focused on non-CBT techniques |

- Allow patient to discuss non-agenda items for the majority of the session (i.e., >25 of 50 minutes)
- Encourage the patient to explore dynamic conflicts that could have given rise to his/her ARFID
- Play with food for the majority of the session
- Encourage parents to 'leave the child alone' or 'not apply pressure' to increase volume or variety (family-supported cases only)

| **11. Overall Adherence Rating** | 1–7 |

*If the therapist did not use cognitive-behavioral strategies for ARFID for the majority of the session or suggested any non-CBT strategies (e.g., allowed patient to discuss non-agenda items for the majority of the session, encouraged the patient to explore dynamic conflicts that could have given rise to his/her ARFID, played with food for most of the session, encouraged parents to 'leave the child alone' or 'not apply pressure' to increase volume or variety), the overall rating should reflect this with an overall adherence score ≤ 5).

CBT-AR Adherence: Stage 3

Lack of Interest Module, Later Sessions

Instructions: Use this scale to rate adherence to instructions in the treatment manual. For each adherence item below, rate the extent to which the therapist completed it using the following scale:

1 = Not at all 2 = Very Little 3 = Little 4 = Somewhat 5 = Moderately 6 = Mostly 7 = Completely

NOTE: Use bulleted items as a general guideline for what the therapist should have done in the session. However, as those are very detailed, your rating should capture only what is marked in bold font.

Question	Rating
1. Set agenda	1–7
Did the therapist...	
• Verbally set the agenda jointly with the patient?	
2. Weigh patient	1–7
Did the therapist...	
• Weigh the patient and share the patient's weight?	
• (*Underweight patients only*) Reinforce changes that have led to successful weight gain, or, if the patient hasn't gained, work with the patient (or family) to create a concrete weight gain plan for the week?	
3. Review at-home practice tasks	1–7
Did the therapist...	
• Review how the patient is doing with regular eating and increasing eating flexibility, and identify further changes that can be made?	
• Review hunger and fullness ratings and identify times of day when he or she feels more hungry than others, and recommend increasing volume specifically at those times?	
4. Conduct further interoceptive exposure	1–7
Did the therapist...	
• Invite the patient to engage in the interoceptive exposure(s) most relevant to his or her eating-related discomfort bloating (pushing belly out), fullness (gulping water), and/or nausea (spinning in a chair)?	
• Have the patient engage in the exposure and provide SUDS ratings?	
• Coach the patient to sit with rather than avoid anxious or uncomfortable feelings and to notice reduction in SUDS during exposures?	
5. Five Steps for highly preferred foods	1–7
Did the therapist...	
• Use the Five Steps handout to invite the patient to describe 5 highly preferred foods that the patient has brought to session?	
6. Patient-generated agenda items	1–7
Did the therapist...	
• Respectfully address patient-generated agenda items, without allowing non-ARFID-related topics to dominate the session?	

(cont.)

Question	Rating

7. Assign at-home practice task

Did the therapist...

- Ask that the patient continue with self-monitoring, regular eating, and increasing eating flexibility as this week's at-home practice tasks?
- Ask the patient to practice any relevant interoceptive exposure exercises at home?
- Ask the patient to bring 5 more preferred foods to the next session for in-session exposure?
- Ask the patient to practice eating highly preferred foods at home this week?

1–7

8. *(Final session of module only, if there are multiple maintaining mechanisms)* Prepare for next maintaining mechanism to target in Stage 3

Did the therapist do one of the following:...

- Ask the patient (or family) to bring small portions of 5 items from the 'willing to learn about' column of the Primary Food Group Building Blocks for the first in-session exposure? *(Sensory Sensitivity module only)*
- Ask the patient (or family) to begin thinking about fears he or she would like to tackle in Stage 3? *(Fear of Aversive Consequences module only)*

9. Did the therapist use any of the following non-CBT techniques?

- Allow patient to discuss non-agenda items for the majority of the session (i.e., >25 of 50 minutes)
- Encourage the patient to explore dynamic conflicts that could have given rise to his/her ARFID
- Play with food for the majority of the session
- Encourage parents to 'leave the child alone' or 'not apply pressure' to increase volume or variety (family-supported cases only)

Please rate how many minutes the therapist focused on non-CBT techniques

10. Overall Adherence Rating

If the therapist did not use cognitive-behavioral strategies for ARFID for the majority of the session or suggested any non-CBT strategies (e.g., allowed patient to discuss non-agenda items for the majority of the session, encouraged the patient to explore dynamic conflicts that could have given rise to his/her ARFID, played with food for most of the session, encouraged parents to 'leave the child alone' or 'not apply pressure' to increase volume or variety), the overall rating should reflect this with an overall adherence score ≤ 5).

1–7

CBT-AR Adherence: Stage 4

Session 1

Instructions: Use this scale to rate adherence to instructions in the treatment manual. For each adherence item below, rate the extent to which the therapist completed it using the following scale:

1 = Not at all 2 = Very Little 3 = Little 4 = Somewhat 5 = Moderately 6 = Mostly 7 = Completely

NOTE: Use bulleted items as a general guideline for what the therapist should have done in the session. However, as those are very detailed, your rating should capture only what is marked in bold font.

Question	Rating
1. Set agenda *Did the therapist...* • Verbally set the agenda jointly with the patient?	1–7
2. Weigh patient *Did the therapist...* • Weigh the patient and share the patient's weight?	1–7
3. Review at-home practice tasks *Did the therapist...* • Review any at-home practice tasks assigned the prior week?	1–7
4. Revisit personalized formulation *Did the therapist...* • Refer the patient back to his or her personalized formulation and discuss what has changed since the start of treatment?	1–7
5. Revisit Primary Food Group Building Blocks *Did the therapist...* • Review the patient's completed Primary Food Group Building Blocks and identify foods that were successfully tasted and/or added to the patient's diet? • Ensure that the patient is currently eating multiple foods in each of the five primary food categories? • Review the Choose My Plate handout and ensure that the patient's recent meals have corresponded more closely to this model than they did before treatment? • Identify areas for future progress (e.g., foods to learn about or continue practicing independently post-treatment)?	1–7
6. Discuss readiness to complete CBT-AR *Did the therapist...* • Share with the patient the CBT-AR criteria for ARFID recovery? • Identify areas where the patient has succeeded? • Identify areas where the patient continues to struggle and, if necessary, discuss potential opportunities for additional support after CBT-AR has completed?	1–7
7. Discontinue self- or parent-monitoring records *Did the therapist...* • Share with the patient that food records are no longer required in CBT-AR Stage 4?	

(cont.)

Question	Rating
8. Patient-generated agenda items *Did the therapist...* • Respectfully address patient-generated agenda items or defer them to the next session, without allowing non-ARFID-related topics to dominate the session?	1–7
9. Did the therapist use any of the following non-CBT techniques? • Allow patient to discuss non-agenda items for the majority of the session (i.e., >25 of 50 minutes) • Encourage the patient to explore dynamic conflicts that could have given rise to his/her ARFID • Play with food for the majority of the session • Encourage parents to 'leave the child alone' or 'not apply pressure' to increase volume or variety (family-supported cases only)	Please rate how many minutes the therapist focused on non-CBT techniques
10. Overall Adherence Rating ***If the therapist did not use cognitive-behavioral strategies for ARFID for the majority of the session or suggested any non-CBT strategies (e.g., allowed patient to discuss non-agenda items for the majority of the session, encouraged the patient to explore dynamic conflicts that could have given rise to his/her ARFID, played with food for most of the session, encouraged parents to 'leave the child alone' or 'not apply pressure' to increase volume or variety), the overall rating should reflect this with an overall adherence score ≤ 5).**	1–7

CBT-AR Adherence: Stage 4

Session 2

Instructions: Use this scale to rate adherence to instructions in the treatment manual. For each adherence item below, rate the extent to which the therapist completed it using the following scale:

1 = Not at all 2 = Very Little 3 = Little 4 = Somewhat 5 = Moderately 6 = Mostly 7 = Completely

NOTE: Use bulleted items as a general guideline for what the therapist should have done in the session. However, as those are very detailed, your rating should capture only what is marked in bold font.

Question	Rating
1. Set agenda *Did the therapist...* • Verbally set the agenda jointly with the patient?	1–7
2. Weigh patient *Did the therapist...* • Weigh the patient and share the patient's weight?	1–7
3. Review progress since last session? *Did the therapist...* • Review progress with weight maintenance (if needed) and incorporation of novel foods (if needed)?	1–7
4. Co-create relapse prevention plan *Did the therapist...* • Work with the patient to co-create a relapse prevention plan that includes ways that the patient's eating has improved, possible triggers for relapse, red flags for relapse, CBT-AR techniques to continue, and post-treatment goals?	
5. Patient-generated agenda items *Did the therapist...* • Respectfully address patient-generated agenda items or defer them to the next session, without allowing non-ARFID-related topics to dominate the session?	1–7
6. End the treatment *Did the therapist...* • End the last session on a positive note by giving the patient credit for his or her treatment successes and expressing optimism about continued progress after treatment has concluded?	1–7
7. Did the therapist use any of the following non-CBT techniques? • Allow patient to discuss non-agenda items for the majority of the session (i.e., >25 of 50 minutes) • Encourage the patient to explore dynamic conflicts that could have given rise to his/her ARFID • Play with food for the majority of the session • Encourage parents to 'leave the child alone' or 'not apply pressure' to increase volume or variety (family-supported cases only)	Please rate how many minutes the therapist focused on non-CBT techniques

(cont.)

Question	Rating
8. Overall Adherence Rating	1–7

If the therapist did not use cognitive-behavioral strategies for ARFID for the majority of the session or suggested any non-CBT strategies (e.g., allowed patient to discuss non-agenda items for the majority of the session, encouraged the patient to explore dynamic conflicts that could have given rise to his/her ARFID, played with food for most of the session, encouraged parents to 'leave the child alone' or 'not apply pressure' to increase volume or variety), the overall rating should reflect this with an overall adherence score ≤ 5).

References

Academy for Eating Disorders Medical Care Standards Committee Guide. (2016). *Eating disorders: A guide to medical care* (3rd ed.). Reston, VA: Academy for Eating Disorders.

American Psychiatric Association. (2013). *Diagnostic and statistical manual of mental disorders* (5th ed.). Arlington, VA: American Psychiatric Association Publishing.

American Society for Enteral and Parenteral and Enteral Nutrition. (2017). *Adult nutrition support core curriculum* (3rd ed.). Silver Spring, MD: ASEPEN.

Andony, L. J., Tay, E., Allen, K. L., et al. (2015). Therapist adherence in the strong without anorexia nervosa (SWAN) study: A randomized controlled trial of three treatments for adults with anorexia nervosa. *International Journal of Eating Disorders*, **48**(8), 1170–1175.

Bailey, R. L., Gahche, J. J., Lentino, C. V. et al. (2010). Dietary supplement use in the United States, 2003–2006. *The Journal of Nutrition*, **141**(2), 261–266.

Barlow, D. H., Leitenberg, H., Agras, W. S., et al. (1969). The transfer gap in systematic desensitization: An analogue study. *Behaviour Research and Therapy*, 7(2), 191–196.

Becker, A. E., Thomas, J. J., & Pike, K. M. (2009). Should non-fat-phobic anorexia nervosa be included in *DSM-V*? *International Journal of Eating Disorders*, **42**, 620–635.

Benini, L., Todesco, T., Dalle Grave, R., et al. (2004). Gastric emptying in patients with restricting and binge/purging subtypes of anorexia nervosa. *The American Journal of Gastroenterology*, **99**(8), 1448–1454.

Benoit, D., Wang, E. E., & Zlotkin, S. H. (2000). Discontinuation of enterostomy tube feeding by behavioral intervention in early childhood: A randomized controlled trial. *Journal of Pediatrics*, **137**, 498–503.

Berry, R. C., Novak, P., Withrow, N., et al. (2015). Nutrition management of gastrointestinal symptoms in children with autism spectrum disorder: Guideline from an expert panel. *Journal of the Academy of Nutrition and Dietetics*, **115**(12), 1919–1927.

Birch, L. L. & Fisher, J. O. (2000). Mothers' child-feeding practices influence daughters' eating and weight. *American Journal of Clinical Nutrition*, **71**, 1054–1061.

Birch, L. L. & Marlin, D. W. (1982). I don't like it; I never tried it: Effects of exposure on two-year-old children's food preferences. *Appetite*, **3**(4), 353–360.

Birch, L. L., McPhee, L., Shoba, B. C., et al. (1987). What kind of exposure reduces children's food neophobia? Looking vs. tasting. *Appetite*, **9**(3), 171–178.

Boettcher, H., Brake, C. A., & Barlow, D. H. (2016). Origins and outlook of interoceptive exposure. *Journal of Behavior Therapy and Experimental Psychiatry*, **53**, 41–51.

Boschen, M. J. (2007). Reconceptualizing emetophobia: A cognitive-behavioral formulation and research agenda. *Journal of Anxiety Disorders*, **21**(3), 407–419.

Boswell, J. F., Anderson, L. M., & Anderson, D. A. (2015). Integration of interoceptive exposure in eating disorder treatment. *Clinical Psychology: Science and Practice*, **22**(2), 194–210.

Breen, F. M., Plomin, R., & Wardle, J. (2006). Heritability of food preferences in young children. *Physiology & Behavior*, **88**(4), 443–447.

Brewerton, T. D. & D'Agostino, M. (2017). Adjunctive use of olanzapine in the treatment of avoidant restrictive food intake disorder in children and adolescents in an eating disorders program. *Journal of Child and Adolescent Psychopharmacology*, **27**(10), 920–922.

Brownell, K. D. & Horgen, K. B. (2004). *Food fight: The inside story of the food industry, America's obesity crisis, and what we can do about it*. Chicago: Contemporary Books.

Bryant-Waugh, R. (2013). Avoidant restrictive food intake disorder: An illustrative case example. *International Journal of Eating Disorders*, **46**(5), 420–423.

Bryant-Waugh, R., Micali, N., Cooke, L., et al. (in press). Development of the PICA, ARFID, and Rumination Disorder Interview, a multi-informant, semi-structured interview of feeding disorders across the lifespan: A pilot study for ages 10 to 22. *International Journal of Eating Disorders*.

Buie, T., Campbell, D. B., Fuchs, G. J., et al. (2010). Evaluation, diagnosis, and treatment of gastrointestinal disorders in individuals with ASDs: A consensus report. *Pediatrics*, **125**(Supplement 1), S1–S18.

Byars, K. C., Burklow, K. A., Ferguson, K., et al. (2003). A multi-component behavioral program for oral aversion in children dependent on gastrostomy feedings. *Journal of Pediatric Gastroenterology and Nutrition*, **37**, 473–480.

Chatoor, I. (2002). Feeding disorders in infants and toddlers: Diagnosis and treatment. *Child and Adolescent Psychiatric Clinics of North America*. 11(2), 163–183.

Chatoor, I. (2009). *Diagnosis and treatment of feeding disorders in infants, toddlers, and young children.* Washington, DC: National Center for Clinical Infant Programs.

Chorpita, B. F., Vitali, A. E., & Barlow, D. H. (1997). Behavioral treatment of choking phobia in an adolescent: An experimental analysis. *Journal of Behavior Therapy and Experimental Psychiatry*, **28**(4), 307–315.

Coniglio, K., Mancuso, C., Izquierdo, A., et al. (2017). I want it now! Reward preferences among individuals with avoidant/restrictive food intake disorder. Poster presentation at the annual Association for Behavioral and Cognitive Therapies conference, San Diego, CA.

Cooke, L. & Webber, L. (2015). *Stress-free feeding: How to develop healthy eating habits in your child.* London: Robinson.

Craighead, L. W. (2006). *The appetite awareness workbook: How to listen to your body and overcome bingeing, overeating, and obsession with food.* Oakland, CA: New Harbinger Publications.

Craske, M. G., Antony, M. M., & Barlow, D. H. (2006). *Mastering your fears and phobias.* Oxford: Oxford University Press.

Craske, M. G. & Barlow, D. H. (2001). Panic disorder and agoraphobia. In D. H. Barlow (Ed.), *Clinical handbook of psychological disorders: A step-by-step treatment manual* (pp. 1–59). New York: Guilford.

Craske, M. G. & Barlow, D. H. (2007). *Mastery of your anxiety and panic: Therapist guide.* Oxford: Oxford University Press.

Dodrill, P. (2014). Feeding problems and oropharyngeal dysphagia in children. *Journal of Gastroenterology and Hepatology Research*, **3**(5), 1055–1060.

Dovey, T. M., Staples, P. A., Gibson, E. L., et al. (2008). Food neophobia and 'picky/fussy' eating in children: A review. *Appetite*, **50**(2), 181–193.

Dunn Klein, M. & Morris, S. E. (2007). *Homemade blended formula handbook.* Tucson, AZ: Mealtime Notions.

Eddy, K. T., Dorer, D. J., Franko, D. L., et al. (2008). Diagnostic crossover in anorexia nervosa and bulimia nervosa: Implications for *DSM-V. American Journal of Psychiatry*, **165**(2), 245–250.

Eddy, K. T., Thomas, J. J., Hastings, E., et al. (2015). Prevalence of *DSM-5* avoidant/restrictive food intake disorder in a pediatric gastroenterology healthcare network. *International Journal of Eating Disorders*, **48**, 464–470.

Emond, A., Emmett, P., Steer, C., et al. (2010). Feeding symptoms, dietary patterns, and growth in young children with autism spectrum disorders. *Pediatrics*, **126**(2), e337–e342.

Fairburn, C. G. (2008). *Cognitive behavior therapy and eating disorders.* New York: Guilford Press.

First, M. B., Williams, J. B. W., Karg, R. S., et al. (2014). *Structured clinical interview for DSM-5 disorders–research version (SCID-5-RV).* Arlington, VA: American Psychiatric Association.

First, M. B., Williams, J. B. W., Karg, R. S., & Spitzer, R. L. (2015). *Structured clinical interview for DSM-5 disorders, clinical version (SCID-5-CV).* Arlington, VA: American Psychiatric Association.

Fischer, A. J., Luiselli, J. K., & Dove, M. B. (2015). Effects of clinic and in-home treatment on consumption and feeding-associated anxiety in an adolescent with avoidant/restrictive food intake disorder. *Clinical Practice in Pediatric Psychology*, **3**(2), 154.

Fisher, M. M., Rosen, D. S., Ornstein, R. M., et al. (2014). Characteristics of avoidant/restrictive food intake disorder in children and adolescents: A "new disorder" in *DSM-5. Journal of Adolescent Health*, **55**(1), 49–52.

Fitzpatrick, K. K., Forsberg, S. E., & Colborn, D. (2015). Family-based therapy for avoidant restrictive food intake disorder: Families facing food neophobias. In K. L. Loeb, D. Le Grange, & J. Lock (Eds.), *Family therapy for adolescent eating and weight disorders: New applications* (pp. 256–276). New York: Routledge.

Forman, S. F., McKenzie, N., Hehn, R., et al. (2014). Predictors of outcome at 1 year in adolescents with *DSM-5* restrictive eating disorders: Report of the national eating disorders quality improvement collaborative. *Journal of Adolescent Health*, **55**(6), 750–756.

Frecka, J. M. & Mattes, R. D. (2008). Possible entrainment of ghrelin to habitual meal patterns in humans. *American Journal of Physiology: Gastrointestinal and Liver Physiology*, **294**(3), G699–G707.

Garner, D. M. (1997). Psychoeducational principles in treatment. In D. M. Garner & P. E. Garfinkel (Eds.), *Handbook of treatment for eating disorders* (pp. 145–177). New York: Guilford.

Golding, J., Steer, C., Emmett, P., et al. (2009). Associations between the ability to detect bitter taste, dietary behavior, and growth: A preliminary report. *Annals of the New York Academy of Sciences*, **1170**, 553–557.

Greer, A. J., Gulotta, C. S., Masler, E. A., et al. (2007). Caregiver stress and outcomes of children with pediatric feeding disorders treated in an intensive inter-disciplinary program. *Journal of Pediatric Psychology*, **33**, 612–620.

Hay, P., Mitchison, D., Collado, A.E., et al. (2017). Burden and health-related quality of life of eating disorders, including Avoidant/Restrictive Food Intake Disorder (ARFID), in the Australian population. *Journal of Eating Disorders*, **5**(1), 21.

Hilbert, A. and van Dyck, Z. (2016). Eating Disorders in Youth – Questionnaire. English version. University of Leipzig (online). Available at: http://nbn-resolving.de/urn:nbn:de:bsz:15-qucosa-197246.

Hunter, P. V. and Antony, M. M. (2009). Cognitive-behavioral treatment of emetophobia: The role of interoceptive exposure. *Cognitive and Behavioral Practice*, **16**(1), 84–91.

Izquierdo, A. M., Plessow, F., Becker, K. R., et al. (2017). Belief bias toward thinness and dieting is present in anorexia nervosa independent of explicit weight/shape concern but not in avoidant/restrictive food intake disorder. Paper presentation at the Eating Disorders Research Society conference, Leipzig, Germany.

Izquierdo, A. M., Thomas, J. J., Mancuso, C. J., et al. (2018). Restrictions apply: Comparing standardized caloric and macronutrient intake among individuals with low-weight eating disorders and healthy controls. Oral paper presentation at the International Conference on Eating Disorders, Chicago, IL.

Jacobi, C., Schmitz, G., & Agras, W.S. (2008). Is picky eating an eating disorder? *International Journal of Eating Disorders*, **41**(7), 626–634.

Kahn, B.E., & Wansink, B. (2004). The influence of assortment structure on perceived variety and consumption quantities. *Journal of Consumer Research*, **30**(4), 519–533.

Kandemir, N., Becker, K. R., Singhal, V., et al. (2017). Impact of low weight severity and menstrual status on bone in adolescents with anorexia nervosa. *International Journal of Eating Disorders*, **50**, 359–369.

Kardas, M., Cermik, B. B., Ekmecki, S., et al. (2014). Lorazepam in the treatment of posttraumatic feeding disorder. *Journal of Child and Adolescent Psychopharmacology*, **24**(5), 296–297.

Kendall, P. C. & Hedtke, K. A. (2006). *The coping cat workbook*. Ardmore, PA: Workbook Pub.

King, L. A., Urbach, J. R., & Stewart, K.E. (2015). Illness anxiety and avoidant/restrictive food intake disorder: Cognitive-behavioral conceptualization and treatment. *Eating Behaviors*, **19**, 106–109.

Kotler, L. A., Cohen, P., Davies, M., et al. (2001). Longitudinal relationships between childhood, adolescent, and adult eating disorders. *Journal of the American Academy of Child & Adolescent Psychiatry*, **40**(12), 1434–1440.

Kumar, R. K., Singhal, A., Vaidya, U., et al. (2017). Optimizing nutrition in preterm low birth weight infants – consensus summary. *Frontiers in Nutrition*, **4**, 1–9.

Kurz, S., Van Dyck, Z., Dremmel, D., et al. (2015). Early-onset restrictive eating disturbances in primary school boys and girls. *European Child & Adolescent Psychiatry*, **24**(7), 779–785.

Lesser, J., Eckhardt, S., Ehrenreich-May, J., et al. (2017). Integrating family based treatment with the unified protocol for the transdiagnostic treatment of emotional disorders: A novel treatment for avoidant restrictive food intake disorder. Clinical Teaching Day presentation at the International Conference on Eating Disorders in Prague, Czech Republic.

Linardon, J., Brennan, L., & de la Piedad Garcia, X. (2016). Rapid response to eating disorder treatment: A systematic review and meta-analysis. *International Journal of Eating Disorders*, **49**, 905–919.

Lock, J. & Le Grange, D. (2015). *Treatment manual for anorexia nervosa: A family-based approach* (2nd ed.). New York: Guilford Publications.

Lock, J., Le Grange, D., Agras, W. S., et al. (2015). Can adaptive treatment improve outcomes in family-based therapy for adolescents with anorexia nervosa? Feasibility and treatment effects of a multi-site treatment study. *Behaviour Research and Therapy*, **73**, 90–95.

Lopes, R., Melo, R., Curral, R., et al. (2014). A case of choking phobia: Towards a conceptual approach. *Eating and Weight Disorders: Studies on Anorexia, Bulimia and Obesity*, **19**(1), 125–131.

Lucarelli, J., Pappas, D., Welchons, L., et al. (2017). Autism spectrum disorder and avoidant/restrictive food intake disorder. *Journal of Developmental & Behavioral Pediatrics*, **38**(1), 79–80.

Lukens, C. T. & Silverman, A. H. (2014). Systematic review of psychological interventions for pediatric feeding problems. *Journal of Pediatric Psychology*, **39**(8), 903–917.

Mancuso, C. J., Becker, K. R., Plessow, F., et al. (2017). But I'm really not hungry: Aberrant ghrelin release in individuals with ARFID and AN. Oral presentation at the Eating Disorders Research Society conference, Leipzig, Germany.

Marchi, M. & Cohen, P. (1990). Early childhood eating behaviors and adolescent eating disorders. *Journal of the American Academy of Child & Adolescent Psychiatry*, **29**(1), 112–117.

Marshall, J., Hill, R. J., Ware, R. S., et al. (2015). Multidisciplinary intervention for childhood feeding difficulties. *Journal of Pediatric Gastroenterology and Nutrition*, **60**, 680–687.

Mascola, A. J., Bryson, S. W., & Agras, W. S. (2010). Picky eating during childhood: A longitudinal study to age 11 years. *Eating Behaviors*, **11**(4), 253–257.

Mascolo, M., Geer, B., Feuerstein, J., et al. (2017). Gastrointestinal comorbidities which complicate the treatment of anorexia nervosa. *Eating Disorders*, **25**(2), 122–133.

McElhanon, B. O., McCracken, C., Karpen, S., et al. (2014). Gastrointestinal symptoms in autism spectrum disorder: A meta-analysis. *Pediatrics*, **133**(5), 872–883.

McNally, R. J. (1986). Behavioral treatment of a choking phobia. *Journal of behavior therapy and experimental psychiatry*, **17**(3), 185–188.

McNally, R. J. (1994). Choking phobia: A review of the literature. *Comprehensive Psychiatry*, **35**(1), 83–89.

Mennella, J. A., Jagnow, C. P., & Beauchamp, G. K. (2001). Prenatal and postnatal flavor learning by human infants. *Pediatrics*, **107**(6), e88–e88.

Methven, L., Langreney, E., & Prescott, J. (2012). Changes in liking for a no added salt soup as a function of exposure. *Food Quality and Preference*, **26**(2), 135–140.

Micali, N., Simonoff, E., Elberling, H., et al. (2011). Eating patterns in a population-based sample of children aged 5 to 7 years: Association with psychopathology and parentally perceived impairment. *Journal of Developmental & Behavioral Pediatrics*, **32**(8), 572–580.

Milos, G., Spindler, A., Schnyder, U., et al. (2005). Instability of eating disorder diagnoses: Prospective study. *The British Journal of Psychiatry*, **187**(6), 573–578.

Misra, M. & Klibanski, A. (2014). Anorexia nervosa and bone. *Journal of Endocrinology*, **221**(3), R163–R176.

Morris, S. E. & Klein, M. D. (1987). *Pre-feeding skills: A comprehensive source for feeding development*. Tucson, AZ: Therapy Skill Builders.

Murphy, J. & Zlomke, K. R. (2016). A behavioral parent-training intervention for a child with avoidant/restrictive food intake disorder. *Clinical Practice in Pediatric Psychology*, **4**(1), 23.

Murray, S. B., Thornton, C., & Wallis, A. (2013). Selective eating in a 9-year-old boy: Family therapy as a first-line treatment. *Clinical Child Psychology and Psychiatry*, **18**(2), 270–275.

Nakai, Y., Nin, K., Noma, S. I., et al. (2016). Characteristics of avoidant/restrictive food intake disorder in a cohort of adult patients. *European Eating Disorders Review*, **24**(6), 528–530.

Nicely, T. A., Lane-Loney, S., Masciulli E., et al. (2014). Prevalence and characteristics of avoidant/restrictive food intake disorder in a cohort of young patients in day treatment for eating disorders. *Journal of Eating Disorders*, **2**(1), 21.

Nicholls, D., Christie, D., Randall, L., et al. (2001). Selective eating: Symptom, disorder or normal variant. *Clinical Child Psychology and Psychiatry*, **6**(2), 257–270.

Nock, M. K. (2002). A multiple-baseline evaluation of the treatment of food phobia in a young boy. *Journal of Behavior Therapy and Experimental Psychiatry*, **33**(3), 217–225.

Norris, M. L., Robinson, A., Obeid, N., et al. (2014). Exploring avoidant/restrictive food intake disorder in eating disordered patients: A descriptive study. *International Journal of Eating Disorders*, **47**(5), 495–499.

Norris, M. L., Spettigue, W., Hammond, N. G., et al. (2017). Building evidence for the use of descriptive subtypes in youth with avoidant restrictive food intake disorder. *International Journal of Eating Disorders*, **51**(2), 170–173.

Nowak-Cooperman, K., & Quinn-Shea, K. (2013). Finding the balance: Oral eating and tube feeding one pediatric hospital's experience with a hunger-based intensive feeding program. *ICAN: Infant, Child, & Adolescent Nutrition*, **5**(5), 283–297.

Office of Dietary Supplements (US). (2016, November 17). Calcium. Bethesda, MD: US National Institutes of Health. Accessed February 6, 2018 at: https://ods.od.nih.gov/factsheets/Calcium-HealthProfessional/

Office of Dietary Supplements (US). (2016, April 20). Folate. Bethesda, MD: US National Institutes of Health. Accessed February 6, 2018 at: https://ods.od.nih.gov/factsheets/Folate-HealthProfessional/

Office of Dietary Supplements (US). (2016, February 11). Iron. Bethesda, MD: US National Institutes of Health. Accessed February 6, 2018 at: https://ods.od.nih.gov/factsheets/Iron-HealthProfessional/

Office of Dietary Supplements (US). (2016, February 11). Riboflavin. Bethesda, MD: US National Institutes of Health. Accessed March 1, 2018 at: https://ods.od.nih.gov/factsheets/Riboflavin-HealthProfessional/

Office of Dietary Supplements (US). (2016, August 31). Vitamin A. Bethesda, MD: US National Institutes of Health. Accessed February 6, 2018 at: https://ods.od.nih.gov/factsheets/VitaminA-HealthProfessional/

Office of Dietary Supplements (US). (2016, February 11). Vitamin B12. Bethesda, MD: US National Institutes of Health. Accessed February 6, 2018 at: https://ods.od.nih .gov/factsheets/VitaminB12-HealthProfessional/

Office of Dietary Supplements (US). (2016, February 11). Vitamin C. Bethesda, MD: US National Institutes of Health. Accessed February 6, 2018 at: https:// ods.od.nih.gov/factsheets/VitaminC-HealthProfessional/

Office of Dietary Supplements (US). (2016, February 11). Vitamin D. Bethesda, MD: US National Institutes of Health. Accessed February 6, 2018 at: https:// ods.od.nih.gov/factsheets/VitaminD-HealthProfessional/

Office of Dietary Supplements (US). (2016, February 11). Vitamin K. Bethesda, MD: US National Institutes of Health. Accessed February 6, 2018 at: https:// ods.od.nih.gov/factsheets/VitaminK-HealthProfessional/

Office of Dietary Supplements (US). (2016, February 11). Zinc. Bethesda, MD: US National Institutes of Health. Accessed February 6, 2018 at: https://ods.od.nih.gov/ factsheets/Zinc-HealthProfessional/

Ollendick, T. H. & Davis, III, T. E. (2013). One-session treatment for specific phobias: A review of Öst's single-session exposure with children and adolescents. *Cognitive Behaviour Therapy*, **42**(4), 275–283.

Ornstein, R. M., Essayli, J. H., Nicely, T. A., et al. (2017). Treatment of avoidant/restrictive food intake disorder in a cohort of young patients in a partial hospitalization program for eating disorders. *International Journal of Eating Disorders*, **50**(9), 1067–1074.

Ornstein, R. M., Rosen, D. S., Mammel, K. A., et al. (2013). Distribution of eating disorders in children and adolescents using the proposed *DSM-5* criteria for feeding and eating disorders. *Journal of Adolescent Health*, **53**(2), 303–305.

Paul, C., Williams, K. E., Riegel, K., et al. (2007). Combining repeated taste exposure and escape prevention: An intervention for the treatment of extreme food selectivity. *Appetite*, **49**, 708–711.

Pinhas, L., Nicholls, D., Crosby, R. D., et al. (2017). Classification of childhood onset eating disorders: A latent class analysis. *International Journal of Eating Disorders*, **50**(6), 657–664.

Pizzo, B., Williams, K. E., Paul, C., et al. (2009). Jump start exit criterion: Exploring a new model of service delivery for the treatment of childhood feeding problems. *Behavioral Interventions*, **24**, 195–203.

Pliner, P., Pelchat, M., & Grabski, M. (1993). Reduction of neophobia in humans by exposure to novel foods. *Appetite*, **20**(2), 111–123.

Pulumo, R., Coniglio, K., Lawson, E. A., et al. (2016). *DSM-5* Presentations of avoidant/restrictive food intake disorder: Are categories mutually exclusive or overlapping? Poster presentation at the Eating Disorders Research Society meeting, New York, NY.

Rhodes, P., Prunty, M., & Madden, S. (2009). Life-threatening food refusal in two nine-year-old girls: Re-thinking the Maudsley model. *Clinical Child Psychology and Psychiatry*, **14**(1), 63–70.

Rolls, B. J., Rowe, E. A., & Rolls, E. T. (1982). How sensory properties of foods affect human feeding behavior. *Physiology & Behavior*, **29**(3), 409–417.

Rowell, K., McGlothlin, J., & Morris, S. E. (2015). *Helping your child with extreme picky eating: A step-by-step guide for overcoming selective eating, food aversion, and feeding disorders*. Oakland, CA: New Harbinger Publications.

Sant'Anna, A. M., Hammes, P. S., Porporino, M., et al. (2014). Use of cyproheptadine in young children with feeding difficulties and poor growth in a pediatric feeding program. *Journal of Pediatric Gastroenterology and Nutrition*, **59**(5), 674–678.

Satter, E. (1987). *How to get your kid to eat. . . But not too much*. Boulder, CO: Bull Publishing Company.

Satter, E. M. (1986). The feeding relationship. *Journal of the American Dietetic Association*, **86**, 352–356.

Savage, J. S., Fisher, J. O., & Birch, L. L. (2007). Parental influence on eating behavior: Conception to adolescence. *The Journal of Law, Medicine & Ethics*, **35**(1), 22–34.

Schermbrucker, J., Kimber, M., Johnson, N., et al. (2017). Avoidant/restrictive food intake disorder in an 11-year-old South American Boy: Medical and cultural challenges. *Journal of the Canadian Academy of Child and Adolescent Psychiatry*, **26**(2), 110.

Sharp, W. G., Jaquess, D. L., Morton, J. F., et al. (2010). Pediatric feeding disorders: A quantitative synthesis of treatment outcomes. *Clinical Child and Family Psychology Review*, **13**(4), 348–365.

Sharp, W. G. & Postorino, V. (2018). Food selectivity in autism spectrum disorder. In L. K. Anderson, S. B. Murray, and W. H. Kaye (Eds.), *Clinical handbook of complex and atypical eating disorders* (pp. 126–146). New York: Oxford University Press.

Solomou, S., & Korbonits, M. (2014). The role of ghrelin in weight-regulation disorders: Implications in clinical practice. *Hormones (Athens)*, **13**(4), 458–475.

Strandjord, S. E., Sieke, E. H., Richmond, M., et al. (2015). Avoidant/restrictive food intake disorder: Illness and hospital course in patients hospitalized for nutritional insufficiency. *Journal of Adolescent Health*, **57**(6), 673–678.

Sysko, R., Glasofer, D. R., Hildebrandt, T., et al. (2015). The eating disorder assessment for *DSM-5* (EDA-5): Development and validation of a structured interview for feeding and eating disorders. *International Journal of Eating Disorders*, **48**(5), 452–463.

Tanaka, S., Yoshida, K., Katayama, H., et al. (2015). Association of Beck Depression Inventory score and Temperament and Character Inventory-125 in patients with eating disorders and severe malnutrition. *Journal of Eating Disorders*, **3**(1), 36.

Thomas, J. J., Brigham, K. S., Zayas, L. V., et al. (2017b). Case records of the Massachusetts General Hospital: An 11-year-old girl with difficulty eating after a choking incident. *New England Journal of Medicine*, **376**(24), 2377–2386.

Thomas, J. J., Hartmann, A. S., & Killgore, W. D. S. (2013). Non-fat-phobic eating disorders: Why we need to investigate implicit associations and neural correlates. *International Journal of Eating Disorders*, **46**, 416–419.

Thomas, J. J., Lawson, E. A., Micali, N., et al. (2017a). Avoidant/restrictive food intake disorder: A three-dimensional model of neurobiology with implications for etiology and treatment. *Current Psychiatry Reports*, **19**(8), 54.

Thomas, J. J., Roberto, C. A., & Brownell, K. D. (2009). Eighty-five percent of what? Discrepancies in the weight cut-off for anorexia nervosa substantially affect the prevalence of underweight. *Psychological Medicine*, **39**, 833–843.

Toomey, K. A., Ross, E., & Kortsha, B. (2014). SOS Basic Training Workshop. Little Rock, Arkansas. Sponsored by the Sensory Processing Disorder Foundation.

Villar, J., Giuliani, F., Barros, F., et al. (2018). Monitoring the postnatal growth of preterm infants: A paradigm change. *Pediatrics*, **141**(2), e20172467.

Waller, G., Cordery, H., Corstorphine, E., et al. (2007). *Cognitive behavioral therapy for eating disorders: A comprehensive treatment guide*. Cambridge: Cambridge University Press.

Williams, K., & Seiverling, L. (2016). *Broccoli boot camp: A guide for improving your child's selective eating*. Kindle Edition.

Williams, K. E., & Foxx, R. M. (2007). *Treating eating problems of children with autism spectrum disorders and developmental disabilities: Interventions for professionals and parents*. Austin, TX: Pro-ed.

Williams, K. E., Paul, C., Pizzo, B., et al. (2008). Practice does make perfect: A longitudinal look at repeated taste exposure. *Appetite*, **51**(3), 739–742.

Williams, K. E., Riegel, K., & Kerwin, M. L. (2009). Feeding disorder of infancy or early childhood: How often is it seen in feeding programs? *Child Health Care*, **38**, 123–136.

Zajonc, R.B. (1968). Attitudinal effects of mere exposure. *Journal of Personality & Social Psychology*, **9**(2p2), 1–27.

Zickgraf, H. F., & Ellis, J. M. (2018). Initial validation of the Nine Item Avoidant/Restrictive Food Intake disorder screen (NIAS): A measure of three restrictive eating patterns. *Appetite*, **123**, 32–42.

Zickgraf, H. F., Franklin, M. E., & Rozin, P. (2016). Adult picky eaters with symptoms of Avoidant/Restrictive Food Intake Disorder: Comparable distress and comorbidity but different eating behaviors compared to those with disordered eating symptoms. *Journal of Eating Disorders*, **4**(1), 26.

Zlomke, K., & Davis, T.E. (2008). One-session treatment of specific phobias: A detailed description and review of treatment efficacy. *Behavior Therapy*, **39**(3), 207–223.

Zucker, N., Covington, V., & Petry, J. (2015). Food scientists: Sensory-based exposure for very young children with a variant of avoidant/restrictive food intake disorder. Workshop presented at the International Conference on Eating Disorders, Boston, MA.

Index